MANAGING CAPITAL FLOWS IN TURBULENT TIMES

MANAGING CAPITAL FLOWS IN TURBULENT TIMES

The Experience of Europe's Emerging Market Economies in Global Perspective

edited by
Zdeněk Drábek and
Stephany Griffith-Jones

M.E. Sharpe
Armonk, New York
London, England

Library of Congress Cataloging-in-Publication Data

Managing capital flows in turbulent times : the experience of Europe's emerging market
economies in global perspective / edited by Zdeněk Drábek and Stephany Griffith-Jones.
p.   cm.
Includes bibliographical references and index.
ISBN 0-7656-0369-1 (alk. paper)
1. Capital movements—Europe, Eastern. 2. Europe, Eastern—Foreign economic relations.
3. Europe, Eastern—Economic policy—1989– .
I. Drábek, Zdeněk. II. Griffith-Jones, Stephany.
HG3891.M365   1999
332′.042—dc21   99-11328
CIP

Printed in the United States of America

The paper used in this publication meets the minimum requirements of
American National Standard for Information Sciences—
Permanence of Paper for Printed Library Materials,
ANSI Z 39.48-1984.

BM (c)   10   9   8   7   6   5   4   3   2   1

Contents

About the Editors and Contributors

Currently a Senior Adviser in the World Trade Organization, Dr. **Zdeněk Drábek** was formerly Minister's Plenipotentiary in the Federal Ministry of Economy in Czechoslovakia and Principal Adviser to the governor of the Czech Central Bank. He served as the Czechoslovak government's chief negotiator for the Association Agreement with the European Union and in GATT ("Uruguay Round") and President of the Federal Agency for Foreign Investment in the former Czechoslovakia. Prior to government service he was Senior Economist at the World Bank (1983–1990) and the chairman of the Economics Department at the University of Buckingham in England (1976–1983). Dr. Drábek has published widely in major professional economics journals and authored or coauthored eleven books.

Stephany Griffith-Jones is a Fellow at the Institute of Development Studies, University of Sussex. She has published fourteen books and numerous articles on international finance and macroeconomic policy. Her most recent book is *Global Capital Flows: Should They Be Regulated?* She has advised many international organizations, including the World Bank and the European Commission, and several national authorities, including the Czech Central Bank and the Brazilian Presidency.

Oldřich Dědek is a member of the Monetary Board and Deputy Governor of the Czech National Bank, a position to which he was appointed in February 1999. Until then he was an economic adviser to the Governor of the Czech National Bank (who served as prime minister in 1998) and a researcher and Deputy Director of the Economics Institute of the Czech National Bank. Dr. Dědek was educated in Prague and has also held a number of visiting fellowships at Western research institutions, including Warwick University and the Federal Reserve Bank of St. Louis.

Pál Gáspár is a researcher at the Financial Research Institute in Budapest. He previously worked in the Institute of World Economy of the Hungarian Academy of Sciences and has been an adviser to the Hungarian Ministry of Finance on macroeconomic issues. Recently, he has been primarily active in a number of multi-country research projects.

Stanislaw Gomulka is Professor of Economics at the London School of Economics and a widely published expert on growth theory, macroeconomics, transition issues, and econometrics. Throughout the 1990s he has been a special economic adviser in Poland, especially to the Governor of the National Bank of Poland and two ministers of finance.

Jan Klacek is currently Chief Executive Officer and Chairman of the Board of *Investicni a Postovni Banka* (Investment and Postal Bank) in Prague, the third largest Czech commercial bank. Prior to accepting that position in late 1998, he was Director of Economics Institute of the Czech National Bank and an economic adviser in the Social Democratic Party. In the 1980s he was Senior Researcher in the Institute of Economics of the Academy of Sciences and taught at the Prague School of Economics. He was educated in Prague and was a visiting scholar at a number of Western universities. He has written widely on macroeconomic and international economic issues.

José García Solanes is Professor of Economics at the Faculty of Economic Sciences, Universidad de Murcia (Spain). He is a leading specialist on international economic and macroeconomic issues in Spain especially on questions related to the Spanish economy. His work has been published in both Spanish and English. In addition to his academic activities he has advised the Central Bank of Spain and other institutions.

John Williamson was educated at the London School of Economics and Princeton University. He taught at the Universities of York and Warwick in England, and at the Pontificia Universidade Catolica do Rio de Janeiro in Brazil. He was a Senior Adviser in the UK Treasury in the late 1960s and at the IMF in the early 1970s. Since 1981 he has lived in Washington, where he has been a Senior Fellow at the Institute for International Economics, from which he is currently on leave to serve as Chief Economist for South Asia at the World Bank.

MANAGING CAPITAL FLOWS IN TURBULENT TIMES

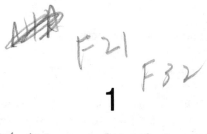

1
BK Title: Introduction

Zdeněk Drábek

Even the most inconspicuous countries may become the targets of unstable capital flows. This is perhaps the most surprising and astonishing experience of the Central European countries in recent years as they unfolded from a highly centralized system of economic planning and management. In the early 1990s, very few people would have guessed that transition economies could become so attractive to foreign investors that they would become targets of speculative attacks. Very few people would have been concerned about the dangers of "excessive" capital inflows into these countries or alarmed about the ensuing instability of capital inflows. The problem was traditionally perceived to be the opposite—shortage of foreign capital and concerns about the most effective ways of attracting foreign investors.

Yet capital surges and a dangerous instability of capital inflows are precisely what have occurred in the region in recent years. It began with the speculative attacks against the Czech koruna, but both Poland and Hungary have experienced similar problems, albeit of smaller magnitude and impact. The results have been almost as dramatic as the more widely publicized cases of Asian countries or Mexico. The strongest impact was felt in the Czech Republic, where economic growth virtually stopped in 1997–98 and the political system has been shaken by a government crisis—both of these events reflecting to a considerable extent the difficulties with the management of capital flows.

Clearly, the recent experience of Central Europe demonstrates that no country in the world is immune to the problems that may arise from capital movements. The loss of confidence has indiscriminately affected even relatively good performers, as we have seen with several countries in Asia. By

4 · ZDENĚK DRÁBEK

the same token, the country may not necessarily be a "superstar" in terms of economic growth and, therefore, opportunities to attract foreign investors. Neither the Czech Republic nor Hungary and Poland were such super performers at the time—say, in the mid-1990s—particularly in comparison to fast-growing countries in Asia and Latin America. Russia, with its negative economic growth over a long period of time, provides an even more striking example of a country that may become attractive to foreign investors under general conditions of economic stagnation. The example of Russia is, of course, somewhat different and more complex, since capital inflows there have been accompanied by massive capital flight. Broadly speaking, often all that is required is the possibility of free entry and exit for foreign investors to take advantage of profitable opportunities in a given market.

What we think should make this book interesting is that it is about the management of capital flows in transition economies in Central Europe. Transition economies are attractive case studies for two reasons. One has been already noted—the ability of these countries to attract foreign capital since, in the past, foreign investors have primarily targeted developed and highly industrialized OECD countries as their markets. This trend has changed fundamentally in recent years. The other reason is transition countries' limited experience with the management of capital flows and their similarly limited experience in the use of market-driven instruments. For these reasons the book should provide valuable lessons not only for all transition countries but also for many developing countries that have suffered from the same kind of "immaturity." We have chosen to spotlight Central European countries for the simple reason that they have been in the forefront of economic reform among transition countries.

Moreover, at least one of the Central European countries under consideration pursued policies that were regarded by most observers as exemplary and generally fully supported by the so-called Washington consensus. The country was the Czech Republic, and its government at the time could simply do nothing wrong. It took the lead among all transition economies in introducing its original mass privatization program. Strong inflationary pressures were subdued relatively quickly and without too much pain using tight monetary policies and responsible fiscal management. The economy has been widely liberalized, including foreign trade and foreign exchange, foreign investment, and domestic prices, and the government rationalized the foreign exchange regime. Clearly, all these measures have made the Czech Republic highly attractive to foreign investors.

The choice of Central Europe is interesting for another reason. Since all three countries under consideration have been subject to capital surges, the obvious question arises: How much have these countries learned from experiences elsewhere? After all, the Czech Republic, Poland, and Hungary were not the first to experience problems of managing capital flows. Many other countries have experienced such difficulties in the past, and therefore we have been able to accumulate a considerable amount of knowledge that should have been helpful to relative newcomers to the world financial markets, such as those from Central Europe.

Unfortunately, studies of capital flows are not easy, partly because we are only now beginning to be reasonably well equipped with economic theory to guide us in our assessments of policies to manage capital flows. Nevertheless, various aspects of capital flow management—such as the question of sequencing and timing of liberalization of capital account—still remain subject to controversies. But the difficulties are even more elementary: a lack of good data. The existing data on capital flows remain suspicious and often subject to a considerable doubts about their reliability. These data are at present reported by a variety of institutions and sources, most notably by the International Monetary Fund, the Bank for International Settlements, and the World Bank. Other sources include various commercial and investment banks, specialized UN agencies, the OECD, and others. Given the multiplicity of sources, it is perhaps not surprising that the data are not always consistent or even comparable. Moreover, the statistical work on capital flows is relatively new. As a result, the range of data tends to be far narrower than what researchers need. This has become apparent in the preparation of our study, where the data we required (e.g., on maturity of investments, new investment products, etc.) were sometimes beyond what statistical offices around the world could provide.

This book is a result of a collaborative effort of economists from the East and from the West. They represent a cross-section of considerable experience from academia, international organizations, central banks, and research institutes. Each one of the contributors has been personally involved in top policy making in their countries and elsewhere, which undoubtedly adds to the credibility of their contributions here. The book includes three country studies covering the Czech Republic, Hungary, and Poland, written by experts from the countries concerned. Several contributors to this volume have provided and analyzed data concerning other transition countries. We have also included two contributions that look at the management of capital flows elsewhere—in Spain and Latin America. Another article provides a general description of capital inflows into the region as well as an analysis of "warning lights" to see whether government responses to capital flows were needed or not. Finally, we have included in the book a general discussion of policy instruments available to governments in situations when they face capital surges.

We have asked the following questions in this book:

1. What have been the main features and the scale of capital flows into Central Europe? What have been the main categories of inflows—FDI, equity investment, securities, bank lending, other? What have been their financial conditions—maturities, costs, other? Did financial innovations take place? Did these innovations carry different risks in comparison to more traditional instruments?
2. Are the capital inflows of permanent or transitory nature? What are the main reasons for the predominance of particular types of capital inflows? Are these reasons mainly due to national or international developments? Are these factors stable?
3. How have the external capital flows been used internally by the countries concerned? What sectors are the main beneficiaries? Could we identify the extent to which foreign capital has been directed toward productive investments, especially in tradables? Has the government and/or private sector been monitoring the microeconomic impact of capital flows? If not, would it have been desirable and/or feasible to do so?
4. What has been the policy response of the monetary and fiscal authorities? What policy instruments have they used? Have all (some) inflows been discouraged? If so, how was it done?
5. Have the authorities used sterilized or nonsterilized interventions? In what proportions were these policies used and through what mechanisms? What was the cost of such sterilization policies as a percentage of GDP? Has the sterilization become so large as to become problematic? How have the authorities responded to these problems?
6. Have fiscal measures been taken to compensate for the inadequacies of monetary sterilization?
7. Have the authorities taken measures to relax controls on capital outflows or to liberalize imports?
8. Has the exchange rate policy been changed as a result of governments' responses to capital surges?
9. What effects have these policy measures had? What lessons can be drawn from the experience? Should alternative policy measures have been used?
10. What have been the main macroeconomic effects of capital flows and of their management? What are the likely macroeconomic effects in the future—especially in terms of output, investment, domestic savings, and inflation? What are the estimated effects of

capital flows (and policies to manage them) in terms of foreign exchange reserves, money supply, interest rates, and both nominal and real exchange rates? What are the likely long-term growth effects, if the level of flows is sustained, if it increases, and if it decreases? Are there risks that these flows could suddenly fall or be reversed? What effect would this have on the financial systems?

11. Are the capital inflows into the countries of Central and Eastern Europe sustainable?

The reader will undoubtedly sense from the above list of questions a certain caution and concern about "excessive" capital flows. Given the recent experiences in Asia and, prior to that, in Mexico and elsewhere in Latin America, we hope these sentiments are not exaggerated. The message we do *not* wish to convey is that "foreign capital is bad" and that protection of domestic markets against foreign capital is in some cases a priori way desirable. One could easily slip into this negative position, particularly in light of the Asian turmoil. Foreign capital is vital for all of these countries, inasmuch as it is already a part of everyday life in developed countries. Moreover, the integration of financial markets around the world has already progressed so far and affected so many countries that no individual country alone can choose to stay outside. Participation in this process is not a question of choice but rather a matter of necessity. Countries simply have to take part in the globalization process if they do not wish to be marginalized and if they wish to have access to foreign capital.

The two chapters following this introduction are general in nature. John Williamson, who is one of the pioneers in the balance-of-payments literature and in the forefront of discussions on the management of capital flows, provides in his article a general overview of policies to manage capital flows. Zdeněk Drábek's chapter examines the overall magnitude of capital inflows into the region and evaluates various warning signals that have been flashing in the countries concerned, urging governments to respond to capital surges. The subsequent four chapters are the country case studies. The Czech Republic is covered in two separate papers by Jan Klacek and Oldřich Dědek, who look at the management of capital inflows and at the policy of liberalizing the market for foreign currencies, respectively. Both Klacek and Dědek were senior advisers in the central bank at the time and are therefore highly qualified to discuss the Czech case. The case study of Hungary is by Pál Gáspár, director of the Financial Institute in Budapest, which specializes in the study of financial markets. Finally, the case study of Poland has been prepared by Stanislaw Gomulka, of the London School of Economics. Gomulka has long been involved with policy-making institutions in Poland, first in the Ministry of Finance and later in the central bank, in both cases as a senior adviser to top management. He, too, therefore has intimate knowledge not only of the issues but also of the internal debates that surround them. In addition, both of the editors—myself and my colleague Stephany Griffith-Jones—have been closely associated with the Czech central bank, myself as a staff member for two years and Griffith-Jones as an adviser.

The book concludes with two chapters by Griffith-Jones and José García Solanes on the relevant experiences of Latin America and Spain, respectively. The main objective of these two papers is to provide an intellectual framework from which we can draw lessons for policy making in Central Europe. These chapters will be particularly of interest to those readers who have direct or indirect impact on policy making in Central Europe, either in various advisory capacities or as academics writing about Central Europe. Both Griffith-Jones and García Solanes have written extensively about capital flows and have personal and deep knowledge of Latin America and Spain, respectively. We conclude the book with a chapter summarizing our findings and offering policy recommendations.

On behalf of my coeditor and all the other contributors to the book, I would like to thank a number of people and institutions who have made this project possible. First of all, we would like to thank the European Commission for financing most of this project under the umbrella of the Action for Cooperation in the Field of Economics (ACE) program. A large part of our budget has been also covered by British Overseas Development Assistance. Additional financing in kind has been received from the Czech National Bank, where we organized one of our seminars, and we are grateful to Oldřich Dědek and the staff of the Czech National Bank for the excellent organization. We would also like to thank the staff of the Institute of Development Studies at the University of Sussex and the Institute of Finance in Budapest for organizing two more workshops in Brighton and Budapest, respectively.

In addition, we have greatly benefited from comments and presentations of distinguished experts who have participated in our Prague, Budapest, and Brighton workshops. They include David Begg, of Birbeck College in London; Helmuth Reisen, of OECD; Guy Pfefferman, chief economist at the World Bank; Stefan Kawalec, former deputy minister of finance in Poland; Jorge Braga de Macedo, of the Portuguese parliament; David Lubin, senior economist at the Hong Kong Shanghai Bank Corporation in London; and other participants in our workshops. We are grateful to Josef Tošovský, governor of the Czech National Bank, and Jan Vit, his deputy, who lent their personal patronage to our Prague seminar.

Our thanks go to Aishah Colautti, from the World Trade Organization, and Jeanne Grant, who have provided excellent secretarial support and to Roberto Castellanos for very efficient proofreading. We are also very grateful for the intellectual support that we have received from our colleagues at the World Trade Organization in Geneva—especially Patrick Low—and from the Institute of Development Studies in Brighton. Our most sincere thanks also go to the book's publishers, M.E. Sharpe, and especially to Patricia A. Kolb and Elizabeth T. Granda for their highly professional help, efficient editorial support, and fast responses to all our questions. This book is dedicated to my wife, Sylvie, who has been by far the biggest support to me. Of course, none of these people and institutions I have mentioned here are responsible for any weaknesses that may remain in the book.

2

The Management of Capital Inflows

John Williamson

This paper is organized as follows. The first section identifies the problems that have been revealed by experience in Latin America during both the lending by commercial banks in the late 1970s and early 1980s and the more recent influx, in the forms of bonds and equity, following the resolution of the debt crisis. The second section catalogues the policy options that can be taken in response to seemingly excessive capital inflows. The third section describes the policy options adopted by six principal Latin American countries during the most recent episode, and sketches the outcomes so far. A brief concluding section lays out some policy implications.

The Problems Caused by "Excessive" Capital Inflows

The main danger posed by large capital inflows is that they may destabilize macroeconomic management. This can happen both through the inflows themselves leading to an appreciation of the real exchange rate and what is called "Dutch disease," and through the inflows cumulating to a stock of debt that the country has difficulty servicing on the contractually agreed terms.[1]

Consider first the problems that arise through a real appreciation induced by capital inflows. It is traditional to distinguish between cases in which such an appreciation is temporary and those in which it is permanent. A temporary real appreciation *that the public expects to be temporary* is unlikely to have major effects on investment, which is presumptively governed by long-run expectations; indeed, the principal effect may be to stimulate an attempt to take advantage of the temporarily low price of foreign capital goods in order to accelerate investment. To the extent that domestically made capital goods (e.g., buildings) and foreign-made capital goods (e.g., machinery) are complements, the investment boom will spill over to increase domestic demand as well. Usually a capital inflow will in any event tend to be associated with a domestic boom, when it results from low foreign interest rates, domestic reforms, or a domestic stock market boom (an exception arises if it is caused by high domestic interest rates resulting from tight monetary policy). Consumption can be expected to rise under similar conditions, for similar reasons (as a result of increasing wealth and complementarity of domestic and imported goods in consumption). And, so long as the public has the rational expectations nowadays posited by many economic theorists, none of this creates a policy problem.

Consider, however, the alternative possibility that the low foreign interest rates or the domestic stock market boom that is responsible for the capital inflow is temporary but that the public does *not* recognize this. Then the decreased profitability of producing tradables will discourage investment in those industries. Either investment will shift toward nontradable industries, which is perhaps the most likely outcome given that the initiating factor was a decrease in the cost of capital, or the mix of expenditure will shift away from investment and toward consumption. When the capital inflow ceases, the economy will find itself in a worse position to service foreign debt than it would have been in given the absence of a capital inflow. It is obvious that in this case a policy of preventing the real appreciation from occurring—of short-circuiting the misleading price signals—would have been beneficial.

Consider now the possibility that the capital inflow is permanent, e.g., because of reforms that make the domestic economy more attractive to foreign investors. There are sharp differences of view among economists about the desirability of resisting a real appreciation that results from a permanent capital inflow. One view is that, just like a resource discovery that induces a real appreciation, such an inflow is a piece of good fortune that permits a country to enjoy a larger real income, which it can take in the combination of increased consumption and increased investment that it prefers.[2] The other view is that the damage to the tradable goods industries caused by the real appreciation can harm the country's prospects for development, given that those industries tend to be the key to long-term growth. While the theory as to why this should be so has never been very satisfactorily developed, it is a view that is held quite strongly by many economists.

In practice, of course, it is often true that neither the public nor the government has a clear view as to whether a capital inflow is going to prove temporary or permanent. A rule of prudence would suggest that positive shocks should be treated as temporary and negative shocks as permanent. A second rule of prudence would suggest that while no government should ever adopt a policy that is not viable if expectations *are* rational, it should also avoid policies whose success is *dependent* upon expectations being rational. The two rules together imply that a prudent government will treat as a problem any capital inflow so large as to induce a real appreciation big enough to threaten the growth of exports.

The other major macroeconomic problem caused by capital inflows is that they may build up a level of debt that the country finds difficult to service on the contractually agreed terms, as happened throughout Latin America in 1982. This raises two issues: identifying how much debt a country can prudently take on, and limiting borrowing to a prudent level when the market wants to lend more. The first of these issues is briefly discussed in an appendix to this paper, while the various ways in which the second may be accomplished are discussed in the next section of the paper.

A number of other problems are sometimes also mentioned as possible undesirable consequences of large capital inflows. Inflows may, for example, lead to a speculative bubble in the stock market. One undesirable consequence of such a bubble is typically a decline in the local savings rate, as individuals discover that their asset accumulation objectives are being achieved without the need for anything so tedious as abstaining from consumption. Another undesirable consequence can be a financial crisis, and the danger of a recession, when the bubble bursts.

Capital inflows may also involve the loss of local control over economic decision making; this is clearest in the case of majority-owned direct investment, although direct investment carries offsetting benefits in terms of access to technology and markets, and the loss of control can in any event often be avoided through joint ventures. Problems may also arise to some degree in the case of portfolio equity investment, if concentrated shareholding is allowed, and even loans, where powerful foreign creditors (notably the IMF when times get difficult) expect to be consulted about the course of economic policy.

On the other hand, there seems no particular reason to be concerned about foreign borrowing leading to dollarization. The latter is caused by economic mismanagement that results in Gresham's Law coming into play to the point where the local currency is undermined. When capital starts to be repatriated, it may seek some form of dollar guarantee, but it seems more natural to blame the resulting dollarization on the preceding mismanagement rather than on the capital reflow. Neither is it right to think of the use of foreign borrowing to finance local expenditure as posing a particular problem. It is even conceivable that, when an economy has idle capacity and is suffering from a foreign exchange constraint, financing local expenditure may be the very best use of foreign borrowing. What matters from the standpoint of preserving creditworthiness is that the new investment should contribute to the production of tradables so as to generate foreign exchange with which to service the debt, and not what the capital is spent on.[3] It is of course important to be alert to the danger of wasting resources on grandiose projects with a derisory rate of return, but that is true whether they are financed from local savings or from foreign borrowing.

These extra possible problems of foreign borrowing are not addressed in detail in the present chapter. They have not been totally absent in Latin America. For example, Chile had a stock market boom in the early 1980s driven by capital inflows, which drastically reduced domestic savings. Many countries were tempted into grandiose projects with poor rates of return by the easy availability of commercial bank finance with no questions asked in the late 1970s, and many of them also paid too little attention to ensuring that sufficient investment was being directed to the tradables industries to be able to service the debt. And worries about foreign control used to be intense. Nonetheless, the rest of the paper focuses on the problems for macroeconomic management posed by large inflows.

Policy Options

Suppose that a government is faced with large capital inflows. It has to choose among the following possible reactions:

i. to allow a nominal appreciation of the currency
ii. to buy up reserves (e.g., by holding the exchange rate fixed) and allow the money supply to expand in consequence (i.e., to engage in unsterilized intervention)
iii. to liberalize restrictions on imports of goods and services
iv. to buy up reserves but sterilize the intervention by selling an equal value of domestic-currency-denominated bonds
v. to increase the reserve ratio applying to bank deposits
vi. to switch government-controlled deposits (e.g., deposits in the postal savings system) from the commercial banks to the central bank
vii. to widen the band of permissible exchange rate fluctuations
viii. to pursue a contractionary fiscal policy
ix. to improve the mobilization of private savings
x. to eliminate any remaining subsidies to inward investment, such as free deposit insurance
xi. to impose or increase controls on capital inflows
xii. to relax controls on capital outflows

The strategic decision is whether to allow the capital inflow to be translated into a current account deficit so as to finance increased domestic investment and/or consumption. If it is decided to "make the transfer," there are three polar mechanisms by which this can be accomplished. The first is the flexible exchange rate mechanism of currency appreciation, which is listed first on the above list. The second is the fixed exchange rate ("gold standard") mechanism, whereby an expanding money supply increases demand and thus causes inflation and real appreciation once again. The third is to relax import restrictions, which will also lead to an increased current account deficit, although with the important difference that this will come about through higher imports and will avoid the discouragement of exports.

However, it was also argued above that there are circumstances—where the inflow is believed to be temporary, where Dutch disease threatens growth prospects, where the debt is growing so large as to threaten to precipitate a debt crisis, or where the outlook is uncertain—where it is rational to resist current account adjustment that would accomplish the transfer. The natural first resort in this instance is to intervene in the exchange market to hold a "fixed" exchange rate and to sterilize the intervention through open market operations (the fourth option).[4] The difficulty with this option is that it is expensive. Especially when domestic interest rates are being held up in order to restrict domestic demand, or because there is a lack of confidence in the domestic currency, the domestic interest rate the central bank will have to pay on the bonds that it issues may be very much higher than the foreign interest rate it will earn on the reserves that it acquires.[5] Moreover, in order to persuade the public to hold bonds equal to the whole of the reserve increase, it may be necessary to increase the domestic interest rate (although this can be avoided by allowing a monetary expansion equal to a part of the reserve increase). If interest rates are allowed to increase, the capital inflow will rise further; even if they are held constant, there will be no market incentive to reduce the inflow.

Financing such inflows can be expensive. For example, in Argentina in July 1994 the interest rate on thirty-day government paper was 10.6 percent per annum, as against 4.5 percent on the comparable U.S. government assets that Argentina might have been holding in its reserves. The interest differential consisted of 2.2 percent exchange risk premium and 3.9 percent country risk premium. Similarly, Mexico had an interest differential of 7.7 percent in September 1994, consisting of 3.8 percent expected depreciation, 1.8 percent exchange risk premium, and 2.1 percent country premium.[6] In Mexico's case, the loss on sterilized intervention is the interest differential minus planned depreciation, or 3.9 percent; in Argentina's case it would be a massive 8.4 percent (although Argentina's currency board system implies that it does not actually undertake sterilized intervention). Other Latin American countries have suffered comparable losses. Larraín (Group of Thirty 1994, p. A-89) reports calculations that the losses on sterilized intervention have been around 0.5 percent of GDP in both Chile and Colombia.

So far as the central bank is concerned, this cost can be avoided by raising the reserve ratio, thus averting the need to issue additional domestic currency bonds while still avoiding an increase in the money supply despite the increase in the monetary base. However, high reserve ratios impose costs of a different sort, diminishing the efficiency of the financial system as borrowers are diverted away from those lenders subject to the high reserve requirements and toward others that escape that requirement. Another way of achieving de facto sterilization without issuing additional bonds is to require government-controlled financial institutions (such as the postal savings system) to switch their deposits from the commercial banks to the central bank. While this proved effective in a number of Asian countries (Fisher and Reisen 1992), it implies either reducing the return to the savers in those institutions or (if the central bank pays the normal domestic interest rate) imposing a financial cost on the central bank.

The seventh possible policy reaction is to widen the band of permissible exchange rate fluctuations. This will allow the capital inflow to push the exchange rate to the top of the band, but is intended to leave the private sector with a presumption that the appreciation is temporary. If that is indeed believed, it will have two helpful effects. The first is that, since foreign investors deduct expected future depreciation from the domestic currency return in order to calculate the expected yield in their own currency, it will reduce the incentive for the capital inflow. The second is that it will minimize the danger that the appreciation will discourage investment in the tradable goods industries, which is presumably influenced mainly by expectations of the long-term real exchange rate.

The eighth policy option is to tighten fiscal policy, either by cutting government expenditure or by raising taxes. This will permit domestic interest rates to be reduced, thus diminishing the incentive for the capital inflow, without losing control of domestic demand and thus risking inflation.

A similar effect could be achieved by institutional measures, as opposed to higher rates of interest, that would increase private savings. The establishment of a postal savings system or of a system for the private provision of pensions are examples of the sorts of measure that might increase savings without requiring higher interest rates.

Capital inflows might also be discouraged by withdrawing any measures that inadvertently subsidize inward investment. The two most common examples are probably insurance of bank deposits and grants to direct investors. The latter are presumably seeking to attract direct investment because of its job-creating or technology-enhancing features, but there is absolutely no reason except accident or inertia why foreigners should get the benefit of free or subsidized deposit insurance.

We are now in the realm of measures intended to repel rather than to finance capital inflows. The classic measures of this type are capital controls. These can take many forms: for example, the prohibition of foreign purchase or holding of domestic assets, requirements to obtain administrative permission for a foreign bond issue, minimum maturity periods for foreign bond issues, a dual exchange rate for capital transactions, taxes on purchases of domestic assets by foreigners or on investment income earned by foreigners, or reserve requirements on deposits held by foreigners. If such controls were easy to enforce, there would be no problem of excessive capital inflows. The dominant question to ask of proposals for such controls is always whether they can be enforced and, if so, at what cost in terms of economic distortions or civil liberties, remembering that additional controls become progressively more likely to produce perverse side effects as there are a larger number of preexisting controls with which they may interact in unforeseen ways. As an example of the limits of such controls in a European country with a well-regarded administrative apparatus, Belgium for many years operated a dual exchange rate system, but problems of evasion began to become significant whenever the two rates diverged by more than 3 percent.

The final entry on my list of possible policy reactions to a capital inflow is to relax controls on capital outflows. There is, however, some evidence that a blanket relaxation of outflow controls can at times have the perverse effect of stimulating a net *inflow* (Labán and Larraín 1993). The reason is that investors can be so reassured that they will have no difficulty in withdrawing their money should they wish to do so that they actually increase their exposure. It may nonetheless be possible to undertake limited liberalization, e.g., by permitting domestic pension funds to invest abroad, while avoiding the danger of provoking a perverse reaction.

Latin American Policy Responses

Table 2.1 shows that, for Latin America as a whole, the recent surge of capital inflows was initially used largely to build up reserves. As the inflow was sustained, however, and even more as it began to subside, the inflow has been increasingly fully transferred.

Both the extent and the manner of this transfer have differed very signifi-

Table 2.1

Latin America: Balance of Payments, 1985–94

Year	(1): Balance of goods, services, and private transfers[a] ($ billion)	(2): Balance on capital account plus net errors and omissions[a] ($ billion)	(3): Increase in reserves ($ billion)	(4): $\frac{(3)}{(2)} \times 100$
1985	−5.5	6.5	1.0	15
1986	−19.8	13.2	−6.6	−50
1987	−11.8	15.0	3.2	21
1988	−13.4	5.7	−7.7	−135
1989	−10.1	12.7	2.6	20
1990	−8.5	23.6	15.1	64
1991	−20.5	38.9	18.4	47
1992	−34.7	53.4	18.7	35
1993	−35.1	39.1	4.0	10

Source: Calvo (1994), drawing on IMF, *World Economic Outlook* data.

Note: [a]Balance on goods, services, and private transfers is equal to the current account balance less official transfers. The latter are treated in this table as external financing and are included in the capital account.

cantly between one country and another. It is natural to divide the six major countries into three categories: those that have used the exchange rate as a nominal anchor in their stabilization programs, namely, Argentina and Mexico; those that have floated, which is only Peru; and those that have managed their exchange rates with a view to maintaining the competitiveness of the export sector, namely, Chile and Colombia and, at least until the recent Plano Real, Brazil.[7]

Table 2.2 provides summary statistics about the recent economic performance of the six countries. It can be seen from column 6 that both of the countries that chose to use the exchange rate as a nominal anchor, Argentina and Mexico, have experienced a substantial real appreciation as compared to the average for 1982–90 (the years of the debt crisis, which were used as a base period that was sufficiently long to minimize the danger that an erratic number in the base period will lead to misleading conclusions).[8] Argentina had stagnant exports (although they have started to grow in 1994, primarily to Brazil under the stimulus of Mercosur) and a significant current account deficit that was overfinanced by capital inflows. Internally it enjoyed spectacular success, with inflation being brought down from 1.59 percent in 1990 to minus 3 percent in the most recent twelve-month period of 1994 for which statistics are given in ECLAC's *Economic Panorama of Latin America 1994* (which happens to be the twelve months to August

Table 2.2

Recent Economic Indicators for Six Latin American Countries

	1. Annual growth in GDP (end 1989 to latest available quarter in 1994) (%)	2. Annual growth in volume of exports, 1991–93 (%)	3. Average current account deficit as % of GDP, 1990–92	4. Average capital inflow as % of GDP, 1990–92	5. Change in investment between 1981–89 and 1990–93 as % of GNP	6. Real effective exchange rate for exports, Jan.–Sept. 1993[a]	7. CPI 1990 (% p.a.)	8. Inflation 1994 (% p.a.)	9. Average tariff protection (%), 1991–92
Argentina	6.0	1,344	4	-0.1	1.3	2.0	159	-3.0	15.0
Brazil	0.5	1,585	3,176	11.2	0.0	1.2	119	-1.0	21.1
Chile	5.8	27	8	10.5	1.0	7.7	84	3.7	11.0
Colombia	3.5	32	22	12.6	-3.0	0.2	83	-1.0	6.7
Mexico	3.1	30	7	8.7	4.9	6.5	137	3.8	4.0
Peru	0.8	7,650	21	5.2	7.3	6.2	204	2.9	15.0

Sources: ECLAC, *Preliminary Overview of the Economy of Latin America and the Caribbean 1993* and *Economic Panorama of Latin America 1994.* Column 5: World Bank, *World Debt Tables, 1993–94.* Column 6: Ffrench-Davis et al. 1994. Column 7: Group of Thirty 1994, table 8. Column 9: Edwards 1993, table 5.2.

Note: [a]Index of the real effective exchange rate for exports using a CPI deflator with 1982–90 average = 100. A larger number signifies a real appreciation.

1994), and strong growth of 6 percent per year. Investment has been recovering, although it fell to an exceptionally low level at the end of the 1980s.

Mexico had a much larger current account deficit than Argentina, again overfinanced by very large capital inflows. It too achieved a respectable reduction in inflation, though its growth performance was less impressive. (The capital inflow was reversed in Mexico during the course of 1994.) Investment was quite strong in the early 1980s, though more recently savings have been declining.

Peru is the only one of the countries to have adopted a floating exchange rate. It has experienced an even stronger real appreciation, which—despite some bounce-back of exports after the chaos of the García government, which left office in 1990—has led to an even bigger current account deficit, which was largely financed by massive capital inflows. Peru again made spectacular progress in bringing hyperinflation under control, although its growth record has been modest until very recently. Growth is currently quite strong.

In contrast, both Chile and Colombia adopted an exchange rate policy that attempted to maintain the gains in competitiveness that they had achieved during the debt crisis, in pursuit of export-led growth. Both of them found this difficult because of the size of the influx of reserves. In the case of Chile, this was because of a massive capital inflow that overwhelmed the modest current account deficit, while in Colombia it was until recently principally the result of a current account surplus. Both of them maintained strong export growth. Chile also enjoyed strong GDP growth backed by a large rise in investment and combined with an impressive reduction of inflation. Colombian performance was less impressive on all three scores. The discovery of a large oil field, which is presently being developed, has led to big capital inflows that have posed an even more intense challenge to the aim of maintaining a competitive exchange rate.

Until the stabilization program (Plano Real) took effect in July 1994, Brazil also followed an exchange rate policy fairly similar to that of Chile and Colombia, focused on offsetting domestic inflation so as to maintain the competitiveness of exports. There had in fact already been some slippage by 1993, but Brazil had nonetheless maintained a respectable rate of export growth and kept its current account in balance. However, internal performance was abysmal, with inflation increasing even further and output and investment stagnant. Things have changed enormously in the last few months: inflation has been brought under control, output is buoyant, the current account remains strong so far, capital inflows have surged, and the currency has been allowed to float up from the 1:1 exchange rate against the dollar at which it was introduced. However, intervention again started (reluctantly) after an appreciation of about 17 percent, and a number of other measures intended to repel capital inflows were adopted, indicating that the authorities maintain their concern with sustaining competitiveness.

It is clear that policies have differed significantly across countries. Argentina and Peru made no attempt to avoid capital inflows being translated into current account deficits: Peru let this happen the quickest way, through currency appreciation, but Argentina's unsterilized intervention produces the same result equally surely (except to the extent that the demand to hold pesos increases). Mexico sterilized much of the intervention and for a time had a large reserve buildup, but its growth has been unimpressive and it now faces a widespread market belief that its currency is overvalued. The interesting question is whether these policies are consistent with robust growth. It is certainly true that Argentina, and more recently Peru, have enjoyed quite strong growth, but the critical question is whether this is just bounce-back growth that will be undermined before long by the weakness of exports. If it is true that the only growth that can be sustained in today's world is export-led, the outlook for Peru under its present policy regime is poor, and the question for Argentina and Mexico is whether Mercosur and NAFTA, respectively, can provide enough export momentum to overcome the hurdle of the strong exchange rate.

Chile is the one country in Latin America where an East Asian rate of growth has become institutionalized, and, since its export performance seems to be a key factor in that achievement, strenuous measures have been taken to avoid overvaluation.[9] Particular interest therefore attaches to the measures that Chile has taken to prevent the massive capital inflows with which it has been faced from undermining its policy stance.

The previous section listed twelve possible policy responses to a capital inflow. Chile has applied a wide range of policies:

(i): Two small reevaluations, of 2 percent and 5 percent, were undertaken in 1991 and 1992, respectively (running counter to the regular crawling depreciation that offsets differential inflation).

(ii) and (iv): Chile has bought reserves on a massive scale, totaling $6.2 billion from the end of 1989 to November 1993 (some 15 percent of 1993 GDP). The authorities report having issued large sums of bonds in order to sterilize their purchases of reserves (Ffrench-Davis et al. 1994, p. 10). Nonetheless, it is an interesting fact (according to the figures in *International Financial Statistics*) that during the period when reserves increased by $6.2 billion (from $3.6 billion at the end of 1989 to $9.8 billion in November 1993), the stock of reserve money increased by almost exactly the same amount, $6.5 billion (from $7.8 billion to $14.3

billion). Of course, this left Chile no room for domestic credit expansion, but the fact is that over the period as a whole it did not actually sterilize.

(iii): The uniform import tariff was reduced from 15 percent to 11 percent in June 1991.

(v): Leiderman and Reinhart (in Group of Thirty 1994, p. A-17) report that Chile increased marginal reserve requirements.

(vi): Switching government-controlled deposits to the central bank could not be applied because there are no such deposits.

(vii): The band for exchange rate fluctuations was widened from +/- 5 percent to +/–10 percent in 1992.[10]

(viii): The budget surplus was increased from 1.8 percent of GDP in 1989 and 0.8 percent in 1990 to 2.2 percent in 1992.

(ix): The switch to private provision of pensions in the early 1980s has given Chile a healthy savings rate, but I am not aware of further measures since 1989.

(x): The subsidies to inward investment provided by debt-equity swaps were already phased out in the late 1980s.

(xi): Chile has retained its minimum term for foreign bond issues. A reserve requirement of 20 percent was imposed against foreign holdings of bank deposits in 1991, and this was increased to 30 percent in 1992. ?A tax of 1.2 percent was imposed on short-term external credits in 1991 (Ffrench-Davis et al. 1994).

(xii): Outward direct investment was liberalized. Pension funds were permitted to place a proportion of their portfolios in foreign assets.

Thus Chile took remarkably broad-ranging actions in its so far successful attempt to avoid Dutch disease.

Colombia has also made strong efforts to limit real appreciation (indeed, the successful presidential candidate in the recent election made a pledge to avoid any further real appreciation). Until 1993 the payments surplus originated largely on current account (at least according to the official statistics), but last year the current account surplus was reinforced by a large capital inflow estimated at 4.3 percent of GDP.

Since early 1993 depreciation has not kept up with the inflation differential, resulting in a real appreciation against the dollar of nearly 20 percent (though less on an effective basis) by mid-1994. ?Intervention has nonetheless been massive, and in the case of Colombia it has mostly been sterilized: Reserve money increased by only $1.5 billion from the end of 1989 to March 1994, while reserves increased by $4.1 billion. A marginal reserve requirement of 100 percent was imposed on the deposits of most financial institutions in January 1991 in order to help restrain credit. However, it seems that policy changed after October 1991, with an attempt to reduce domestic interest rates so as to reduce the incentive for capital inflow, implying a greater willingness to allow reserve increases to expand the money supply (Ffrench-Davis et al. 1994, p. 13). Perhaps this helps explain the limited success in reducing inflation.

Colombia adopted an extensive trade liberalization program in 1989–90. Quantitative restrictions were almost entirely abolished in 1990, and a five-year program of tariff reduction was announced. In the event, the whole of the tariff reductions planned for the following four years were brought forward to 1991 (Urrutia 1994). The motivation was explicitly the desire to curb a large reserve buildup without hurting the growth of nontraditional exports.

Another important measure was a de facto widening of the band within which the exchange rate can fluctuate. This was accomplished by replacing cash intervention in the exchange market by the supply of dollar-denominated, non-interest-bearing exchange certificates with a maturity of one year, coupled with an undertaking to keep the discount in a band between 5.5 percent and 12.4 percent (Ffrench-Davis et al. 1994, p. 13). This in effect gives a 7 percent band for the exchange rate. It also had the advantage of giving one-off help in sterilizing.

The country also pursued an austere fiscal policy during this period, achieving a budget surplus of some 3 percent of GDP by the end of the Gaviria government.

Colombia still maintains controls on capital inflows, although these have been liberalized in recent years. A further liberalization was undertaken in 1992, when the minimum maturity of external loans was reduced from five years to one. In the other direction, a 3 percent tax on transfers and foreign earnings from personal service abroad was imposed in 1991, and in 1992 the central bank increased the commission for the purchase of foreign exchange from 1.5 percent to 5 percent (Ffrench-Davis et al. 1994, p. 13).

Finally, Colombia liberalized certain capital outflows in 1992. Exporters were authorized to keep a part of their foreign earnings abroad, and residents were authorized to hold up to £500,000 abroad without prior permission.

Brazil is the third country that has endeavored to avoid translating capital inflows into current account deficits. It too has applied a wide range of policies to that end. It is in fact the heaviest sterilizer of any of the three: Between the end of 1989 and May 1994, reserves increased by no less than $332.4 billion, while (under the pressure of near hyperinflation) the dollar value of the stock of reserve money actually contracted by $1 billion. Since stabilization was achieved with the introduction of the real on 1 July 1994, the money supply has been expanding rapidly. Brazil has also experienced a surge of capital inflows, which have been met with a battery of measures.

In the first place, while a floor has been placed under the value of the real by a commitment to sell dollars at a price of 1:1, the exchange rate has been allowed to appreciate. The authorities did not initially indicate any upper limit on how far the rate would be allowed to float, but they began to resist further appreciation when the dollar had reached a price of about 83 centavos. Thus there seems to be a de facto band of a little under 20 percent, on top of the real appreciation that had already been experienced before the Plano Real started (see Table 2.2).

Second, imports have been liberalized under a program that began in 1990 and that has seen the abolition of virtually all quantitative restrictions, drastic general tariff reductions, and the negotiation of a free trade area with three neighboring countries (Mercosur). Further tariff reductions have taken place in recent months, especially in sectors where the government regards price increases as abusive. (As the final column of Table 2.2 shows, at least until recently Brazil had the highest tariffs of the six countries in the early 1990s, averaging just over 20 percent in 1991–92.)

In addition, a reserve requirement of 15 percent was imposed against new credits in October. And the fiscal deficit has been eliminated, at least for the time being.

Measures have also been taken to discourage capital inflows. A 1 percent tax was imposed on foreign investment in the stock market in October. The tax on Brazilian companies issuing bonds overseas was increased from 3 percent to 7 percent, and that on foreign capital invested in fixed income funds was raised from 5 percent to 9 percent at the same time. Limits were placed on the ability of exporters to accept prepayment. On the other side of the account, Brazilian pension funds were for the first time allowed to place up to 10 percent of their portfolio in foreign assets, and all restrictions on spending by tourists were abolished.

Policy Considerations

An important debate is currently under way in Latin America about the relative merits of the policies pursued in Argentina and Peru, on the one hand, versus Chile, Colombia, and (tentatively) Brazil on the other. The former group allowed the capital inflows to be translated into current account deficits; the last three have tried to resist losing competitiveness, with the danger that loss poses of undermining export-led growth. (Mexico is an intermediate case: It allowed the capital inflow to finance a current account deficit but has sought to sterilize the outflow experienced in 1994, with the result that its reserve position is currently looking fragile.)

As of now, the most successful countries in each group are clearly Argentina and Chile. Argentina's situation still looks fragile because of its uncompetitive exchange rate and weak balance-of-payments situation, although there are some positive recent signs even in those areas. Chile has been a spectacular success story in recent years, but it nonetheless also continues to have problems that threaten its ability to sustain the policy course that it has been following, notably the pressure of capital inflows on the exchange rate. The choice between those two strategies depends on fundamental views about whether a macroeconomic policy oriented to the maintenance of a competitive exchange rate is capable of improving on laissez-faire.

What are the lessons of Latin American experience for those who believe that it does indeed make sense for the government to try to maintain a competitive exchange rate? I suggest the following:

- Resisting or neutralizing large capital flows is not easy and can be expensive.
- Nevertheless, there is a wide range of instruments that are relevant. It is simply not true that there is no alternative but to bow to the wisdom of the market, or even that the only things that can help are to tighten fiscal policy or to liberalize imports (though both of those can indeed help).
- The best policy is to employ many instruments and avoid expecting any one to provide a panacea. Sterilized intervention and increased reserve requirements can provide useful short-term relief. The band should be widened, imports should be liberalized, and fiscal policy should be tightened so that domestic interest rates can be reduced. There are a number of ways that capital inflows can be discouraged through controls or taxes, although it is critically important to recognize that all controls leak and will be evaded if the incentive to do so is strong; the most common mistake is to expect too much of capital controls. Certain capital outflows can be liberalized. Together, these measures offer some prospect of enabling a government to keep macroeconomic control without losing the potential of an export boom.

Setting a Prudent Limit on Foreign Indebtedness

There is no very satisfying method of estimating the safe level of debt. The best approach still seems to be that based on various rules of thumb about the relationship of debt or debt service to variables that influence the ability to service debt, such as exports, GDP, or the capital stock. The most famous such rules state that the debt/export ratio should not exceed 200 percent, that the debt service ratio (i.e., the ratio of debt service to exports) should not exceed 25 percent, and that the debt/GDP ratio should not exceed 40 percent. Such rules of thumb doubtless ought to be combined in some way, but in the meantime they do at least provide a starting point for analysis.[11]

What do these rules of thumb imply about sustainable (desirable) current account deficits? A little algebra can show. Let D = foreign debt and Y = nominal income (expressed in dollars, as the debt mostly is), and use a hat over a variable to signify its rate of change, so that D/D is the proportionate rate of change of debt. Consider a developing country that can expect a long-term growth rate of real income of 5 percent; then its expected long-term growth of nominal income measured in U.S. dollars (the international currency) will be 8 percent if one assumes an average 3 percent dollar inflation. In steady state the rate of growth of debt must be the same as the rate of growth of nominal income. Then the prudent steady-state current account deficit according to the debt/GDP rule of thumb would be $\hat{D}/Y = (D/Y) (\hat{D}/D). = 0.08 \times 0.4 = 0.032$, i.e., the steady-state current account deficit should not exceed 3.2 percent of GDP. Of course, a country that starts out with a debt/GDP ratio lower than 40 percent can run a greater deficit for a while, but it is a good idea to prevent the deficit from getting too much larger because of the difficulty of adjusting back as the debt limit approaches. (It is appropriate to focus on the debt/GDP ratio for a country with an export/GDP ratio in excess of 20 percent, and on the debt/export ratio for a country with an export/GDP ratio below 20 percent, to ensure that both constraints are satisfied.)

Of course, a country's vulnerability to capital outflow depends not just on the level of debt but also on the type of liability that is contracted. Foreign direct investment is the least vulnerable to sudden withdrawal. Portfolio equity investment has an important self-equilibrating property: A loss of confidence will lead to a decline in stock prices that will automatically serve to decrease the incentive for further withdrawals. Long-term bonds have the advantage that the principal can be liquidated only as the bonds mature. Bank loans have the advantage that it is relatively feasible to renegotiate the terms of the contract when the need arises. Nevertheless, both bonds (especially those with a short maturity) and bank loans expose countries to a significant risk of confronting a debt crisis, with consequences that the 1980s showed can be severe.

In view of these differences, is it appropriate to count the stock of non-debt foreign claims on the economy—notably foreign direct investment and foreign holdings of equity claims in domestic companies—on a par with debt itself? They too generate a need for foreign earnings so as to maintain debt service, so it would seem wrong to ignore such claims entirely. Perhaps the most reasonable procedure is to treat a dollar of a foreign nondebt claim as something less than a dollar's worth of debt, e.g., to give it a 50 percent weight. In any event, such figures can provide no more than a very rough guide as to how much borrowing is more than the economy can safely handle, a figure that will also vary with the proportion of the capital inflow that is being translated into investment in general and investment in tradables in particular.

Notes

The material in this chapter was originally presented in Prague at the June 1995 workshop on managing capital flows in Central and Eastern Europe.

1. The term "Dutch disease" was originally used to describe the difficulties encountered by manufacturing in the Netherlands following the development of natural gas on a large enough scale to prompt a major appreciation of the real exchange rate. It has since been used to refer to any situation in which a natural-resources boom, large amount of foreign aid, or capital inflows cause real appreciation that jeopardizes the prospects of manufacturing.

2. Note, however, that it has been argued by Ground and Bianchi (1988) that a resource boom is inherently temporary, because the rents that it generates will ultimately be bid away. This suggests that on some time scale the factors making for Dutch disease should always be considered as temporary. Nevertheless, if the resource boom or the capital inflow is expected to last for ten or twenty years, it would seem to make sense to adjust the balance of payments to increase absorption rather than to finance the inflow, *if* such an increase in absorption is indeed in the long-run interest of the country in question (see discussion in text).

3. There is no particular need for the individual project financed by foreign borrowing to generate foreign exchange, but it is of fundamental importance that the economy as a whole produce an adequate proportion of tradables to permit debt service to be maintained without throwing the economy into recession or straining the country's ability to borrow.

4. The term *fixed* should be interpreted in this context to include a crawling peg or other forms of managed rate.

5. This also applies to the interest rate that a central bank pays on bonds that it sells from its portfolio.

6. I am grateful to my colleague Jeffrey Frankel for supplying me with these figures.

7. Actually there is a seventh major country, Venezuela, but this is excluded from the following comparison because it has not experienced an excessive capital inflow in recent years. (It is still trying to pursue rather old-fashioned policies, including a Bretton Woods–style policy of holding a fixed exchange rate until being forced into a reluctant devaluation.)

8. A radically different conclusion would be suggested for Argentina if the WPI rather than the CPI were used as deflator, where the index would be a hypercompetitive 59 rather than 159. (It makes little difference for the other countries.) Anecdotal evidence suggests strongly that it is the CPI figure that should be treated as correct; the reason for the implausible WPI figure is not known.

9. A part of the explanation of recent Chilean policy would seem to be the recollection of its attempt to stop inflation by using the exchange rate as a nominal anchor from 1979 to 1982. That attempt was fed by a large capital inflow that financed a massive current account deficit, reaching some 14 percent of GDP in 1981—a policy rationalized

at the time by the argument that the fiscal accounts were in surplus and that private foreign borrowing could not create problems (an argument repeated in 1988 in the United Kingdom by Nigel Lawson). In the end, the currency had to be devalued and GDP fell by about 15 percent in a savage recession that also cut real wages as much as 35 percent. Chile adopted a radically different macroeconomic policy stance as it climbed out of that recession.

10. There were also other changes in exchange rate management, which had previously been based on a dollar peg that had crawled in order to offset the excess of inflation in Chile over that in the United States. These involved the introduction of discretionary intervention within the band and a switch to a basket peg.

11. As was done in some of the literature of the 1970s, e.g., Cline and Frank 1971 and Petersen 1977.

References

Calvo, Guillermo (1994). "The Management of Capital Flows: Domestic Policy and International Cooperation," in *International Monetary and Financial Issues for the 1990s,* volume IV (Geneva: UNCTAD).

Cline, William R., and Charles R. Frank (1971). "Measurement of Debt Servicing Capacity: An Application of Discriminant Analysis," *Journal of International Economics.*

Edwards, Sebastian (1993). *From Despair to Hope: Latin America and the Caribbean a Decade After the Debt Crisis.* Draft manuscript (Washington, DC: World Bank).

Ffrench-Davis, Ricardo, Daniel Titelman, and Andras Uthoff (1994). *International Competitiveness and the Macroeconomics of Capital Account Opening.* ECLAC Working Paper no. 29 (Santiago: ECLAC).

Fischer, Bernhard, and Helmut Reisen (1992). *Towards Capital Account Convertibility.* Paris: OECD Development Centre Policy Brief no. 4 (TK: OECD).

Ground, Richard L., and Andrés Bianchi (1988). "The Economic Development of Latin America," in *A Comparative Study on Economic Development Between Asia and Latin America,* ed. A. Bianchi and T. Nohara (Tokyo: Institute of Developing Economies).

Group of Thirty (1994). *Latin American Capital Flows: Living with Volatility.* Study group report (Washington: Group of Thirty).

Labán, Raúl, and Felipe Larraín (1993). "Can A Liberalisation of Capital Outflows Increase Net Capital Inflows?" Documento de Trabajo no. 155 (Santiago: PUC).

Petersen, H.J. (1977). "Debt Crisis of Developing Countries: A Pragmatic Approach to an Early Warning System," *Konjunkturpolitik.*

Urrutia, Miguel (1994). "Colombia," in *The Political Economy of Policy Reform,* ed. J. Williamson (Washington: Institute for International Economics).

F32 P33
879

3

The Sustainability of Foreign Capital Flows into Central and Eastern Europe

An Analysis of Indicators of Instability of Capital Flows

Zdeněk Drábek

The last few years have witnessed a massive inflow of foreign capital into the Czech Republic, Hungary, and Poland. The inflow has paralleled to some extent similar capital flows into other emerging markets, and the obvious question, therefore, is whether the capital flows into these countries of Central and Eastern Europe (CEECs) are sustainable. The question is obviously very important because foreign capital can and should play a major role in financing the transformation of the CEECs into market economies and in providing modern technology and know-how. This question is becoming particularly important at the present time, which some writers see as a period of rising scarcity of global capital that is available for investment (Reisen 1995).

The question of sustainability of foreign capital flows has been recently examined in a number of studies (Dehesa 1994, Dadush et al. 1994, Hernandez and Rudolph 1995, Akyüz and Cornford 1994, and others). None of these studies, however, deals specifically with countries in transition, and to the extent that such countries are covered, the treatment is aggregate rather than country-specific. The purpose of this paper is, therefore, to assess the sustainability of the rapid inflow of foreign capital into three CEECs—the Czech Republic, Hungary, and Poland. At the time of writing this chapter, Slovakia was not the subject of much interest to foreign investors, but is also included here. These countries have been generally considered to be the "big three"—the three most attractive countries in the region of the former CMEA, which should make them interesting as case studies for future expansion of foreign capital into other economies in transition.[1]

In this respect, it is important that governments know or at least are warned in advance that the supply of foreign capital may dry up. In general, there are four main reasons why it is important for governments to be able to detect early in the process any indications of potential difficulties. First, historical experience, particularly the recent capital flight from Mexico, teaches that massive capital inflows may be dramatically reversed, so the sustainability of capital inflows is not at all self-evident. Second, the stability of economic policies may be jeopardized as a result of the reversal of capital flows. For example, governments may find it much more difficult to maintain liberal trade policies in the presence of capital flight. Moreover, the reversal of economic policies provoked by capital flight may in turn further discourage capital inflows. Third, it is sometimes assumed that capital inflows sufficient to finance current account deficits will make domestic policies and foreign capital inflows sustainable in the future. This implicitly further assumes that the size of the current account deficit can be infinitely large and that it is the sole determinant of instability of capital inflows. Finally, it is also sometimes assumed that governments do not need to prepare in any way for shifts in capital flow. This is a dangerous proposition, as is now increasingly recognized. In real life, most governments will normally need and want some indicators of potential trouble—"warning signals."

The purpose of this paper is to examine the sustainability of capital flows into CEECs. This will be done by proposing and analyzing various indicators of potential instability of capital flows. It is clear that policy makers have to operate with a set of indicators that would provide the "warning signals" noted above. With the rising concerns about instability of capital flows, various indicators have recently been proposed by several writers, such as Williamson (1999), Goldstein (1996), Griffith-Jones (1996), and Milesi-Fereti and Razin (1996). These indicators can be methodologically divided into two groups: characteristics of capital flows and determinants of capital flows. But here the agreement among experts usually ends about which of these indicators should be used. While there is a broad similarity in their approaches, the actual techniques and indicators used are not identical. For these reasons, this chapter will also identify the main differences in the individual approaches and provide explanations why the differences exist.

The chapter consists of three parts. The first part contains a brief methodological discussion of various symptoms of potential instability of foreign capital inflows. Methodologically, the symptoms are divided into two groups—domestic economic conditions and characteristics of foreign capital inflow. The main purpose of this part is to identify the most relevant domestic elements of potential instability of foreign capital inflows in the CEECs. The second part begins with a brief description of data problems. The objective of this part of the chapter is, however, an examination of the main characteristics of foreign capital inflows in the three Central and East European countries. Domestic fundamentals together with an important structural constraint are analyzed in the third part in order to see whether we can identify any domestic economic symptoms of instability. Whether the symptoms are temporary phenomena or whether they will take time to disappear will crucially depend on the efficiency of markets and on the policies pursued by the countries concerned. The chapter ends with a short section containing conclusions and some policy recommendations.

A Typology of Symptoms of Instability of Foreign Capital Flows

Limitations of Economic Theory

The sustainability of foreign capital inflows depends on the determinants of foreign investments, and thus on the stability of these determinants. The determinants can be, in turn, grouped into external and internal factors. This paper deals only with internal factors, that is, with the conditions prevailing in the country receiving foreign investment. This separation is not unusual even though most relevant studies deal with the supply side—as, for example, Graham 1995, which discusses the role of multilateral investment rules, or Dryer et al. 1995, which discusses the role of policies in the countries in which foreign investment originates.

Theoretically, the concentration on internal factors may seem to be a serious omission in the analysis of sustainability of foreign investment. It has been argued by Griffith-Jones and Papageorgiou (1993), for example, that portfolio capital flows are strongly affected by factors completely outside the policy considerations in the recipient country. In addition to the role of monetary policies in the capital-supplying countries, discussed further below, the most important external factor of portfolio flows is the psychology of investors. As we have recently seen in the case of the Mexican and Asian crises, the supply of foreign capital to different countries can be adversely determined by the "contagion effect" as foreign investors withdraw their investment not only from the economy in crisis but also other, stronger countries. The point is also supported by important empirical evidence (e.g., Calvo 1994, Fernandez-Arias and Spiegel 1994, and Dooley et al. 1994), even though this is now challenged in other empirical studies (Hernandez and Rudolph 1995). Most writers agree that the crucial determinant of foreign portfolio capital flows is the level of interest rates. In particular, the sensitivity of short-term portfolio capital flows is strongly influenced by differences in the level of interest in the home (capital-supplying) and host (capital-receiving) countries. The important role of interest rates in the home countries has presumably been the main reason why most analyses so far (Dadush et al. 1994, in addition to those already mentioned above) have focused on the external factors.

However, recent empirical studies have suggested that external factors account for only about 30 to 50 percent of the fluctuations in foreign capital movements.[2] A similar conclusion is reached by Hernandez and Rudolph (1995), who find that internal factors are crucial in attracting foreign capital. In addition, domestic conditions are obviously important for determining the level of domestic interest rates, which strongly depend on domestic factors in the absence of perfect capital mobility. Overall macroeconomic conditions are, therefore, very important, and affect even portfolio capital flows. Furthermore, the domestic conditions of host countries are also important in determining the investment decisions of portfolio managers. Here again there are at least three reasons to make the point. First, investment decisions of portfolio managers are heavily influenced by the ratings issued by ratings agencies. Second, both the IMF and the World Bank as well as other regional banks put a considerable emphasis on economic fundamentals for their own lending activities. Since these institutions often act as a catalyst to private capital, it follows that their assessment of economic conditions in a particular country is very important to attract foreign investment. Last but not least, foreign firms themselves are very likely to assess the economic conditions in the host countries before investing.

The determination of foreign direct investment (FDI) has been approached in the literature rather differently. Most students of FDI would probably argue that the determinants of FDI are different from those of portfolio capital flows in spite of the fact that in theory, the crucial role again should be played by interest rates. In fact, however, many markets for foreign capital have historically been highly restricted and therefore imperfect. For this reason, the link between interest rates and return on foreign direct investment has been found to be very tenuous.[3]

While many internal factors can affect foreign investments, economic theory provides rather limited guidance on the role of these factors. In general, explanations of capital flows and, in particular, those of foreign direct investment are clouded by many difficulties. First, as noted above, the determinants of foreign direct investment are different from those of portfolio foreign investment. Discussion of foreign capital flows must therefore recognize this distinction and treat these two types of foreign capital differently. Second, there are different theories.[4] Starting with Dunning (1958), a number of writers have identified the ability of multinational corporations to transfer technologies and other intangible assets as the main factor in foreign direct investment abroad. Vernon (1966) stressed the importance of "new product technology" as a determinant of international trade and foreign direct investment. Writers such as Buckley and Casson (1976) have provided yet another stream of theoretical arguments, suggesting that there are economies to be realized by internalizing within a single firm production and marketing functions. Third, because empirical evidence is also limited, the explanatory power of some theories has turned out to be very limited.[5] As a result, it is virtually impossible to generalize; most studies suggest that country-specific conditions are most important. Fourth, the behavior of foreign direct investment can change over time. For example, external debt and sovereign risk have been identified as major impediments to LDCs' attractiveness to FDI in the past.[6] However, recent experience with Mexico, Brazil, and Argentina all but contradicts this argument. A positive credit rating, even from reputable institutions, is clearly not sufficient to prevent crises.[7]

In addition, there is a strong presumption that official development assistance should not be treated under the same heading of capital flows as, say, portfolio investment. It could be argued that the determinants of official capital inflows, which are quite important in a number of developing and transition countries, are determined differently than private portfolio investment. Furthermore, no economic theory has so far attempted to explain surges in foreign capital flows. For example, the rapid growth in foreign capital inflows at the end of the 1970s and again at the end of the 1980s took most economists by surprise. The economic literature has even today very little to say about the surges. Needless to say, however, there have been a number of attempts to explain the surges on the basis of "stylized facts," such as Ffrench-Davis and Griffith-Jones 1995 and IMF 1995c.

The Basic Questions

For the reasons noted above, analysts usually have to adopt a pragmatic approach. In analyzing the host countries' domestic factors of foreign capital flows, the first important question is which domestic conditions should be considered. In theory, there are three internal economic conditions we should examine. First, according to the standard argument, macroeconomic balances—that is, the conditions that are often identified as the "economic fundamentals"—must be "right" in order to attract foreign investments. Normally, the role of macroeconomic conditions in determining inflow of foreign capital is dominant.[8] Second are structural conditions, such as poorly developed financial sectors that may not be able to efficiently absorb the rising flows of foreign capital.[9] An inefficient and/or poorly developed financial sector is arguably the most serious constraint on capital inflows. Finally, economic policies must be such that they convince foreign investors there is a certain degree of stability of economic conditions, and that these conditions will be maintained within the time horizon of the investor. In other words, the policies should be stable, transparent, predictable, and credible. Examples may include privatization and a foreign investment legislation but also credible macroeconomic policies.[10]

In the short run, domestic economic growth can probably continue even in the presence of low savings and heavy external debt. This is because of better utilization of existing resources and higher yields on new investments as the economy begins to recover. In the medium and long run, however, the story could change. A low and/or declining rate of domestic savings is likely to push down the rate of domestic investment and hence economic growth. As shown by Feldstein and Harioka (1980) and more recently by Reisen (1995), domestic investment tends to closely match domestic savings in the long run.[11] At the same time, countries' future ability to service their rising debt will depend on the rates of return to investments that are undertaken at present. The crucial question is, therefore, how the borrowed resources are used—for investment or consumption, and if for investment, whether they are used effectively (see below). Moreover, the countries' ability to service their debt will depend on the growth of their exports. Prudent policy should, therefore, also consider savings behavior, the efficiency of investment, and export performance as additional indicators of potential country risk. We will not be able to analyze all the indicators, but we shall at least address some major issues examining the savings-investment balance and the performance of exports.

The next important question is, therefore, which economic fundamentals and other economic conditions are relevant. For reasons related to ambiguities in the determinants of foreign capital flows, noted above, the answer is not at all straightforward. The standard approach is to consider the following macroeconomic issues: (a) *Inflation and inflationary pressures.* An analysis of inflationary pressures is important. This is particularly so in the CEECs because inflation had been suppressed for several decades in these countries, and the subsequent price liberalization has, therefore, released forces that are not easily predictable. In addition, inflationary pressures influence the extent to which existing exchange rates can be sustained; they provide signals about the country's competitiveness; and they have an effect on national savings and investment. (b) *The level and structure of external debt.* This is perhaps the most important indicator of the country's creditworthiness. The higher the external debt, *ceteris paribus,* the greater the difficulties in servicing the existing debt obligations. Also, the shorter the maturity of the debt, the more difficult it is to service it. At the same time, the faster the growth of GDP, the better the country's ability to service its debt. (c) *The balance between (national) savings and (domestic) investment.* High national savings rates indicate the country's ability to support a high level of domestic investment. A relatively low level of national savings increases dependence on foreign savings to finance domestic investment and increases the country's vulnerability to capital movements. (d) *Stability of comparative advantages.* An unstable pattern of comparative advantages will discourage long-term investors and in extreme cases may prevent any foreign direct investments. All these economic variables are usually the important elements in the analysis of country risk and a country's creditworthiness.

Next, one should also decide what other economic conditions related to efficiency of markets and domestic policies in the host countries should be considered. There are many examples of microeconomic and structural policies that could potentially become or are already serious impediments for growth in the CEEC region. For example, none of the countries in the region has so far successfully addressed the problems of agriculture. There are also serious infrastructural constraints that inhibit future growth. Examples include, again in all countries, outdated and poorly targeted transport systems, high energy consumption and environmental concerns about existing energy uses and future energy investments, and a highly inadequate telecommunications network. The scope and speed of privatization will be, of course, important in attracting foreign capital. But, arguably, the most serious and, in terms of foreign capital, most urgent issue is the ongoing process of financial sector liberalization and the establishment of those financial industries that have been grossly neglected under central planning. An efficient, sufficiently large, and well-regulated financial sector is *conditio sine qua non* not only to attract foreign capital but also to finance modern and effective market institutions such as those discussed above.[12]

Credible economic policies represent another crucial element of stability of capital flows. For example, an overvalued exchange rate is unlikely to be sustainable over a long period of time in the light of its adverse impact on the country's competitiveness. A fixed exchange rate may also not be sustainable in the presence of higher domestic inflation relative to inflation abroad. Incomes policies may be the origin of strong inflationary pressures as well. Government budgetary policies may also be inflationary and generate strong biases against the private sector. These are examples of macroeconomic policies, but government may also pursue poor policies on a microeconomic level, such as privatization, social policies, regional policies, and others.

While a complete analysis of the sustainability problem should also include a discussion of economic policies, such a discussion is too lengthy in the context of one paper. This is partly because of the institutional diversity of the countries concerned. I have, therefore, decided to limit the present discussion in this chapter to macroeconomic issues. Policy issues arising from capital inflows into the region will be discussed in a separate paper.

Indicators of Symptoms of Instability of Capital Flows in the CEECs

Following the discussion in the previous section, we shall translate the symptoms of instability into specific indicators. The procedures will be slightly different but complementary to the methodology adopted recently by Milesi-Fereti and Razin (1996) and Griffith-Jones (1996). Different writers may emphasize different indicators, but the interesting point is that even different methodologies often lead to the same conclusions.

It is customary to identify the symptoms of instability in terms of the following characteristics of foreign capital flows. (i) *The level of foreign capital inflows.* The level of such inflows may be excessive, for example, in terms of the host country's overall money stock or GDP. Since foreign capital adds to the host country's overall level of external indebtedness, one should also relate the foreign capital inflows to the level and structure of external debt. (ii) *Distribution between direct and portfolio foreign capital.* The distinction between direct and portfolio foreign capital is very important. Foreign direct investment typically refers to multinational corporations' long-term strategies and reflect decisions that are unlikely to be reversed in the short run. Portfolio investments are, by contrast, more likely to be unstable. They are typically made to maximize returns during relatively short periods during which attractive conditions prevail. They are typically also much more liquid than foreign direct investment, which further facilitates their movements across frontiers. (iii) *Structure of foreign direct investment.* This may also make a difference for the stability of capital flows. Here it may be useful to distinguish between "greenfield" investment and investments into equity. The difference lies in the commitment to invest into physical capital in the case of the former. The latter may not involve any such investment, and as a result may be more liquid. (iv) *Structure of portfolio investment.* The maturities of portfolio investment may vary widely and with them, therefore, the ability of foreign investors to liquidate their investments in the short run (e.g., Chuhan et al. 1996). (v) *Investors' base.* If this is narrow, the chances of instability of capital flows increase.

In addition to the characteristics of capital flows, we can identify a number of other important macroeconomic indicators that may serve to signal potential problems for future capital flows: the *consumer price index* as an indicator of inflation, combined with an analysis of underlying forces of inflation—productivity-adjusted growth of wages and the rates of seigniorage as an indicator of expansionary monetary policies; examination of the *external debt liabilities* of each country as well as of the debt burden as measured in terms of the size of international reserves and the level of exports; changes in the balance between national savings and domestic investment and their levels, with particular attention being paid to government savings and to savings of the private sector; and various indicators to characterize the country's comparative advantage, including *relative wages* and the speed with which they are changing.

The Level and Structure of Capital Inflows in the CEECs

Data Problems

Comparative analysis is difficult for a variety of reasons.[13] Definitional and data problems are particularly serious. Foreign direct investments are often recorded on both "disbursement" and "commitment" bases, with the former identifying the actual money disbursements and the latter referring to commitments made for future disbursements. State foreign promotion agencies usually report the latter, while central banks provide statistics on the former. The differences between the series are typically large. While the central bank figures may often be more useful, they are not always provided in the detail needed for the analysis of the impact of capital on domestic beneficiaries. The definition of direct and portfolio investments and that of short- and long-term capital may also differ from country to country—unless the country concerned adheres to established standards, such as those of the IMF or the OECD.

This comment leads to the second general problem, which is the lack of sufficiently detailed data. Studies of the impact of foreign capital, for example, must take into account the effect of foreign investment on final users. However, data on foreign investment by end use are normally not available or are not provided in sufficient detail. In addition, money is fungible. As a result, it is extremely difficult to do an efficiency analysis of project finance. Geographical distributions of sources of bonds as well as of their purchasers are also not normally available, which seriously affects comparative analysis of bond issues as well as the analysis of risk distribution. Even the Czech Republic, which has a relatively good record of providing statistics on foreign capital, does not publish sufficiently detailed data on the structure of debt instruments and foreign direct investments, the geographical distribution of portfolio flows, or the end use of foreign capital. A part of the problem is that statistical authorities do not typically collect information on geographical origin of foreign capital except in the case of foreign direct investment. Moreover, even if the figures were available, their interpretation would not be straightforward since the actual origin of capital supplied by portfolio funds may not be known.

The third problem is the general lack of statistics on portfolio investments in the CEECs. Only the Czech Republic regularly provides official figures (ECE 1995, p. 152). The lack of statistics is a particularly serious problem in the case of Poland. As we shall see further below, the Polish authorities have reported a fairly large inflow of so-called inward portfolio investment in 1995 even though a significant portion of this inflow represented earnings of Polish exporters in the border trade that were converted into zlotys in the foreign exchange offices. Strictly speaking, such transactions would not normally qualify as portfolio investment, but they are recorded as such for statistical purposes. Nevertheless, even Poland has been experiencing a significant inflow of foreign capital since the second half of 1995.

The fourth problem is the lack of comparability of data between countries. This follows to some extent from what has been already said. But additional problems exist. For example, the geographical composition of foreign direct investment reported by Poland includes "multinational corporations" as one item on the list of "countries." The procedure is quite clearly unusual even though one can understand the motivation of the statistical authorities for this procedure.

The Level and Structure of Foreign Capital in the CEECs

A crucial question about capital inflows is whether the inflows (1) do not exhibit certain characteristics that could make them highly unstable and sensitive to changes in expectations or in economic fundamentals, (2) effectively contribute to the country's competitiveness, and (3) support future investment rather than consumption. As noted above, there is no general agreement about all the characteristics.[14] Nevertheless, most writers will probably agree, with certain caveats, that the characteristics of potentially unstable foreign capital may include (a) a large share in short-term investments, and (b) a low share of foreign direct investments. Moreover, (c) the so-called greenfield investments are usually preferable as more stable than equity (direct) investments, which can exit relatively fast.

The level of foreign investment in some of the CEECs is already at a level that could turn out to be dangerously high. Let us begin with an assessment of the level of foreign capital inflows on a comparative basis.

The country in the region with by far the largest gross inflow of foreign capital has been Hungary (Table 3.1). During the period 1990–95, Hungary received a cumulative amount of foreign capital amounting to about U.S. $41 billion on a gross basis. In 1995 alone, the total amount of gross foreign capital inflows amounted to more than U.S. $13 billion. Next in line was the Czech Republic. The comparable figure for 1994 was almost U.S. $4 billion, and the preliminary figure for 1995 was almost U.S. $8 billion. In Slovakia, net capital inflows were less than U.S. $1 billion in 1995, or about one-eighth of the corresponding Czech figure. Gross capital inflows for Poland are also not available, but the corresponding net figure for 1995 was almost U.S. $3 billion.

An alternative way of comparing the level of capital inflows is on the basis of *net* figures, after allowing for capital outflows. Here the picture is radically different. The largest capital inflows recently have been in the Czech Republic (U.S. $8.2 billion in 1995), which exceeded those of Hungary (U.S. $7 billion). The large difference between the gross and net figures in Hungary is due to large amounts of debt service payments.[15] Net capital inflows to Poland were negative until 1994, mainly due to large debt service obligations, but 1994 represented a major turnaround in Poland. Net capital outflows turned into inflows of U.S. $1.2 billion in 1994, and the figure reached almost U.S. $3 billion in 1995, as noted above. Net capital inflows to Slovakia have been marginal, partly because of the fairly low figure for gross inflows and partly because of the country's debt service obligations.

Another way of assessing the level is to calculate the share of foreign investment in domestic output (GDP), domestic savings, gross domestic capital formation, money supply, or GDP. These indicators show quite clearly that the shares are very high in the Czech Republic, Hungary, and Slovakia and remain relatively lower in Poland. For example, the share of foreign direct investment in GDP in the Czech Republic is probably comparable to the corresponding share in Brazil, another country with a significant exposure to foreign capital and where the share of foreign investment was estimated at 5 percent. This can be seen from Table 3.3, which reproduces recent estimates made by the EBRD. The figures have been calculated on the basis of the current exchange rate rather than purchasing power parities (PPP). Due to large differences between both rates, the latter would show considerably higher shares in GDP than those calculated from current exchange rates. Unfortunately, the data have been estimated only for FDI excluding portfolio capital. If we include portfolio capital, the share net total foreign capital in GDP would amount in the Czech Republic in 1995 to 17.5 percent in current prices. The corresponding number for Hungary is also quite high—16 percent. In contrast, the corresponding shares in Poland and Slovakia were small—1.3 percent and 5.2 percent, respectively (Table 3.2).

The role of foreign money is even more pronounced in the monetary area. The numbers are particularly high in the Czech Republic when we measure the exposure to foreign capital as the share of foreign capital in domestic savings and money supply, but the importance of foreign capital both as a contribution to domestic savings and as the source of money supply was high in the other countries. As the figures in Table 3.2 demonstrate, the foreign component of domestic money stock was growing considerably faster than total money supply. The pattern became particularly pronounced in 1995. As we shall see further below, the growth of money supply in the Czech Republic was generated in 1995 primarily by the growth of foreign assets, while the growth of aggregate domestic credit amounted to only about 5 percent, well below the growth of net foreign assets or the growth of nominal GDP (about 17 percent). The contribution of foreign capital to total savings has been equally impressive even though the actual numbers must be treated with extreme caution in view of the well-known difficulties in measuring savings and making international comparisons. In the Czech Republic, for example, foreign capital accounted for almost 80 percent of national savings in 1995. The comparable figure in Hungary was even higher—more than 90 percent.

Direct Versus Portfolio Foreign Investments

Another indication of the potential instability of foreign capital flows may be a heavy dependence on portfolio rather than foreign direct investment. The distinction between direct and portfolio investments is crucial. There are also strong reasons to believe that the effects of foreign direct investment (FDI) on employment and wages are much stronger than those of trade.[16] FDI is an important vehicle for the transfer of technology, contributing relatively more to growth than domestic investment (Borensztein et al. 1995). In addition, whatever the technology gains through foreign direct investments, these are usually captured by joint ventures.[17] This implies that FDI plays a highly stabilizing and growth-conducive role. FDI tends to be long-term and, therefore, less volatile. In addition, FDI is non-debt-creating, hence avoiding the dangers and pressures of debt service.

Table 3.1

CEECs: Foreign Capital Inflows, 1990–1995 (millions of U.S. $)

	1990	1991	1992	1993	1994	1995
Former CSFR[a]						
Total capital inflows (gross)	326	47	–6	—	—	—
Total capital inflows (net)	—	592	947	—	—	—
FDI	—	—	—	—	—	—
Portfolio	—	—	—	—	—	—
Other medium- and long-term capital	899	1,732	321	—	—	—
Short-term capital	–573	–2,277	–1,274	—	—	—
Czech Rep.[a,j]						
Total capital inflows (gross)[d]	—	—	2,200	3,000	3,900	7,700
Total capital inflows (net)	—	—	2[c]	3,025	3,371	8,226
FDI	—	—	983[c]	552	749	2,526
Portfolio	—	—	–26[c]	1,601	855	1,362
Other medium- and long-term capital	—	—	320[c]	816	1,109	3,367
Short-term capital	—	—	–1,275[c]	56	659	971
Slovakia[e]						
Total capital inflows (gross)	—	—	—	—	—	—
Total capital inflows (net)	—	—	–85	262	714	911
FDI	—	—	100	–373[f]	250	395
Portfolio	—	—	—	—	—	—
Other medium- and long-term capital	—	—	251	562	659	571
Short-term capital	—	—	–436	73	–195	–55
Hungary[a]						
Total capital inflows (gross)[b]	1,966	4,918	3,680	9,186	7,535	13,070
Total capital inflows (net)	–689	2,453	437	6,091	3,255	7,012

FDI	311	1,459	1,471	2,328	1,097	4,410
Portfolio	–	–	–	–	–	–
Other medium- and long-term capital	–107	1,611	–1,039	3,304	1,198	1,191
Short-term capital	–893	–617	5	459	960	1,411
Poland						
Total capital inflows (gross)	–6,678[g]	–8,515[h]	–1,255[h]	–999[h]	1,196[h]	2,957[hi]
Total capital inflows (net)						
FDI	–	117	284	580	542	900[h]
Portfolio	–	–	–	–	–	–
Other medium- and long-term capital	–4,153	–6,059	–292	–471	31	465[i]
Short-term capital	–2,525	–2,573	–1,247	–1,108	623	1,592[i]

Sources: Economic Bulletin for Europe of the United Nations Economic Commission for Europe (UNECE); Czech National Bank Monthly Bulletin; Balance of Payments Report on Slovakia, Geneva: WTO, 1996; National Bank of Hungary Monthly Report; Balance of Payments Report on Poland, Geneva: WTO, 1996.

Notes: [a] In convertible currencies only.

[b] Calculated by Gáspár (1996).

[c] Estimated as the share of the Czech Republic in the former CSFR.

[d] Calculated by Klacek (1996).

[e] Including transactions with the Czech Republic.

[f] Including U.S. $529 million of Slovak shares in Czech companies acquired through the "first wave" of voucher privatization in the former CSFR. The counterpart is presented as a capital transfer.

[g] Foreign currency earnings generated through border trade are defined as "short-term" capital flows.

[h] Excluding debt relief, amounting to U.S. $4,382 million in 1991, U.S. $202 million in 1992, U.S. $7,900 million in 1994, and U.S. $1,592 million in 1995.

[i] Estimates.

[j] Excluding transactions with Slovakia. Total capital flows (net) between the Czech Republic and Slovakia were U.S. $2,737 million in 1993, U.S. $3,122 million in 1994, and U.S. $8,275 million in 1995.

Table 3.2

CEECs: Foreign Capital, Domestic Savings, and Money Supply, 1994–1995

		Czech Rep.	Hungary	Poland	Slovakia
I. Foreign Capital (in million U.S. $)					
	1995	8,226	7,012	2,957	911
	1994	3,371	3,255	1,196	714
II. Gross National Savings and Money Supply (in billion local currency)					
Gross national savings	1995	260,580	984,500[a]	–	–
	1994	208,538	539,524	37,030	–
M1	Dec. 1995	431,083	887,400[b]	37,439	148,400
	Dec. 1994	403,973	895,600	27,450	123,820
	Dec. 1993	268,969	811,700	19,646	116,615
M2	Dec. 1995	1,085,662	2,355,400	104,352	356,900
	Dec. 1994	839,623	1,994,900	77,302	298,272
	Dec. 1993	697,319	1,758,600	55,924	263,968
Exchange Rate (local currency/U.S.$):	1995	26.6	125.7	2.424	29.7
	1994	28.8	105.1	2.273	32.0
III. Memorandum (percent)					
Foreign capital/savings					
	1995	84.0	89.5	–	–
	1994	46.6	63.4	7.3	–
Foreign capital /Δ savings					
	1995	420.5	198.1	–	–
	1994	394.7	238.8	19.7	–
Foreign capital/M1					
	1995	50.8	99.3	19.1	18.2
	1994	24.0	38.2	9.9	18.5
Foreign capital/Δ M1					
	1995	807.1	410.3	71.8	110.1
	1994	71.9	407.7	34.8	317.1
Foreign capital/M2					
	1995	20.2	37.4	6.9	7.6
	1994	11.6	17.1	3.5	7.7
Foreign capital/Δ M2					
	1995	88.9	244.5	26.5	46.1
	1994	68.2	144.8	12.7	51.6
Foreign capital/GDP					
	1995	17.5	16.0	2.4	5.2
	1994	9.4	7.9	1.3	5.2

Source: IMF, *International Financial Statistics1996*, Table 1.
[a]Estimate from Gáspár (1996).
[b]End of the third quarter figures.

As Table 3.1 shows, significant differences exist among the CEECs with regard to the structure of foreign capital flows. In Hungary, the majority of foreign capital has come in the form of FDI. In contrast, the majority of foreign capital in the Czech Republic has been in the form of portfolio investment and foreign borrowing as "other medium- and long-term capital." In Poland there has been a significant surge in both direct and portfolio foreign capital since 1994, with the latter tending to exceed the amount of FDI. In Slovakia, portfolio foreign investment is somewhat larger than FDI, but the numbers are much smaller. Moreover, the growth of FDI has been very unstable, with the amounts changing quite significantly from year to year.

Structure of FDI

FDI is normally considered desirable foreign capital in terms of its stability characteristics. However, one important distinction is that FDI may include either greenfield investment or investment linked to acquisitions of existing assets (e.g., via privatization). The point is that acquisition of equity in excess of a certain percentage, depending on specific legislative conditions in a given country, will be classified as FDI. The distinction could be important in that equity investments tend to be much more liquid than investments in factories or other physical assets.

Unfortunately, the data distinguishing between greenfield and equity FDI are not readily available for the countries concerned. We would venture to suggest, however, that most FDI in Hungary, Poland, and Slovakia has involved acquisition of portfolio investments rather than construction of new physical assets, or "greenfield." The pattern is probably the same in the Czech Republic.

The country in which FDI has played the most important role is Hungary, as can be seen from Table 3.1. But Hungary has been an attractive country for foreign investment even on a larger scale, and even compared to FDI in countries outside the region. This can be seen from comparisons of FDI as a share in GDP and FDI per capita (Table 3.3). The Hungary per capita FDI figures are by far the highest in the region—U.S. $432 in 1995 compared to the second-ranking Czech Republic, where the comparable figure stood at U.S. $243 in the same year. Hungary's per capita figures are also far above the comparable figures in all other transition economies. The same conclusion can be reached from the comparison of the share of FDI in GDP, which has been calculated by the EBRD both in current dollars and in terms of purchasing power parity. The share stood in Hungary at 3.8 percent in 1993, and the comparable figure using the PPP-based denominator was almost double that—6 percent. These are large figures, and considering

44

Table 3.3

Foreign Direct Investment in Eastern Europe, the Baltics and the CIS, 1989–1995

	FDI inflows (U.S. $ millions)		Cumulative FDI inflows 1989–1995	Percentage of cumulative FDI	FDI inflows per capita		Ratio of FDI to GDP[a] 1995
	1994	1995			1989–1995	1995	1995
Eastern Europe							
Albania	53	70	200	0.7	63	22	3.5
Bulgaria	105	100	302	1.0	36	12	0.8
Croatia	98	68	251	0.8	53	14	0.4
Czech Republic	850	2,500	5,481	18.2	532	243	5.6
FYR Macedonia	24	14	38	0.1	18	7	0.3
Hungary	1,146	4,453	11,466	38.0	1,113	432	10.2
Poland	542	900	2,423	8.0	63	23	0.7
Romania	341	367	879	2.9	39	16	1.0
Slovak Republic	187	180	623	2.1	117	34	1.1
Slovenia	88	150	505	1.7	253	75	0.8
Total/Average	*3,434*	*8,802*	*22,168*	*73.4*	*229*	*88*	*2.4*
The Baltics							
Estonia	214	204	637	2.1	413	132	5.8
Latvia	155	160	409	1.4	164	64	3.5
Lithuania	60	55	228	0.8	61	15	0.8
Total/Average	*429*	*419*	*1,274*	*4.2*	*213*	*70*	*3.4*

The CIS

Armenia	3	19	22	0.1	6	5	1.4
Azerbaijan	50	206	276	0.9	37	28	11.7
Belarus	10	7	85	0.3	8	1	n.a.
Georgia	8	6	92	0.3	17	1	n.a.
Kazakhstan	635	723	1,831	6.1	110	43	3.8
Kyrgyzstan	45	88	143	0.5	32	20	5.5
Moldova	18	63	95	0.3	22	15	3.5
Russia	1,000	1,500	3,100	10.3	21	10	0.4
Tajikistan	12	13	29	0.1	5	2	n.a.
Turkmenistan	100	100	215	0.7	54	25	10.6
Ukraine	91	120	581	1.9	11	2	0.4
Uzbekistan	85	120	287	1.0	13	5	1.5
Total/Average	*2,057*	*2,965*	*6,756*	*22.4*	*24*	*10*	*0.6*
Total/Average	5,920	12,186	30,198	100.0	76	30	1.5

Source: EBRD 1996.

Note: [a]Nominal GDP figures for Tajikistan and Turkmenistan in 1995 were set equal in per capita terms to the 1994 observation for Kazakhstan.

that the FDI growth further accelerated in 1994–95, the important role of FDI on the macro level is quite evident.

Portfolio Foreign Investment: Short Versus Long Maturities

As mentioned above, the vulnerability of countries to foreign capital increases with a rising share of short-term debt and/or portfolio capital in the total. The explanation is based on the rationale that short-term investors have a better possibility of exit than those who commit their resources for a longer period of time. Even though the empirical evidence is not entirely straightforward, I shall accept the widely held belief that short-term capital is indeed more unstable.[18]

The exposure to short-term capital can be analyzed with the help of data showing the term structure of the countries' liabilities. We shall discuss these in more detail later; here it may suffice to refer to Table 3.4, which shows the term structure of the country's foreign liabilities. In addition, using Table 3.1, it is clear that short-term foreign investment has become very important in the Czech Republic and Poland. In the Czech Republic, the share increased from 25.4 percent in 1992 to 30.5 percent in 1995 (Table 3.4). This means, therefore, that not only does the Czech Republic get a relatively high proportion of foreign investment in the form of potentially unstable portfolio investment, but a large proportion of that portfolio investment and other forms of indirect investment is short-term. On the other hand, the positive feature of changes in external liabilities is the fact that the share of short-term capital in total outstanding debt has been recently stabilized and, according to preliminary reports, even fell in 1996.

The picture is somewhat different in the other three countries (Table 3.4). The short-term liabilities have been either falling (Poland, primarily due to debt arrangements with external creditors) or stable (Hungary and Slovakia). More important, the share of short-term debt in total outstanding debt has been falling in all three countries, and it is the highest in Slovakia—more than 22 percent. The main reason for the relatively low share of short-term debt in Poland and Slovakia has been the restricted access to private capital markets and their heavy borrowing from official creditors or to private creditors who primarily provide long-term funds against guarantees from the government. Poland, in particular, has until recently been able to tap only the resources of multilateral and bilateral official creditors (almost 80 percent of the total external debt—Table 3.5C). The dominant share in total long-term debt was owed to bilateral official creditors, while multilateral creditors accounted for about 5 percent of total long-term debt in 1994. In contrast, Hungary's exposure to bilateral official

Table 3.4

CEECs: Maturity Structure of External Debt (millions of U.S. $)

	1990	1991	1992	1993	1994	1995	Indices (Total = 100)	
							1994	1995
Czech Rep.								
Gross external debt	6,371	7,211	7,082	8,496	10,694	16,549	167.9	259.8
Short-term	2,400	2,143	1,798	2,002	2,888	5,045	120.3	210.2
Medium- and long-term	3,971	5,068	5,284	6,494	7,806	11,504	196.6	289.7
Share of short-term in gross external debt (%)	37.7	29.7	25.4	23.6	27.0	30.5	–	–
Hungary								
Gross external debt	21,270	22,658	21,438	24,560	28,521	31,655	134.1	148.8
Short-term	2,941	2,177	2,286	2,005	2,397	3,203	81.5	108.9
Medium- and long-term	18,329	20,481	19,152	22,555	26,124	28,453	142.5	155.2
Share of short-term in gross external debt (%)	13.8	9.6	10.7	8.2	8.4	10.1	–	–
Poland								
Gross external debt	49,163	53,585	48,649	45,328	42,160	43,900	85.8	89.3
Short-term	9,595	7,566	4,532	2,656	845	–	8.8	–
Medium- and long-term	39,568	46,019	44,117	42,672	41,315	–	104.4	–
Share of short-term in gross external debt (%)	19.5	14.1	9.3	5.9	2.0	–	–	–
Slovakia								
Gross external debt	1,992	2,639	2,829	3,476	4,067	5,678	204.2	285.0
Short-term	503	492	567	715	753	–	149.7	–
Medium- and long-term	1,489	2,147	2,262	2,761	3,314	–	222.6	–
Share of short-term in gross external debt (%)	25.3	18.6	20.0	20.6	18.5	–	–	–

Sources: World Bank, *World Debt Tables* 1996, Czech National Bank, The National Bank of Hungary, Balance of Payments Reports.
Note: Convertible currencies only.

Table 3.5A

Czech Republic: Structure of Long-Term External Debt, 1990–1994

Long-term Debt (LDOD) millions of U.S. $

	1990	1991	1992	1993	1994
TOTAL	3,971	4,154	3,920	5,422	7,806
Official creditors	252	575	988	1,136	1,338
Multilateral	179	484	699	776	939
Bilateral	73	91	290	361	399
Private creditors	3,719	3,578	2,922	4,074	6,084
Bonds	436	628	571	1,256	1,687
Commercial banks	1,573	1,598	1,418	1,514	2,586
Other private	1,710	1,352	933	1,305	1,811
Private nonguaranteed	0	2	11	212	384
Bonds	0	0	0	0	0
Commercial banks	0	2	11	212	384

Long-term Debt (LDOD), percent of total

	1990	1991	1992	1993	1994
TOTAL	100.0	100.0	100.0	100.0	100.0
Official creditors	6.3	13.9	25.2	21.0	17.2
Multilateral	4.5	11.7	17.8	14.3	12.1
Bilateral	1.8	2.2	7.4	6.7	5.1
Private creditors	93.7	86.1	74.5	75.1	77.9
Bonds	11.0	15.1	14.5	23.1	21.6
Commercial banks	39.6	38.5	36.2	27.9	33.1
Other private	43.1	32.5	23.8	24.1	23.2
Private nonguaranteed	0.0	0.0	0.3	3.9	4.9
Bonds	0.0	0.0	0.0	0.0	0.0
Commercial banks	0.0	0.0	0.3	3.9	4.9

Source: World Bank, *World Debt Tables,* Washington, 1996.

borrowing has been much smaller (well under 5 percent of total long-term debt), but its exposure to multilateral official borrowing has been correspondingly higher—about one-fifth of total long-term outstanding external debt. Direct commercial bank exposure through commercial lending has declined dramatically in Poland and in Slovakia. Instead, private but guaranteed lending has been increasingly provided through purchases of sovereign debt (bonds), which further diminished the risk to investors. In contrast, the exposure of Hungary and the Czech Republic to external borrowing from private sources have been rising rapidly recently. This includes not only private loans guaranteed by the respective governments but also borrowing without any guarantees. While the size of external debt due to private creditors is almost three times as large in Hungary in comparison to the Czech Republic, the speed with which external debt has increased is

Table 3.5B

Hungary: Structure of Long-Term External Debt, 1990–1994

Long-term Debt (LDOD), millions of U.S. $

	1990	1991	1992	1993	1994
TOTAL	18,006	19,188	18,485	20,995	24,478
Official creditors	2,715	3,857	3,835	3,906	4,288
Multilateral	2,555	3,337	3,226	3,219	3,465
Bilateral	160	520	609	688	823
Private creditors	15,292	15,075	14,009	15,871	17,802
Bonds	4,657	6,009	6,780	10,069	13,394
Commercial banks	9,647	8,134	6,419	5,131	3,930
Other private	988	932	809	671	479
Private nonguaranteed	0	257	642	1,218	2,388
Bonds	0	0	0	0	0
Commercial banks	0	257	642	1,218	2,388

Long-term Debt (LDOD) percent of total

	1990	1991	1992	1993	1994
TOTAL	100.0	100.0	100.0	100.0	100.0
Official creditors	15.1	20.1	20.7	18.6	17.5
Multilateral	14.2	17.4	17.4	15.3	14.1
Bilateral	0.9	2.7	3.3	3.3	3.4
Private creditors	84.9	78.6	75.8	75.6	72.7
Bonds	25.8	31.3	36.7	48.0	54.7
Commercial banks	53.6	42.4	34.7	24.4	16.0
Other private	5.5	4.9	4.4	3.2	2.0
Private nonguaranteed	0.0	1.3	3.5	5.8	9.8
Bonds	0.0	0.0	0.0	0.0	0.0
Commercial banks	0.0	1.3	3.5	5.8	9.8

Source: World Bank, *World Debt Tables,* 1996.

much faster in the Czech Republic. In sum, both Poland and Slovakia remain relatively sheltered against dangers arising from excessive exposure to private debt. The external positions of Hungary and the Czech Republic have become more exposed to private debt, with Hungary more so than the Czech Republic.

Investors' Base

Investors' base is another factor of stability of portfolio capital flows. It is possible to argue that the narrower the investors' base, the more likely it is that capital inflows may be subject to a high degree of instability. The investors' base can be narrow in at least two different senses—geographical

Table 3.5C

Poland: Structure of Long-Term External Debt, 1990–1994

Long-term Debt (LDOD), millions of U.S. $

	1990	1991	1992	1993	1994
TOTAL	39,059	45,166	43,297	41,988	39,974
Official creditors	27,715	34,032	32,974	32,597	31,185
Multilateral	524	878	1,167	1,471	1,957
Bilateral	27,191	33,154	31,807	31,125	29,228
Private creditors	11,344	11,000	9,922	8,850	7,925
Bonds	0	0	0	0	7,322
Commercial banks	9,760	9,715	9,108	8,640	362
Other private	1,584	1,285	814	211	241
Private nonguaranteed	0	135	401	541	864
Bonds	0	0	0	0	0
Commercial banks	0	135	401	541	864

Long-term Debt (LDOD), percent of total

	1990	1991	1992	1993	1994
TOTAL	100.0	100.0	100.0	100.0	100.0
Official creditors	71.0	75.3	76.2	77.6	78.0
Multilateral	1.4	1.9	2.7	3.5	4.9
Bilateral	69.6	73.4	73.5	74.1	73.1
Private creditors	29.0	24.4	22.9	21.1	19.8
Bonds	0.0	0.0	0.0	0.0	18.3
Commercial banks	25.0	21.5	21.0	20.6	0.9
Other private	4.0	2.9	1.9	0.5	0.6
Private nonguaranteed	0.0	0.3	0.9	1.3	2.2
Bonds	0.0	0.0	0.0	0.0	0.0
Commercial banks	0.0	0.3	0.9	1.3	2.2

Source: World Bank, *World Debt Tables*, 1996.

composition and the range of instruments. The statement on the role of investors' base is more intuitive than one based on a strong theory or convincing empirical evidence. A potential problem is, of course, that a wide investors' base is itself not a guarantee of stable investment climate even if other conditions prevail. Many investors are likely to invest in countries *only because* somebody else has already done so and the investors are merely following suit. This so-called herding behavior is in fact quite well known and common among portfolio managers. A wide investors' base may therefore be as unstable as a narrow one. Moreover, it is also quite well known that the psychology of investors may differ from investor to investor and from country to country. For example, pension funds may be

Table 3.5D

Slovakia: Structure of Long-Term External Debt, 1990–1994

Long-term Debt (LDOD), millions of U.S. $

	1990	1991	1992	1993	1994
TOTAL	1,489	1,748	1,793	2,204	2,672
Official creditors	126	284	458	525	737
Multilateral	89	239	334	355	507
Bilateral	36	45	124	170	230
Private creditors	1,363	1,464	1,335	1,679	1,922
Bonds	0	74	74	348	552
Commercial banks	857	886	781	708	663
Other private	506	504	480	623	708
Private nonguaranteed	0	0	0	1	13
Bonds	0	0	0	0	0
Commercial banks	0	0	0	1	13

Long-term Debt (LDOD), percent of total

	1990	1991	1992	1993	1994
TOTAL	100.0	100.0	100.0	100.0	100.0
Official creditors	8.4	16.2	25.5	23.8	27.6
Multilateral	6.0	13.6	18.6	16.1	19.0
Bilateral	2.4	2.6	6.9	7.7	8.6
Private creditors	91.6	83.8	74.5	76.2	71.9
Bonds	0.0	4.3	4.1	15.8	20.6
Commercial banks	57.6	50.7	43.6	32.1	24.8
Other private	34.0	28.8	26.8	28.3	26.5
Private nonguaranteed	0.0	0.0	0.0	0.0	0.5
Bonds	0.0	0.0	0.0	0.0	0.0
Commercial banks	0.0	0.0	0.0	0.0	0.5

Source: World Bank, *World Debt Tables*, 1966.

interested in longer-term investments and may therefore make firm commitments to stay in the country even in the face of temporary fluctuations in the market. The size of the investors' base, therefore, will be used here only as a subsidiary argument.

Unfortunately, we have no data on the geographical structure of the supply of portfolio capital in these countries and very limited data on the structure of the countries' liabilities. The latter has been covered in the previous section to the extent permitted by the availability of data. For the sake of illustration, however, all we can do is to examine the geographical structure of foreign direct investment, and that is not the same as the geographical structure of portfolio investments. Since the data on the structure

Table 3.6A

Poland: Geographical Composition of the Stock of Foreign Direct Investment, 1994

Country	Equity and loans	
	$ million	%
United States	1,413.7	32.7
Multinational corporations	808.3	18.7
Germany	386.4	8.9
Italy	365.8	8.5
France	268.1	6.2
Netherlands	240.4	5.6
Austria	159.7	3.7
United Kingdom	112.2	2.6
Switzerland	112.0	2.6
Sweden	86.7	2.0
Denmark	60.2	1.4
Canada	49.3	1.1
Spain	47.0	1.1
Norway	46.9	1.1
Belgium	38.3	0.9
China	25.0	0.6
Finland	21.9	0.5
Russia	20.0	0.5
Japan	13.8	0.3
Singapore	13.0	0.3
Ireland	7.0	0.2
Australia	6.3	0.1
South Korea	5.0	0.1
South Africa	3.4	0.1
Yugoslavia (former)	3.0	0.1
Turkey	3.0	0.1
Luxembourg	2.3	0.1
Greece	2.1	0.0
Total	4,320.8	100.0

Source: Polish Agency for Foreign Investment.
Note: The data cover investments of more than $1 million.

of debt instruments is also limited, we shall restrict our discussion to the case of the Czech Republic.

As Table 3.6 shows, the geographical base of foreign direct investors is rather narrow in all the CEECs—about 60 to 80 percent of foreign direct investments come from three or four countries. The country with the highest degree of concentration of foreign direct investment appears to be the Czech Republic, with the other countries having the geographical base of their investors somewhat more diversified.

Table 3.6B

Hungary: Geographical Composition of the Stock of Foreign Direct Investment, 1994–1995

	1994		1995	
	U.S. $ million	Share (%)	U.S. $ milion	Share (%)
Germany	151.6	28.4	159.1	22.3
United States	112.0	21.0	101.8	14.3
Austria	84.4	15.8	142.0	19.9
Netherlands	30.1	5.6	79.4	11.1
France	25.3	4.7	37.1	5.2
United Kingdom	20.9	3.9	32.0	4.5
Italy	20.6	3.9	33.3	4.7
Belgium	17.2	3.2	14.7	2.1
Japan	13.7	2.6	13.4	1.9
Switzerland	10.4	2.0	27.4	3.8
CIS	8.8	1.7	12.9	1.8
Australia	7.1	1.3	1.2	0.2
Luxembourg	5.7	1.1	13.0	1.8
Sweden	3.7	0.7	7.9	1.1
Canada	3.2	0.6	6.2	0.9
South Korea	2.0	0.4	2.8	0.4
Israel	1.7	0.3	1.9	0.3
Liechtenstein	1.3	0.2	3.8	0.5
Denmark	1.3	0.2	4.1	0.6
Finland	1.0	0.2	1.5	0.2
Greece	0.9	0.2	0.6	0.1
Ireland	0.8	0.2	2.3	0.3
Cyprus	0.5	0.1	1.1	0.2
Spain	0.5	0.1	1.0	0.1
China	0.3	0.1	0.1	0.0
Turkey	0.1	0.0	0.2	0.0
Other	8.1	1.5	13.0	1.8
TOTAL	533.2	100.0	713.8	100.0

Source: Hungarian Central Statistical Office.

Symptoms of Macroeconomic Instability in the CEECs

In these sections we shall examine the second group of indicators of potential instability of capital inflows. They concern the question of domestic macroeconomic, or fundamental balances to ascertain whether they are "right" or whether they are a matter of concern. Assessment of this is crucial to evaluations of countries' creditworthiness (Ul Hague et al. 1996). The fairly successful drive in all four countries to reduce inflation may give the impression that the authorities in all of these countries have been

Table 3.6C

Slovakia: Geographical Composition of the Stock of Foreign Direct Investment, 1992–1995

	1992		1993		1994		1995	
	mill. Sk.	Share (%)	mill. Sk.	Share (%)	mill. Sk.	Share (%)	mill. Sk.	Share (%)
Czech Republic	0	0.0	1,210	11.2	2,510	15.2	3,556	16.3
Germany	1,803	27.3	2,632	24.5	3,405	20.6	4,693	21.4
Austria	1,648	24.9	2,256	21.0	3,702	22.4	3,831	17.5
United States	1,268	19.2	1,385	12.9	2,389	14.4	2,504	11.4
United Kingdom	–	–	–	–	438	2.6	1,580	7.2
Netherlands	394	6.0	438	4.1	804	4.9	1402	6.4
France	42	0.6	1,133	10.5	1,154	7.0	1,286	5.9
Sweden	340	5.1	463	4.3	521	3.1	522	2.4
Italy	357	5.4	373	3.5	422	2.6	449	2.1
South Korea	323	4.9	323	3.0	323	2.0	323	1.5
Netherlands Antilles	0	0.0	0	0.0	302	1.8	302	1.4
Switzerland	54	0.8	100	0.9	127	0.8	249	1.1
Canada	188	2.8	198	1.8	199	1.2	200	0.9
Hungary	47	0.7	49	0.5	59	0.4	118	0.5
Other countries	143	2.2	196	1.8	187	1.1	867	4.0
Total	6,607	100.0	10,756	100.0	16,542	100.0	21,882	100.0

Source: PlanEcon, Washington, DC.

Table 3.6D

Czech Republic: Geographical Composition of the Stock of Foreign Direct Investment, 1990–1994

	1990–1994		1994	
	$ mill.	Shares (%)	$ mill.	Shares (%)
FRG	1,113.0	36.2	417.6	48.4
United States	651.1	21.2	39.4	4.6
France	355.6	11.6	77.0	8.9
Austria	216.6	7.0	79.5	9.2
Belgium	188.6	6.1	32.5	3.8
Switzerland	136.7	4.4	39.3	4.6
Other countries	415.8	13.5	177.1	20.5
Total	3,077.4	100.0	862.4	100.0

Source: Czech National Bank.

Note: Largest investments under "Other Countries" came mainly from Italy, Great Britain, and The Netherlands.

successful in eliminating fundamental imbalances that existed around 1990 (Drábek et al. 1994). There are also other indicators that point in the same direction, such as a low level of unemployment, a high level of international reserves, and a balanced budget in the Czech Republic and a fairly strong recovery in all the CEECs as well as the relative success in containing the hyperinflationary pressures that existed in the early 1990s. Nevertheless, the macroeconomic picture may not be as sound and stable as might appear from these indicators. The picture is quite clearly blurred in the case of Poland, Hungary, and Slovakia, where unemployment has been well into double-digit figures, albeit beginning to fall. But even the successes of anti-inflationary policies are not as straightforward as they might appear, as we shall see further below.

It is impossible to give a precise meaning to the concept of "fundamental imbalances." What we can do, however, is to look for symptoms of instability from various sources of evidence. For example, if domestic growth of important expenditures is not matched by growth of domestic savings and this leads to a corresponding current account deficit, the external borrowing that is needed to finance the deficit may become at a certain point "excessive." At such a point foreigners will no longer be willing to finance the deficit at the going rate of interest. Alternatively, the country's external debt may be so large that it leads to difficulties in debt servicing. Asset prices are normally also affected by capital inflows, which may create difficulties for the recipient countries.[19] Furthermore, a major imbalance between *ex ante* savings and *ex ante* investment will be reflected in the pressures on interest rates. Indeed, the high level of interest rates in the Czech Republic, together with successful macroeconomic stabilization, has undoubtedly been the most important factor of capital inflows.

The last comment that is necessary before we actually analyze the data regards another aspect of "fundamental imbalances." It is my belief that it is not enough simply to observe an imbalance as sign of fundamental disequilibrium. It is equally important to ascertain that the disequilibrium is not temporary and thus that it is indeed fundamental. For this reason, each indicator of fundamental disequilibrium is accompanied and supported by a discussion of the underlying causes.

Sticky Inflation

A high and/or unstable rate of inflation is normally a deterrent for foreign investments because it reduces the real rates of return on investments and because it increases the uncertainty about future returns, respectively.[20] Moreover, in the world of free capital flows, a persistently higher rate of inflation than in other countries will necessitate a higher level of nominal interest rates there than abroad.

The anti-inflationary policies have clearly not yet been completed, and this can be seen from Figure 3.1. The inflation rate has been reduced dramatically in all four countries, but the rates have remained "sticky" over the last two or three years. In Poland, the inflation rate was stuck at the level of around 30 percent (Lipinski 1994), and the Polish authorities found it difficult to push inflation lower until the second half of 1995. A similar story can be told about Hungary, where the inflation rate was "stuck" at the level of about 20 percent and rising, and the Czech Republic, with an underlying inflation rate of about 10 percent. All the CEECs showed some, albeit slow, decline in the rate of inflation in the course of 1996. However, inflation remains considerably higher than in Western Europe or in the OECD countries in general.

The origins of inflationary pressures remain fundamentally unchanged. These pressures can be analyzed in at least two separate ways. The first approach is to examine the growth of wages relative to the growth of productivity. This should be done by looking at the changes of unit labor costs, but unfortunately the data are not readily available. We shall rely, therefore, on data on industrial earnings, which represent a reasonable proxy for costs of labor in the economy as a whole. The data are shown in Figure 3.2, and they offer a very interesting but worrisome picture. All four countries experienced rapid growth of industrial earnings during 1993–95. In all four countries,

Figure 3.1 **Quarterly Inflation in Central and Eastern European Countries, 1993–1995**

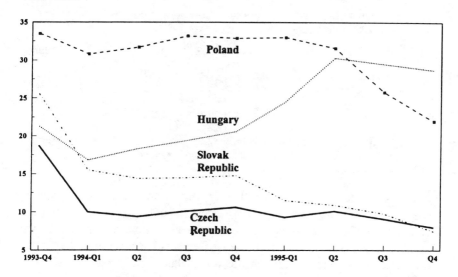

Source: Bank for International Settlements.

Figure 3.2 **Industrial Earnings in Central and Eastern European Countries, 1993–1995**

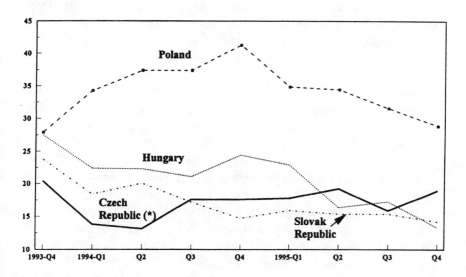

Source: Bank for International Settlements.

*Data for the fourth quarter go only through November 1995.

Table 3.7

CEECs: Labor Industrial Productivity in Central and Eastern European Countries, 1990–1995 (annual percentage growth)

	1990	1991	1992	1993	1994	1995
Czech Republic	−0.2	−9.2	−3.9	0.7	1.8	4.3
Hungary	−0.2	−2.5	5.5	2.8	4.2	2.3
Poland	−7.9	−1.2	7.1	4.4	5.9	6.6
Slovakia	−1.7	−7.3	−1.8	−0.6	5.9	5.5

Source: M. Hajek et al., Makro-ekonomická Analýza České Ekonomiky, 1995 (Prague: Czech National Bank, Economics Institute, Research Report no. 51, 1996).

growth of wages has been faster than growth of inflation. The discrepancy has been by far the greatest in the Czech Republic, while in Poland and Hungary the wage settlements appear to have been more reasonable.[21]

In assessing the effect of wage settlements on inflation, the crucial question is the extent to which the wage claims have been matched by the growth of productivity. Here the problem with data is even more serious, partly because the relevant data are not freely available and partly because the data are typically subject to various methodological shortcomings. We shall rely on data of gross output per worker in constant prices (Table 3.7). These problems notwithstanding, however, the productivity trends appear quite clear. That is, the growth of productivity, albeit accelerating in the post-1990 period, has been far slower than the growth of wages in all of these countries. This clearly explains why inflation rates have remained "sticky."[22]

The second approach is to examine the impact of monetary policy and see whether the policy has helped to fuel domestic inflation with an excessively fast growth of money supply. This amounts to asking the following question: Was the growth of money, including the growth brought about by inflow of foreign capital, inflationary, or did it simply respond to a strong growth of demand for money? One way of answering the question is to quantify the rate of seigniorage. Excessive seigniorage indicates the existence of strong inflationary pressures generated by the central bank and the rate at which it prints money. A high rate of seigniorage only indicates the risk of inflation, since the seigniorage may be transitory or may be accommodating the growth of demand for money.[23]

As Table 3.8 shows, the rates of seigniorage were relatively very low in all four countries during the period 1993–95. This would suggest that the authorities have benefited relatively little from seigniorage and that mone-

Table 3.8

CEECs: Seigniorage 1993–1995

	1993	1994	1995
Czech Republic	(0.062)	0.126 (0.032)	0.139 (0.002)
Hungary	0.074 (0.021)	0.04 (0.012)	0.051 (0.009)
Poland	0.082 (0.025)	0.083 (0.031)	0.056 (0.018)
Slovak Republic	(–0.62)	0.076 (0.004)	0.06 (0.034)

Note: Calculated on the basis of two definitions—the first defines money in terms of M2, the second in terms of M1. The estimates based on M1 definition are provided in parentheses. Seigniorage is shown as a ratio to GDP and was calculated with the help of formulas based on Fischer (1982).

tary policies were not inflationary. Normally, a rate higher than 2 indicates a high risk of inflation and a rate higher than 3 indicates a serious macroeconomic imbalance.[24] Our estimates of seigniorage indicate, therefore, that monetary policies tended to be tight.[25] The low seigniorage level has probably reflected a strong demand for money in both the private and public sectors. It appears that only in the Czech Republic did demand for money in the public sector weaken, as the government maintained a surplus in the budget and net credit to the government declined in both 1993 and 1994.[26] At the same time, however, demand for money in the private sector might have dramatically increased. Privatization, the establishment of new firms, the increase of demand for money by foreigners due to privatization, and growth in the number of foreign trade agents have all contributed to the growth in demand for money. The net effect of these factors is difficult to estimate, and the existing empirical literature does not provide any convincing answers.[27] Nevertheless, the possibility of rapidly rising demand for money in these countries in the examined period cannot be excluded.

Rapid Growth of External Debt

None of the countries appears to have major difficulty servicing its external debt. Nevertheless, the current picture is to some extent misleading. Poland has found itself in the position of having a reasonable level of external debt because of a fairly generous rescheduling agreement with its creditors. Hungary, in turn, has retained its access to external borrowing primarily on the account of continued support from the IMF without asking for debt rescheduling.[28] The main reasons for future concerns are twofold—a large existing stock of debt in Hungary and Poland and massive borrowing by the

Czech Republic and Slovakia, a large part of which has been short-term, as we have seen above.

Whether external debt is heavy or not depends on (1) current foreign exchange earnings, which crucially affect the country's ability to service its external debt, (2) the level of international reserves, and (3) new borrowing, that is, on the level of the current account deficit. Among these three indicators, the relative size of the current account deficit is arguably most important. A more rigorous analysis of macroeconomic instability must therefore include an analysis of debt profiles for each country.

As Table 3.9 indicates, external debt remains very large in Hungary and Poland. Both countries remain among the most indebted countries in the world, especially if external debt is measured on a per capita basis or in terms of a common denominator such as exports (or GDP). Moreover, new borrowing in Hungary increased dramatically in 1994 and 1995, as the current account deficit increased to 9.4 percent of GDP in 1994—substantially above the corresponding current account deficit in Mexico at the time of the recent crisis. Even though the deficit was almost halved in 1995, it remained dangerously high. In contrast, the current account position in Poland has recently been much stronger, and if a large part of the unofficial trade in the border areas is included in the official statistics, the current account was in surplus in 1994 and 1995.

Neither the Czech Republic nor Slovakia was in the same category, but both have increased their external indebtedness at a relatively alarming speed. The gross debt of the Czech Republic amounted to less than U.S. $8 billion in the beginning of 1993. By the end of 1994 gross external debt already stood at U.S. $10.7 billion, and by the end of 1995 the corresponding figure was above U.S. $16.6 billion, about a 55 percent increase.[29] In terms of total exports, the gross external debt of the Czech Republic was considerably less than in Hungary and Poland but rising dramatically. Between the end of 1993 and the end of 1995 external debt in current U.S. dollars increased by almost 75 percent, while dollar exports increased by only 29 percent. In addition, while the growth of external debt was initially—until the end of 1994—associated with a balanced current account, the current account position significantly deteriorated in 1995. Current account turned into a large deficit—2.9 percent of GDP—which had to be financed by foreign capital inflows. This is still less than what some writers such as J. Williamson consider to be a threshold for a real danger—about 5 percent.[30] However, the current account position further deteriorated to almost 8 percent in 1996. Moreover, it is clear that the speed with which the current account position has deteriorated is worrying (Figure 3.3). In brief, while the initial growth of indebtedness in the Czech Republic was fully

Figure 3.3 Czech Republic: Monthly Changes in Trade and Current Account, 1995–1996

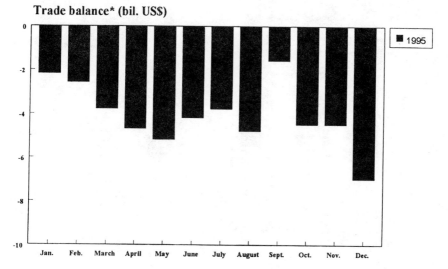

Trade balance* (bil. US$)

Source: Bank for International Settlements.
Note: *Annualized rate.

reflected in the rise of international reserves, the 1995 turnaround meant that foreign capital increasingly had to finance the current account deficit. By 1996 the deficit on current account was growing rapidly while capital inflows slowed down and international reserves slightly declined.

The Slovak story is similar, even though the country's current account position may appear to be relatively stronger. First, the external debt is also relatively higher than in the Czech Republic. Second, and perhaps more important, the current account position has been at least partially maintained by additional restrictive measures that have been introduced by the authorities. The measures included the introduction of an import surcharge in 1994, and the authorities have also attempted to introduce new health and other standards on imports, the effect of which was to slow down imports, particularly from the Czech Republic. Restrictive measures have been also adopted by Polish and Hungarian authorities, who introduced various restrictive measures in the course of 1994–95. All of these additional steps to increase protection against imports suggests that the external position of the these countries has not been stabilized. Finally, official reserves remain relatively low—much lower than in the other three CEECs.

Moreover, the vulnerability of the Czech Republic to the deteriorating current account position also emerges from the composition of external

Table 3.9

Financial Indicators for Selected Central and East European Countries and Mexico, 1994 and 1995
(million U.S. dollars and percent)

Country	Current account		Current account/GDP[b]		Gross debt		Gross debt/exports		Net debt/exports[c]		Short-term debt	
	1994	1995	1994	1995	1994	1995	1994	1995	1994	1995	1994	1995
Croatia	103	−1,712	0.6	−10.3	2,304	3,700	54.1	79.9	−0.1	9.4	74	345
Czech Rep.	−50	−1362	−0.1	−2.9	10,694	16,549	75.0	76.5	31.9	2.5	2,888	5,045
Hungary	−3,911	−2,480	−9.4	−5.7	28,521	31,655	269.4	246.1	205.8	153.1	2,397	3,203
Poland	−944	−2,299	−1.0	−1.9	42,160	43,900	248.7	191.9	213.2	126.5	845	—
Romania	−428	−1,336	−1.5	−3.8	5,492	6,425	89.3	85.5	55.4	64.5	966	1,120
Slovakia	665	649	4.8	3.7	4,067	5,678	60.8	66.2	34.7	26.3	753	—
Slovenia	540	−36	3.8	−0.2	2,290	2,956	33.5	35.4	11.6	13.6	93	—
Mexico[a]	−23,399	−28,785	−6.6	−7.9	118,469	128,302	236.7	228.1	186.2	216.6	27,281	31,599

Country	Short-term debt/gross debt 1994	1995	Official reserves 1994	1995	Current account/reserves 1994	1995	Official reserves/imports 1994	1995	Short-term debt/reserves 1994	1995
Croatia	3.2	9.3	2,307	3,265	4.5	−52.4	5.3	5.2	3.2	10.6
Czech Republic	27.0	30.5	6,145	13,843	−0.8	−9.8	4.9	6.6	47.0	36.4
Hungary	8.4	10.1	6,727	11,968	−58.1	−20.7	5.6	9.3	35.6	26.8
Poland	2.0	–	6,029	14,961	−15.7	−15.4	4.1	7.3	14.0	–
Romania	17.6	17.4	2,086	1,579	−20.5	−84.6	3.8	2.2	46.3	70.9
Slovakia	18.5	–	1,745	3,418	38.1	19.0	3.2	4.7	43.2	–
Slovenia	4.1	–	1,499	1,821	36.0	−2.0	2.5	2.4	6.2	–
Mexico[a]	23.0	24.6	25,299	6,441	−92.5	−446.9	4.1	0.9	107.8	490.6

Sources: Bank for International Settlement, *World Debt Tables* (World Bank), PlanEcon, National Bank of Hungary, Czech National Bank, Balance of Payments Reports, World Trade Organization).

Notes: [a]Data for Mexico are 1993 and 1994. [b]Current account/GNP for Mexico. [c]Net debt equals gross debt less official reserves.

debt. The short-term debt was U.S. $2.9 billion at the end of 1994. According to the figures of the Bank for International Settlements, short-term foreign lending to the Czech Republic continued strongly in 1995. External liabilities increased by about U.S. $5.9 billion between the end of 1994 and the end of 1995. As noted above, a large proportion of the increase came from short-term borrowing—short-term debt increased by U.S. $2.2 billion, representing almost 31 percent of the total gross debt. The corresponding figures for Hungary, Poland, and Slovakia were much smaller—U.S. $0.6 billion, minus U.S. $0.2 billion (a decline in the stock of liabilities) and U.S. $0.2 billion, respectively.[31] As Table 3.9 shows, the percentage of total external debt that is short-term debt in the Czech Republic already exceeds that of Mexico at the time of its financial crisis. According to preliminary official data, the share somewhat declined in 1996.

In sum, the external account position is "fragile" in all four CEECs. In Poland and Hungary, this is because of the large external debt, combined in Hungary with large new borrowings due to the need to finance current account deficits. In the Czech Republic and Slovakia, external debt is much lower but rapidly increasing, especially in the Czech Republic, as a result of new borrowing. This, together with the fact that a large proportion of the debt is short-term, is increasing the country's vulnerability. Only Slovakia's external debt position has so far been kept under tight control, but this was achieved with the help of administrative controls. That country's official reserves also remain relatively low.

Consumption Adjustment?

As Tables 3.10A–C indicate, all countries under consideration have adjusted, but the patterns of their adjustment are different. In Poland, a major adjustment effort was undertaken between 1991 and 1994, resulting in a significant decline in the savings-investment imbalance as a proportion of GDP and subsequently turning into a current account surplus of 2.3 percent of GDP in 1994. Most of the adjustment was achieved through a relative decline in domestic consumption, which dropped sharply between 1991 and 1994. The investment share in GDP is estimated by the IMF to have also dropped to 15.3 percent in 1994, a fall of more than 6 percent since 1991. During the period under consideration, the role of foreign investment was minor, but the situation changed fundamentally after Poland's agreement with commercial creditors in 1993–94, when the inflow of foreign investment sharply accelerated.

In contrast, Hungary's savings-investment balance began to sharply deteriorate in 1991 when the balance, a proxy for the current account deficit, turned

Table 3.10A

Hungary: Sectoral Savings and Investment Balances, 1990–1995
(in percent of GDP)

	1990	1991	1992	1993	1994	1995
Gross national savings	25.7	17.4	14.1	10.4	13.6	17.9
Households	8.6	14.9	12.4	7.7	9.3	10.0
Enterprises	12.4	−1.1	0.2	2.8	4.8	−2.0
Government	4.8	3.6	1.5	0.0	−0.6	9.9
Gross national investments	24.0	19.8	15.5	19.9	21.6	21.4
Households	3.6	5.4	4.4	4.7	4.5	4.3
Enterprises	17.0	10.2	5.0	9.8	12.2	13.6
Government	3.4	4.1	6.0	5.3	5.0	3.4
Nonfinancial balance[a]	1.8	−2.4	−1.4	−9.4	−8.1	−3.5
Households	5.0	9.4	7.9	3.0	4.8	6.6
Enterprises	−4.6	−11.4	−4.8	−7.1	−7.3	−6.5
Government	1.4	−0.5	−4.5	−5.4	−5.6	−3.5

Source: Gáspár 1996.

[a]The nonfinancial balance is a proxy for foreign savings, or the current account in the balance of payments. The nonfinancial balance is on a national accounts basis and differs from the current account in the balance of payments, which is on a settlements rather than a customs basis.

Table 3.10B

Poland: Savings Investment Balance, 1991–1994
(in percent of nominal GDP)

	1991	1992	1993	1994
Foreign savings (capital inflow)	2.8	0.3	0.7	−2.3
Current account deficit	2.8	0.3	2.7	1.1
Unrecorded trade	−	−	−2.0	−3.4
Gross national savings	18.7	17.3	14.9	17.6
Government	−5.1	−4.5	−1.1	−0.9
Nongovernment	23.9	21.8	16.0	18.5
Gross domestic investments	21.5	17.6	15.6	15.3
Government	4.1	3.4	3.4	3.1
Nongovernment	17.4	14.2	12.2	12.2

Source: IMF.

Notes: External current account deficit is indicated with a positive sign. Government savings are calculated as the residual between current revenues and current expenditures (including interest payments). The nongovernment sector was obtained as the residual. The current account deficit was measured on an accrual basis, i.e., external interest payments are on a commitment basis.

Table 3.10C

Czech Republic: Savings Investment Balance, 1990–1995
(in percent of GDP)

	Average 1987–89	1990	1991	1992	1993	1994	1995
Savings	31.2	29.9	36.7	27.4	20.2	20.1	21.5
Investments	27.8	28.6	29.9	27.0	18.0	20.5	25.5
Current account balance	3.3	1.3	6.8	0.4	2.2	–0.4	–3.9

Source: PATRIA, Economic Research, Prague, 4 December 1995.

into a deficit of 2.4 percent of GDP from a surplus of 1.8 percent. After a temporary improvement in 1992, the imbalance dramatically increased in 1993–94, reaching almost 9 percent by the end of 1994. The deterioration has been entirely due to a dramatic fall in the savings rate, which the IMF estimates to have dropped from more than 25 percent in 1990 to just over 17 percent in 1995. The growing imbalance was first mitigated by a decline in the investment rate between 1990 and 1992, but the investment rate somewhat recovered in the subsequent two years. In sum, foreign savings (and investments) appear to have financed mainly domestic consumption, preventing a major drop; only partially did they finance domestic investment.[32]

For the Czech Republic, the evidence seems to suggest that foreign borrowing tended to finance both consumption and investments. According to estimates by the investment house PATRIA, investment ratios remained high during 1990–92, declined sharply in the following two years, but recovered in 1995. On the other hand, savings rates dropped even more significantly than investment rates between 1990 and 1995, suggesting a sharp rise in the ratio of domestic consumption to GDP and increased dependence on foreign savings to finance domestic investments.[33] These findings have important policy implications. To the extent that the investment figures are believable (and there are reasons to suspect the quality of the data, as noted above), the rise in external debt does not pose a serious danger in that external borrowing has been used for financing domestic investments. However, foreign savings have represented a rapidly growing proportion of the total resources available to finance these investments. In addition, it is unclear at the present time whether current investment will result in higher returns in the future. This will depend on various factors such as the distribution of investment into tradables and nontradables, the maturity of investment, the implementation of investment projects, and so on. Thus, the crucial question is whether the investment figures can be believed. If not, the growth of foreign debt could turn out to be highly dangerous in the future.

The Czech experience can be, therefore, contrasted with what happened in Hungary in that foreign capital did finance domestic investments. In Hungary, however, capital inflows have been increasingly used to finance private consumption.[34] Moreover, rising consumption and its financing through foreign capital, if sustainable, may not theoretically be all bad if it reflects a more permanent move to a long-run equilibrium. In Hungary, the main problem has been the budget and thus the government's poor savings performance.[35] While private consumption has been adversely affected by recent adjustments, government spending on various social programs—public consumption—has turned out to be much more difficult to cut.

Instability of Comparative Advantages

Equally important for future macroeconomic stability will be the performance of exports. The growth of exports is crucial for a country's ability to service its external debt and to stimulate growth of output. Some economists even consider export-led growth to be the key condition for success of any development strategy. So far, export performance remains a matter of concern in all four countries—even in Poland and Slovakia, despite their current account surpluses in 1995. The export performance will depend on the extent to which a given country will be able to specialize and exploit its comparative advantages, and it is precisely the uncertainty about the comparative advantages of the CEECs that is another reason for potential macroeconomic instability in the future.

The uncertainty has three sources: First, it is unclear what the current pattern of comparative advantages is. On a broad level, the differences between, say, the OECD countries and the CEECs are relatively straightforward, the former having a comparative advantage in technology and R&D.[36] On a more disaggregated level, however, the picture is less clear. A number of studies have so far failed to firmly establish on an empirical basis the actual pattern of comparative advantages.[37] At the same time, empirical studies have identified significant differences in trade structure of the EU (as a proxy for developed countries) and the CEECs, indicating fundamental differences in comparative advantages (Dobrinsky 1994). Many observers consider the area as having a comparative advantage in its relatively low-priced labor—throughout Eastern Europe, wages are estimated to be on average 90 percent lower than in the West. In 1994, hourly labor costs for unskilled labor were about $7 in the former East Germany,

$1.88 in Hungary, and $1.58 in Poland. This is compared with $16.29 in Italy and $11.60 in Spain. Such comparisons have led some to conclude that labor cost differentials are enormous and must be the main attraction for foreign investors.[38]

However, the argument could be misleading; the wage differentials must be considered in tandem with the differentials in labor productivity. Nevertheless, if CEEC labor is, say, ten times less productive than comparable labor in the West, the productivity-adjusted wages in the CEECs are most likely still attractive for foreign investors, but the question is by how much.[39]

The second reason for the uncertainty about the comparative advantages of the CEECs is that the current labor cost advantages are arguably not a long-term phenomenon. The pattern of comparative advantages in the CEECs is likely to shift in the future, and the change is likely to be very fast. For example, various surveys of enterprise behavior indicate that some investors do not indeed view the current low-cost structure as permanent.[40] Again, there are at least two reasons for this argument: (1) the costs of labor should include benefits that labor receives but which are paid for either by companies or by government, and (2) according to the purchasing power parity, medium-term exchange rates are highly undervalued in the Czech Republic and Slovakia, perhaps less so in Hungary and Poland. The real costs of labor have been rising dramatically in the Czech Republic, as indicated by the rapidly rising real effective exchange rate.[41] Some countries such as the Czech Republic have already experienced a change in the structure of their exports relative to that of the EU, indicating that the pattern of comparative advantages is changing (see Dobrinsky 1994, p. 16).

The third reason is the macroeconomic situation, which remains unstable in all CEECs (Drábek 1996). The instability has different origins in addition to undervalued exchange rates, noted earlier. They range from fiscal imbalances to serious structural and institutional deficiencies. The fragility of the banking sector and other financial markets arguably constitutes the highest threat to macroeconomic stability in the Czech Republic. By the end of 1996 the authorities faced and had to absorb the costs of restructuring thirteen banks, including two of the seven largest banks, which were put either under forced administration or into liquidation.

Conclusions

The rapid inflow of foreign capital into the CEECs has been clearly highly beneficial for these countries. The capital helped finance current account deficits and domestic investment, and it has led to a considerable strengthening of international reserves. In the Czech Republic and Hungary, foreign capital has also played a crucial role in helping the government implement the objective of privatizing a large part of state assets within a relatively short period of time. However, while the contribution of foreign capital has undoubtedly been positive, the speed and the amount of foreign capital have also put a considerable strain on the financial system as well as on the government policies instituted to cope with the inflows. In the absence of international regulations of capital flows or their taxation, the governments have taken numerous measures to contain the adverse impact of "excessive" capital inflows, but the types of measures as well as their effectiveness have been controversial.[42] We certainly do not have full confidence either in the stability of these countries' economic policies or that they are in position to open up fully to market competition, be it in the context of full membership in the European Union or in general.

The government policies pursued by countries in Central and Eastern Europe were risky, if not outright dangerous, in one important respect: They opened up capital accounts with a speed and vigor that do not have many precedents and that have even gone against the conventional wisdom.[43] The policies have encouraged inflow of foreign capital on a scale that may not be sustainable in the long run. Capital inflows tend to be inflationary; they accentuate the distortions in the pattern of investment spending and severely complicate stabilization policies. Exposure to foreign capital has been high mainly in the Czech Republic but also in Hungary and Slovakia. It is still not the case in Poland. This exposure is reflected in a high share of foreign capital in GDP in comparison to other countries, a large impact of foreign capital on money supply, and a high contribution to domestic savings. The large exposure to foreign capital in the Czech Republic is further complicated by the fact that a large proportion of foreign capital has come in the form of short-term and portfolio capital, the movement of which can be reversed relatively rapidly. In contrast, the exposure of Hungary and Slovakia to portfolio and short-term capital is much lower, which makes these countries, together with Poland, relatively less exposed to the risks of capital reversals. Here there are relatively strong capital flows, which are stable in nature but do fluctuate from year to year.

There have been other warning signals suggesting to the policy markets that capital inflows may not be sustainable. These signals relate to the evolution of domestic fundamentals, which remain fragile. This is reflected in the higher rates of inflation in all the CEECs, and these inflationary pressures remain "sticky" and in some sense permanent due to excessive growth of wages (which is turning out to be difficult to curb) and pressures emanating from the government budget in all countries except the Czech Republic. All countries have been experiencing rising external debt pressures—Poland and Hungary due to their existing debt burdens and the Czech Republic due to rapidly rising external borrowing. Foreign investors are also getting rather confusing signals about the pattern of comparative advantages of the countries. What is even more worrying is that of these four countries, only Poland has demonstrated a significant domestic macro-economic adjustment, as reflected in the sharp decline in the share of consumption in GDP. After an initial but relatively small decline of consumption, the other countries have quickly set out on the road of compensatory growth of domestic consumption. Moreover, since investment rates are beginning to recover in all these countries, the result has been a further squeeze of domestic savings rates. It appears from the available evidence, therefore, that foreign capital inflows have been increasingly financing the growth of domestic consumption. Clearly, such a pattern of domestic spending could be quite dangerous.

The inflow of foreign capital has presented the governments with a difficult dilemma. Should the governments pursue a wait-and-see policy, or should they manage the flows? First of all, maintaining fiscal incentives to attract foreign investment under these circumstances does not make any economic, financial, or even political sense in a situation of abundance of foreign capital. Second, the no-intervention approach would have been appropriate provided the increased capital inflow was necessary to meet a rapidly expanding demand for money (there are reasons to believe that various factors strongly acted to stimulate the growth of demand for money, such as the desire of firms to expand output or of agents to adjust their portfolios to a new structure of relative prices), but we have some evidence that demand for money has been relatively stable in these countries (Begg 1997). Moreover, it is unlikely that the factors generating a shift in the demand for money will continue to operate with the same force in the future. Thus, any new expansion of the money supply is likely to create a danger of fueling further the inflationary pressures. The Czech Republic faces the additional problem that the economy is operating near full capacity, and additional capital inflows are unlikely to be accompanied by simultaneous capacity expansion in the short term.

The governments therefore have been justified in managing the flows. The majority view in the Czech Republic has been to approach the expansion of capital inflows by increasing the flexibility in the management of foreign exchange with the hope that this will lead to a revaluation of the currency and slow down the inflow of foreign capital. Also, a greater flexibility in the exchange rate policy should increase the foreign exchange risk to foreign currency traders and thus somewhat lower their foreign exchange activities. It is too soon to say what effects the measure will have. However, a revaluation of the currency is precisely the opposite of what is recommended in light of the country's yawning current account imbalance. An alternative measure may be capital controls. However, capital controls are also problematic—they are difficult to implement and may be damaging to governmental credibility. Another problem with capital controls is that while they can have a mitigating influence on output/employment variations, they are not necessarily effective at containing inflation. The empirical evidence shows that capital controls have been more effective in containing output/employment variations and much less effective in containing inflation variations.[44] The scope for fiscal adjustment existed, but the political constraints were too serious, especially in the Czech Republic, where the government budget was more or less permanently in surplus. Monetary responses have been tried, as shown by Klacek and Gáspár in this volume, but their effectiveness was limited. Moreover, monetary responses to capital inflows were ineffective since they operated under conditions of minimal foreign exchange risks which only further encouraged short-term capital inflows (Reinhart and Dunaway 1996; Montes 1996).

Thus, the only sensible policy must be the establishment of conditions that can be maintained stably over a long period of time. This means, first of all, a reduction of inflation in all four countries. Without significantly lower inflation, interest rates will continue to be above the level of interest rates in other financial markets and will attract foreign capital. This means, therefore, further significant steps to reduce the pressures emanating from fiscal and parafiscal operations, especially in Hungary, Poland, and Slovakia. This also means taking steps toward further moderation in wage settlements and toward liberalization of the remaining price controls in the Czech Republic. Among the long-term measures needed, it will be very important to continue financial sector reform in the Czech Republic and Slovakia, especially by increasing competition in the banking sector, by taking further steps toward the final resolution of the bad-debt problem, and by strengthening bank regulations.

Reducing inflation will take time, however, and short-term measures may have to be adopted in these countries. My instinct leads me to argue that the most effective policies are those that are determined by economic fundamentals. These fundamentals suggest that the exchange rate should be devalued if the external imbalance becomes dangerously large; it could be also addressed through greater exchange rate flexibility. It is obviously debatable whether the imbalance is already at that level, since all four countries are currently able to finance their current account deficits with external capital. What is important, however, is that devaluation would achieve two things at the same time. Most important, it would restore the competitiveness of domestic industries, which has been eroded especially in the Czech Republic and Slovakia, and it would increase the necessary element of risk for foreign investors, which were investing virtually risk-free under the regime of fixed nominal exchange rates. Radical changes in the exchange rate regime would, therefore, go a long way toward discouraging the growth of speculative capital.

Notes

The views expressed in this paper are personal and should not necessarily be attributed to the World Trade Organization. I have benefited from discussions and comments at the regional workshops on management of foreign capital flows in Budapest, 20–21 May 1996, and in Brighton, University of Sussex, 26–27 March 1997. The comments of Stephany Griffith-Jones and John Williamson and the statistical assistance of Maika Oshikawa, Catherine Osmers, and Anna Yankova are also gratefully acknowledged.

1. See, for example, Welfems 1992; Engholm 1994, chapter 6. For a useful background reading see also Bosworth and Offer 1995.

2. See IMF 1995b, which briefly reviews the contribution of internal and external factors on p. 53.

3. See, for example, the recent paper by Graham 1996, pp. 22–23, which also provides empirical evidence on the weak link between foreign direct investments and rates of return. Another relevant source is Dreyer et al. 1995.

4. For a survey see, for example, Rayome and Baker 1995. For a survey of literature see, for example, Hill 1990. The determinants of FDI in the CEECs have been discussed at length in, for example, Engholm 1994, and they will not be discussed at length in this paper. At any rate, not all are suitable for an analysis of aggregate foreign direct investments, as is the case of this study.

5. For a brief summary, see EBRD 1994.

6. See, for example, Nunnekamp 1991.

7. At the time of writing, the Standard and Poor's rating of the Czech Republic was A, the highest in the region. It was BBB- for Slovakia, Hungary, and Poland.

8. See Mainardi 1992 and Engholm 1994, chapter 6. In a similar vein, perhaps only political stability has been found to play an even more important role than macroeconomic economic conditions. See Lucas 1993.

9. Some policies may be important as argued, for example, in Gaster 1992.

10. See Ibarra 1995. An interesting twist to the argument would be to suggest, as Abel and Bonin do, that economic policies will be viable only if they simultaneously assure rapid privatization and significant inflow of foreign capital. See Abel and Bonin 1994, p. 73. This issue, however, will not be considered in this paper. For further details see also Aitken and Harrison 1994.

11. Both studies provide powerful empirical evidence of this argument, in which only aid-dependent Africa stands outside the pattern.

12. The absence of these conditions can have serious consequences. The latter are documented in some detail in Drábek 1995.

13. See, for example, Griffith-Jones 1999 and Dehesa 1994.

14. See, for example, Claessens et al. 1995, which argues that the evidence of greater instability of short-term capital flows is not straightforward, quite the opposite to the widely held view and the position taken in this paper.

15. We shall be returning to the discussion of external debt below.

16. See Baldwin 1995.

17. Aitken and Harrison 1994.

18. As I have noted above, I am aware that the argument of greater vulnerability in the presence of short-term capital is not that straightforward. The empirical evidence in fact does not always confirm this conclusion, as suggested by Claessens et al. 1995. In contrast, Turner 1991, for example, shows empirically that capital flows into developed countries tend to be more long-term and, therefore, stable.

19. For recent experiences, see Schadler et al. 1993.

20. While inflation can be a powerful disincentive for foreign investments, there may be situations in which inflation is not a deterrent for investment. The fact that low to moderate inflation may have no detrimental effect on output has been recently forcefully argued in Bruno and Easterly 1995. They argue that ideal macroeconomic conditions have been less important in small countries, that is, foreign investment took place even in the presence of inflation, but the inflation had to be predictable. *Pari passu*, it could be argued that foreign investment can take place where growth is slow but has good prospects.

21. The fast growth of wages has clearly been a major concession to the electorate after the drop of real wages in the early 1990s and in the aftermath of high unemployment and/or inflation. The population's income expectations are quite strong. Given the current rate of growth of wages, about 18 percent per annum, we estimate that the current level of wages in the Czech Republic will be equal to that of Germany within thirteen years. Clearly the income gap is too large.

22. In the Czech Republic, the trend was established in 1992, when the faster decline of real wages than that of productivity was reversed. See Flek and Buchtikova 1993 and Janáčková 1993.

23. The calculation of the rates of seigniorage is based on the definition of Fisher. It was calculated as $[M1(t) - M1(t-1)]/GDP(t) - g(t) [M(1) GDP](t)$, where M1 refers to the stock of money, GDP is gross domestic product, g is the real growth of GDP, and t refers to the time period.

24. See, for example, the relevant discussion in World Bank 1994, pp. 49 ff.

25. The findings partially confirm estimates carried out by other researchers. See Budina, Hanousek, and Tůma 1995, which estimates seigniorage to have reached the level of 2 in the Czech Republic and to have been "slightly higher" in Poland during the period 1990–93.

26. We shall return to this issue later in the text. The figures for the government budget are somewhat misleading. They constitute only a part, albeit the most important one, of the public sector and its borrowing requirements. The post-1990 decentralization and liberalization payments arrangements have resulted in increased scope for financing by other public sector institutions such as local governments and the Fund for National property. For more detailed information on local budgets see, for example, Mervart 1993. For details on central bank lending to the government, see Kotulan 1995, p. 34.

27. One of the unresolved questions is whether the factors noted had a permanent impact on demand for money or whether they only represented once-and-for-all change. An attempt to estimate demand for money in the Czech Republic was made by Klacek and Smidková 1995.

28. The current situation is marred by difficult negotiations about the future stabilization program, and especially about the government budget deficit.

29. A better indicator of the external debt position would be, of course, a figure for net external debt. While the foreign assets of the Czech Republic are quite large, a significant percentage is held in Iran, Iraq, Libya, and other countries with similar payments difficulties, and these must be therefore treated as doubtful at best.

30. See Williamson 1999.

31. All these figures come from *Economic Indicators for Eastern Europe, Monthly Release* (Basel: BIS, 27 December 1995).

32. See also the chapter by Gáspár in this volume.

33. The decline in savings rates seems to be a general pattern all across the region of countries in transition, as confirmed from other studies. See, for example, Conway 1995.

34. The point was also strongly argued in Calvo et al. 1995. However, that working paper does not provide comprehensive evidence.

35. See Abel and Bonin 1994, pp. 74 ff.

36. This is, of course, the traditional argument about the pattern of foreign trade of the CEECs. For a more recent exposition of this see, for example, Dobrinsky 1994.

37. The studies have been reviewed in Drábek and Smith 1995.

38. See, for example, Engholm 1994, p. 147. See also the study of wage differentials produced by Deutsche Bank in its regular reports and reported in an article in *Financial Times*, 1 September 1995.

39. In his recent statement to the IEWS Board, a multinational public policy research institute, David de Purry, cochairman of the Asea Brown Boveri (ABB) Group, has made this point very clear: "At ABB we began shifting labour-intensive activities from Western to Central and Eastern Europe in 1989. . . . Each hour a Polish worker spends on the job costs us $2.50, compared with U.S. $30 in Germany. While it is true that productivity in Western Europe is higher, the productivity differential does not compensate for the huge differences in wages." *Institute for East West Studies News,* vol. 2, issue 4 (December/January 1996), p. 2.

40. See EBRD 1994, p. 135, but also OECD 1994, p. 9.

41. This is clearly reflected in the comparison with the Western standards. The difference between money wages and productivity is substantial, as noted above. See also discussion further below.

42. These are, of course, highly controversial issues, well covered by Dooley 1995 and Griffith-Jones and Papageorgiou 1993. For a brief summary of the international taxation issues, see Greenaway 1995. Dooley identifies second-best arguments for government interventions to control capital flows, such as speed of adjustment of different markets, speculative attacks, price and wage rigidities, instability of relative prices, and capital market distortions. He also reviews the literature dealing with first-best policies arguments and the existence of multiple equilibria.

43. Only recently did the managing director of the IMF, Michel Camdessus, reaffirm the cautious approach to full convertibility in his public letter to the *Wall Street Journal.* See "IMF Way to Open Capital Accounts," *Wall Street Journal,* 29 September 1995; see also IMF 1995a.

44. See Razim and Yen 1995. As pointed out in IMF 1995b and Ffrench-Davis and Griffith-Jones 1995, a certain degree of discouragement of short-term capital flows, combined with an appropriate package of other measures such as fiscal tightening, can play a positive role in managing large surges in capital flows, or at least be conducive to an effective balance-of-payments management.

References

Abel, I., and J. Bonin (1994). "Direct Foreign Investment and Servicing the Debt." *Russian and East European Finance and Trade,* vol. 30, no. 2 (March-April 1994), pp. 71–88.

Aitken, B., and A. Harrison (1994). Do Domestic Firms Benefit from Foreign Investment? Washington, D.C.: World Bank, Policy Research Working Paper no. 1248, February.

Akyüz, Y., and A. Cornford (1994). Regimes for International Capital Movements and Some Proposals for Reforms; Geneva: UNCTAD, Discussion Paper no. 83, May.

Baldwin, R. (1995). The Effect of Trade and Direct Foreign Investment on Employment and Relative Wages. Cambridge, Mass.: NBER, Working Paper no. 5037.

Begg, D. (1997). "Monetary Policy in Central and Eastern Europe 1990–96: Progress and Pitfalls in Transition," *Oxford Review of Economic Policy,* vol. 13, no. 2.

Borensztein, E., J. de Gregorio, and Jong Wha Lee (1995). How Does Foreign Investment Affect Economic Growth? Cambridge, MA: NBER, Working Paper no. 5057.

Bosworth, B.P., and G. Ofer (1995). *Reforming Planned Economies in an Integrating World Economy.* Washington, D.C.: Brookings Institution.

Bruno, M., and W. Easterly (1995). Could Inflation Stabilization Be Expansionary? Washington, D.C.: World Bank, *Transition,* pp. 1–3.

Buckley, P.J., and M.C. Casson (1976). *The Future of the Multilateral Enterprise.* London: Macmillan.

Budina, N., J. Hanousek, and Z. Tůma (1995). Money Demand and Seigniorage in Transition. Prague: CERGE, Working Paper no. 48, April.

Calvo, G.A. (1994) "The Management of Capital Flows: Domestic Policy and International Cooperation." In *International Monetary Issues for the 1990s,* vol. 4. Geneva: UNCTAD.

Calvo, G.A., R. Sahay, and C. Vegh (1995). Capital Flows in Central and Eastern Europe: Evidence and Policy Options. Washington, D.C.: IMF Working Paper 95/37, May.

Chuhan, P., G. Perez-Quiroz, and H. Popper (1996). International Capital Flows: Do Short-Term Investment and Direct Investment Differ? Washington, D.C.: World Bank, Policy Research Working Paper no. 1669.

Claessens, S., M. Dooley, and A. Warner (1995). "Portfolio Capital Flows: Hot or Cold?" *The World Bank Economic Review,* vol. 9, no. 1 (January).

Conway, P. (1995). Saving in Transition Economies. Washington, D.C.: World Bank, Policy Research Working Paper no. 1509, September.

Dadush, U., A. Dhareshwar, and R. Johannes (1994). Are Private Capital Flows to Developing Countries Sustainable? Washington, D.C.: World Bank, Policy Research Working Paper no. 1397, December.

Dehesa, G. de la (1994). The Recent Surge in Private Capital Flows to Developing Countries: Is It Sustainable? Madrid: Per Jacobsson Lecture, 1994 (for IMF).

Dobrinsky, R. (1994). Trade Restructuring in Transition Economies: An Analysis Based on Trade with the European Union. New York: United Nations, Department for Economic and Social Information.

Dooley, M. (1995). A Survey of Academic Literature on Controls over International Capital Transactions. Cambridge, MA: NBER, Working Paper no. 5352.

Dooley, M., E. Fernandez-Arias, and K. Kletzer (1994). Is the Debt Crisis History? Washington, D.C.: World Bank, Policy Research Working Paper no. 1327, July.

Drábek, Z. (1995). "Non-Banking Financial Sector and the Link to Foreign Investment." In Griffith-Jones and Drábek 1995.

Drábek, Z. (1996). "The Stability of Trade Policy in the Countries in Transition and Their Integration into the Multilateral Trading System." *The World Economy,* vol. 19, no. 6 (November).

Drábek, Z., K. Janáček, and Z. Tůma (1994). "Inflation in Czechoslovakia in 1985–1991." *Journal of Comparative Economics,* vol. 18.

Drábek, Z., and A. Smith (1995). Trade Performance and Trade Policy in Central and Eastern Europe. London: CEPR Discussion Paper no. 1182.

Dreyer, J. et al. (1995). Industrialized Countries' Policies Affecting Direct Foreign Investment in Developing Countries. London: PAS Research Paper Series, 1995.

Dunning, J. (1958). American Investment in British Manufacturing Industry. London: George Allen and Unwin.

EBRD (1994). Transition Report. London: EBRD, October.

EBRD (1995). Transition Report. London: EBRD, October.

ECE (1995). Economic Survey of Europe 1994–1995. Geneva: United Nations Economic Commission for Europe.

Engholm, C. (1994). The Other Europe. New York: McGraw Hill.

Feldstein, M., and C. Harioka (1980). "Domestic Savings and International Investment." Economic Journal, vol. 90, pp. 314–329.

Fernandez-Arias, Eduardo, and Mark M. Spiegel (1996). North-South Customs Union and International Capital Mobility. Washington, DC: World Bank, International Economics Department, Policy Research Working Paper no. 1573.

Ffrench-Davis, R., and S. Griffith-Jones, eds. (1995). Coping with Capital Surges: The Return of Finance to Latin America. Boulder and Ottawa: Lynne Rienner and International Development Research Center.

Flek, V., and A. Buchtiková (1993). Income Policy and Wage Development in the Czech Republic. Prague: Czech National Bank, Research Report no. 12.

Gaster, R. (1992). "Protectionism with Purpose: Guiding Foreign Investment." Foreign Policy, no. 88 (Fall), pp. 91–106.

Goldstein, M. (1996). Presumptive Indicators/Early Warning Signals of Vulnerability to Financial Crisis in Emerging Market Economies. Washington, D.C.: Institute for International Economics, January.

Graham, E.M. (1995). Foreign Direct Investment in the World Economy. Washington, D.C.: IMF Working Paper WP/95/59.

Graham, E.M. (1996). Global Corporations and National Governments. Washington, D.C.: Institute for International Economics, May.

Greenaway, D. (1995). "Sand in the Wheels of International Finance." Economic Journal, vol. 105 (January), pp. 160–161.

Griffith-Jones, S., and Z. Drábek, eds. (1995). Financial Reform in Central and Eastern Europe. London: St. Martin's Press.

Griffith-Jones, S. (1996). International Capital Flows and Their Management. Brighton: University of Sussex, Institute of Development Studies, 1996.

Griffith-Jones (1999). "Capital Flows to Latin America: Lessons for Central and Eastern Europe." Chapter 8 in this volume.

Griffith-Jones, S., and V. Papageorgiou (1993). Globalization of Financial Markets and Impact of Flows to LDCs: New Challenges for Regulation. Paper prepared for the FONDAD conference in The Hague, 21–23 June.

Hernandez, L., and H. Rudolph (1995). Sustainability of Private Capital Flows to Developing Countries. Washington, D.C.: World Bank, Policy Research Working Paper no. 1518.

Hill, H. (1990). "Foreign Investment and East Asian Economic Development." Asian-Pacific Economic Literature, vol. 4, no. 2 (September), pp. 21–58.

Ibarra, Luis A. (1995). "Credibility of Trade Policy Reform and Investment: The Mexican Experience." Journal of Development Economics, vol. 47 (June), no. 1, pp. 39–60.

IMF (1995a). Capital Account Convertibility: Review of Experience and Implications for IMF Policies. Washington, D.C.: International Monetary Fund, Occasional Paper no. 131, October.

IMF (1995b). *World Economic Outlook 1995*. Washington, D.C.: IMF.
IMF (1995c). *World Capital Markets*. Washington, D.C.: IMF.
Janáčková, S. (1993). Balance of Payments of the Czech Republic, Productivity and the Rate of Exchange. Prague: Czech National Bank, Research Report no. 11.
Klacek, J., and K. Šmidková (1995). The Demand for Money Function: The Case of the Czech Economy. Prague: Czech National Bank, Research Report no. 41.
Kotulán, A. (1995). Ražebné a Fiskální Ražebné: Problémy Měření. Prague: Czech National Bank, Research Report no. 44.
Lipinski, J. (1994). "Mozliwost skutecznej polityki antyinflacyjnej." *Gospodarka Narodowa*, 10 (54), pp. 1–6.
Lucas, R.E.B. (1993). "On the Determinants of Direct Foreign Investment: Evidence from East and South East Asia." *World Development*, vol. 21, no. 3 (March), pp. 391–406.
Mainardi, S. (1992). "Foreign Investment in Latin America and South Asia: Relevance of Macroeconomics and Policy-Related Factors." *Giornale degli Economisti e Anali di Economia*, vol. 51, nos. 5–8 (Maggio-Agosto), pp. 259–80.
Mervart, J. (1993). Státní Dluh: Fiskální a měnové aspekty. Prague: Czech National Bank, Research Report no. 10.
Milesi-Fereti, G.M., and A. Razin (1996). Sustainability of Persistent Current Acccount Deficits. Cambridge, Mass.: NBER Working Paper no. 5467, February.
Montes, M.F. (1996). Country Responses to Massive Capital Flows. Helsinki: WIDER, Working Paper 121, September.
Nunnekamp, P. (1991). "Developing Countries' Attractiveness for Foreign Direct Investment—Debt Overhang and Sovereign Risk as Major Impediments?" *The Pakistan Development Review*, vol. 30, no. 4 (Winter), pp. 1145–1158.
OECD (1994). *Assessing Investment Opportunities in Economies of Transition*. Paris: OECD.
Rayome, D., and J.C. Baker (1995). "Foreign Direct Investment: A Review and Analysis of the Literature." *International Trade Journal*, vol. 9, no. 1 (Spring), pp. 3–37.
Razim, A., and Chi-Wa Yuen (1995). Can Capital Controls Alter the Inflation–Unemployment Trade-off? Cambridge, Mass.: NBER Working Paper no. 5239, August.
Reinhart, C.M., and S. Dunaway (1996). *Dealing with Capital Flows.* Helsinki: WIDER, 1996.
Reisen, H. (1995). Developing Country Savings and the Global Capital Shortage. Paris: OECD Development Center, September.
Schadler, S., et al. (1993). Recent Experiences with Surges in Capital Inflows. Washington, D.C.: IMF Occasional Paper no. 108, December.
Washington, D.C.: International Monetary Fund, Working Paper WP/91/23, March.
Turner, Philip (1991). "Capital Flows in the 1980s: A Survey of Major Trends." Basel: *BIS Economic Papers,* no. 30.
Ul Hague, M.S. Kumar, N. Mark, and D. Mathieson (1996). "The Economic Content of Indicators of Developing Country Creditworthiness." IMF, *Staff Papers*, vol. 43, no. 4 (December 1996), pp. 688–724.
UNIDO (1990). Foreign Direct Investment Flows to Developing Countries: Recent Trends, Major Determinants and Policy Implications. Vienna: UNIDO, 10 July.
Vernon, R. (1996). "International Trade and International Investment in the Product Cycle." *Quarterly Journal of Economics*, vol. 83, no. 1.
Welfens, P. (1992). *Market-Oriented Systemic Transformations in Eastern Europe*. New York: Springer-Verlag.
Williamson, J. (1999). "The Management of Capital Inflows." Chapter 2 of this volume.
World Bank (1994). *Adjustment in Africa*. Washington, D.C.: World Bank.

P32
079
F31
F32
P21

4

Economic Transformation, Exchange Rate, and Capital Inflows in the Czech Republic

Jan Klacek

In this chapter I intend to characterize, against a background of medium-term development, distinctly new current trends of the Czech economy as it enters the post-transformation stage. These changes represent a challenge for a new political response in terms of macroeconomic policies, calling for action in the unprecedented conditions of the economies in transition.

The first part of the chapter identifies new trends and the issues with which the monetary policy was faced for controlling inflation under the condition of a rapidly growing money stock. The inflow of foreign capital as a central issue posed to the control of money stock is analyzed in the second part. The degree of sterilization is tested, and empirical estimates of the monetary policy reaction functions are discussed.[1]

Macroeconomic Position and Current Trends

In the period 1993–96 one can observe rather positive outcomes as to the degree of macroeconomic stability of the Czech economy, detailed in reports by the international institutions and research institutes such as the World Bank, IMF, OECD, J.P. Morgan, Planecon, Datakopint, and WIIW. Ratings of sovereign debt by Moody's and Standard and Poor's have been repeatedly upgraded, and the Czech Republic is ranked as investment grade by these agencies. These ratings also placed the country on the list of

Table 4.1

Economic Indicators, 1990–1996

	1990	1991	1992	1993	1994	1995	1996
GDP (growth rate in percent)	−1.2	−14.2	−6.4	−0.9	2.6	4.8	4.4
Industrial output (growth rate in percent)	−3.3	−24.4	−7.9	−5.3	2.1	9.2	6.8
Consumer price index (in percent)	9.9	56.7	11.1	20.8	10.0	9.1	8.8
Rate of unemployment (in percent)	−0.8	4.1	2.6	3.5	3.2	2.9	3.5
Government budget Deficit − / Surplus + (as percent of GDP)	−0.1	−2.1	−0.2	0.1	1.0	−0.2	−0.5[+]
Money supply − M2* (in billion CZK, end of year)		27.3	23.0	20.5	21.5	22.8	9.5[+]
Official reserves (in billion USD)			0.80	3.90	6.2	14.0	12.4
External debt (in billion USD)			7.1	8.5	10.3	16.5	19.5[+]
Average exchange rate CZK/USD	17.95	29.48	28.26	29.15	28.7	26.55	27.34[+]

Sources: Czech National Bank (CNB), Central Statistical Office (CSU), and Ministry of Finance.

*M2 = Currency, demand deposits, time and savings deposits, foreign currency deposits.

[+]Preliminary.

investment opportunities considered by global institutional investors such as big insurance and pension funds. The positive outcomes as well as open issues are illustrated by the main indicators in Table 4.1.

Transition to Economic Growth

Among the new phenomena, the foremost place belonged to the reemergence of economic growth. In the initial period of liberalization and systemic changes, beginning in 1991, a sharp decline of economic activity was experienced. The rate of decline slowed down considerably in 1992–93, and only in 1994 did an economic recovery start. The growth of GDP by 2.6 percent and that of industrial output by 2.1 percent in 1994 accelerated through 1995, when industrial output rose by 9.2 percent and GDP by 4.8 percent. Economic growth was stimulated by a rising aggregate demand, namely, demand by households and investments into fixed capital; it is, however, also accompanied by a very strong demand for imports. The acceleration of economic growth is located especially among small- and medium-sized companies, which accounted for 17 percent of industrial output.[2] The upturn in economic activity is, however, observed also among the medium- and large-sized companies that came out of the privatization process.

Even though the rise in the level of economic activity seemed to represent a new trend, our assessment was still that of fragile economic growth. We were led to this standpoint by a large number of changes in data by the Statistical Office and the resulting low level of their transparency. In the Czech manufacturing industry we still saw conditions insufficient to ensure the start of robust economic growth. In the context of underlying economic trends of the 1990s, robust economic growth is usually defined as growth above 5 percent in the average over the long term. Only this pace of economic growth is consistent with the required catching up in economic level in relation to the developed European economies. Under these conditions the catching up could take place in the first decades of the twenty-first century. We note that among the transition economies such conditions so far have been satisfied only in the unified Germany, where the former states of East Germany have enjoyed a unique extent of aid and support.

The dynamics of the Czech economy are conditioned in the short term by the lack of technological as well as other institutional prerequisites necessary for a substantial rise in the level of total factor productivity. Here we refer among other things to the barriers of underdeveloped financial sector and first of all capital market.

Unemployment and Rigidities in the Labor Market

In the period of economic upturn a rising frequency of conflicting phenomena can be observed in the labor market. The period of transformation of the Czech economy has been typically associated with an extremely low rate of unemployment, ranging between 3 and 4 percent. In 1994, when the economic recovery started, the unemployment rate declined further, to 3.2 percent, and it dropped to 2.9 percent in 1995. A rational explanation of this "miracle" lies first of all in a number of unprecedented conditions that characterized the Czech economy at the start of transformation.

The initial disadvantage of a nonexistent private sector and underdeveloped services translated itself soon after the economic reforms were launched into an advantageously high capacity to absorb the majority of labor dismissed from overdimensioned agriculture and heavy industry. Even in regions hit by large closures, unemployment did not exceed 7 percent, and the

the figure stayed below 1 percent in a number of big towns. The unusually low average unemployment helped in reducing the social costs of transformation and strengthening the social consensus. In the mid-1990s, however, low unemployment—or, to put it more precisely, a rigid labor market—ranks among the major barriers of acceleration of economic activity. The rigid structure of the labor market also intensifies pressures to increase wages and in an interplay with other factors contributes to an excessively high growth of unit labor costs so that this short-term "comparative advantage" is quickly absorbed. The inadequately high growth of wage income is one of the new factors making the control of inflation rather difficult.

Control of Inflation and Growth of Money Stock

A top priority of macroeconomic policies adopted so far was the anti-inflationary goal. The restrictive monetary and fiscal policies prevented an inflationary spiral in an unprecedented situation of radical liberalization of the inherited rigid price structure and the quick opening of the economy in 1991. In a similar way, inflation was put under control in the period of a civilized split of Czechoslovakia into two independent and sovereign states in 1993, when a systemic introduction of VAT took place simultaneously. The annual inflation rate leveled off at 10 percent in 1994. This disinflationary development of the economy as it passed through its transformation was the result of coordinated restrictive macroeconomic policies involving effective control over the money supply.

Since mid-1994 the conditions for the control of money stock have, however, undergone a significant change. The money stock M2 increased by 21.5 percent in 1994, much more than the year before and twice as much as the inflation rate (see Table 4.1). The central bank was faced with the issue of effective control of the money stock for a second consecutive year. The rising difficulties in enforcing the disinflationary trend are linked to several factors. First of all, the core inflation, i.e., the inflation rate after accounting for price deregulation and tax adjustments, is persistently sticky at 5 to 7 percent on an annual basis. Another factor is a shift of priorities toward economic growth, which makes the trade-off between inflation and economic growth rather difficult. Also the former political will to coordinate fiscal policy with monetary policy has visibly vanished.

In 1995 the government and the parliament decided to spend almost all the budgetary surplus from the previous fiscal year. On the top of this, in July 1995 the government made a decision to increase budgetary expenditures out of higher-than-budgeted revenues in order to cover wage demands by railroad workers, teachers, and physicians, who all requested higher sala-

Table 4.2

Foreign Trade Balance and Balance of Payments (in million USD)

	1993	1994	1995
Foreign Trade			
Exports	13,077	14,295	21,754
Imports	12,734	14,731	25,433
Balance	343	−436	−3,679
Balance of Payments			
Current account	114.6	−15.9	−1,892
Capital account	3,024.8	3,031.6	7,686.8

Sources: Czech National Bank, Central Statistical Office.

ies and threatened to strike if their demands were not met. The former coordination of the fiscal and monetary policies seems not to be continued, and the change comes just when the foreign capital flows into the country and becomes the major component of the growth of the money stock, as we will analyze in the second part of the chapter. The central bank has a limited set of instruments to manage monetary policy under these conditions, and the sterilization policies tend to be very costly, which mainly applies to the issues of the bank's bills. The sterilization measures are not sufficiently efficient from the point of view of the control of the money stock, due to the uncertainty involved. The dilemma for the policy option lies in finding not only a short-term solution but simultaneously an efficient medium-term one.

Rising Deficit of Trade Balance

Another new trend was the emergence and subsequent quick rise of a deficit in the trade balance, which turned the current account of the balance of payments into a deficit (see Table 4.2). A surplus in the trade balance in 1993 was followed by a minor deficit in 1994; subsequently, the deficit rose very fast, as exports increased by 52.1 percent and imports jumped by 79.3 percent in 1995. According to the official view, the trade deficit and, in particular, the strong demand for imports could be interpreted as caused by the ongoing economic upturn. Due to the capital account's favorable position, the rising deficit had not represented a critical phenomenon from the short-term point of view. Nevertheless, policy makers should be worried more by a pronounced decline of export performance, which occurs in the context of the rather healthy development of external economic conditions in Europe. The flatness of Czech exports reflects particularly the low competitiveness of the Czech manufacturing sector and the fact that the positive export effects of a massive devaluation of the Czech koruna in 1990 were exhausted. The nominal exchange rate has been fixed at a stable level for four and a half years.

As domestic inflation was distinctly higher in comparison with the partner countries, the koruna underwent a process of real appreciation followed by the expectations of currency appreciation. The rising deficit of the current account, on the other hand, created the risk of a sharp devaluation. We think that in the present macroeconomic situation an efficient solution cannot be derived from simplified considerations of the exchange rate. Given the fact of an economy in transition, it seems helpful to consider an implementation of a policy package, including exchange rate measures.

In the Czech economy's present situation the core of the package should aim at reestablishing former consistency and/or a higher degree of coordination of fiscal policy with monetary policy. This includes a modified exchange rate policy involving some degree of flexibility, which would allow the level of the exchange rate to be to a certain extent determined by market forces, but within controlled boundaries, providing an anti-inflationary anchor.

Inflow of Foreign Capital and Issues of Sterilization Policies

The Czech Republic belongs to a group of economies in transition that have gone through the stage of attracting foreign capital and have entered the period of managing abundant capital inflows. While at the beginning of 1993, after the split of Czechoslovakia, foreign exchange reserves were at a level of US $200 million, the massive accumulation that followed pushed foreign exchange reserves to US $14.0 billion at the end of 1995 (see Figure 4.1). The buildup of foreign exchange reserves in the period 1994–95 is attributable to a surplus on the capital account as the current account turned into a deficit. Since 1994 the Czech National Bank (CNB) has resorted to sterilization policies in order to contain inflationary pressures stemming from the intensive capital inflow.

Structure of Capital Inflows

The factor of a growing capital inflow could be seen on both the demand and supply sides. The growing demand for foreign capital was particularly connected to the need for long-term capital resources caused by the privatization process and the subsequent restructuring of the enterprise sphere. A relatively low interest rate was especially motivated by the comparative advantages of the Czech economy (particularly lower wage production costs), the macroeconomic balance, and—connected to this—the

Figure 4.1 **Official Foreign Exchange Reserves** (in billion USD)

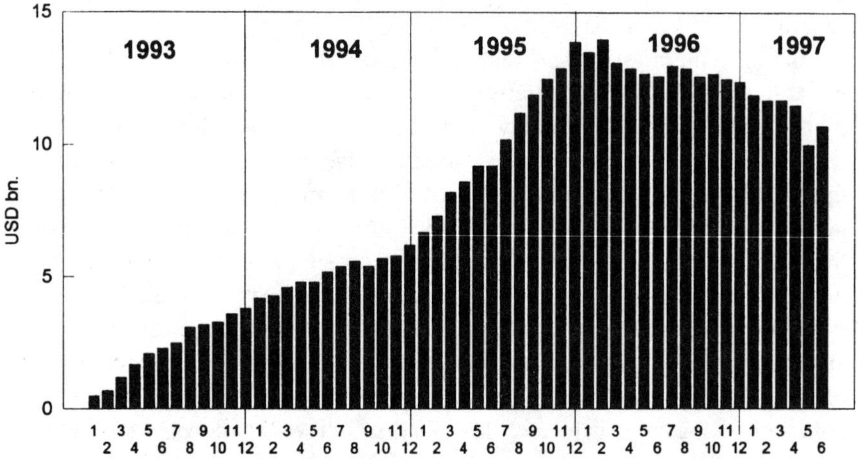

Source: Czech National Bank.

stability of the foreign exchange rate, the substantial potential for portfolio investment, and expanding room for direct investment.

While during the first two years of transformation, capital inflow from official foreign sources dominated (the IMF, European Union, World Bank, and G-24 governments), private capital became important during the transformation process.

In 1994, capital inflow was already dominated by financial credits drawn by commercial banks and enterprises. The volume of net drawing of foreign financial credits other than official during the first years of transformation was not substantial (approximately US $100–200 million per year) and was particularly related to construction activities. These credits started to gain in importance beginning in 1992; in 1995, their gross drawing totaled US $3.7 billion.

From the monetary and economic points of view, the drawing of foreign credits by the banks and enterprises can be seen as:

- a cheaper foreign source of long-term financing because of an insufficient supply of long-term resources on the domestic financial market
- a replacement of foreign direct investments by joint ventures (this is also due to an effort to avoid higher domestic taxation of profits)
- a source of additional demand for construction capacity and growth in this area

Also, the structure of portfolio investments experienced noticeable

Table 4.3

Composition of Net Capital Inflows (in billion USD)

	1993	1994	1995	1996
Direct investments	0.52	0.84	2.53	1.39
Portfolio investments	1.06	0.82	1.61	0.72
Long-term capital	0.53	0.86	3.31	2.72
Short-term capital	0.53	-0.07	0.23	-0.76
Capital inflows in total	2.64	2.44	7.69	4.07

Source: Czech National Bank.

changes. Unlike the previous period, when the inflow of resources from portfolio investments was ensured only through issues of central bank bonds on the international capital markets, in the mid-1990s the capital inflow from this source was used by municipalities and private subjects. In 1995 and 1996 international institutions such as the EBRD, IIF, and European Investment Bank also issued for the first time bonds denominated in Czech koruna.

By the end of 1995 the value of Czech securities denominated in koruna owned by foreign investors amounted to US $2.7 billion. Of this amount, approximately 61 percent was shares, 23 percent state bonds, including those of the National Property Fund, and 16 percent enterprise bonds. By their nature they belong to the short-term capital category. In 1995 the portfolio investment share of the net capital inflow amounted to approximately 21 percent.

Capital inflows underwent a major structural shift. Over the period 1992 to 1995 the structure of foreign capital inflow shifted from official sources to private ones, from direct investments to portfolio investments and direct credits, and, more important, from medium- and long-term forms of capital inflows toward short-term ones. (The sale of Telecom as a part of its privatization in 1995 itself represents US $1.2 billion in foreign direct investment, which inflated the total figure of FDI in that year.)

Impact on Money Stock

In a situation of massive capital inflow to a country, the stock of money tends to be determined by foreign investors and their decision making rather than by the central bank. While the capital account of the balance of payments of the Czech Republic was in surplus in the range of 9.1, 6.6, and

Table 4.4

Broad Money and Net Foreign Assets (NFA) (in billion CZK, end of period)

	1992	1993	1994	1995
M2	598.60	720.40	870.40	1,038.00
NFA	35.50	89.6	168.2	275
Percentage change[a]	—	44.4	52.4	63.8

Sources: Annual Report 1995, Czech National Bank 1996.
Note: [a]The ratio of incremental net foreign assets (NFA) to broad money (M2).

Table 4.5

Capital Account and GDP (in billion USD)

	1992	1993	1994	1995
(1) Capital account of balance of payments	0.002	2.9	2.4	7.7
(2) GDP	33.0	31.70	36.20	45.60
(1) as percentage of (2)	0.0	9.1	6.6	16.9

Source: Annual Report, Czech National Bank 1996.

Table 4.6

Rate of Growth of M2 and Inflation Rate (in percent)

	1992	1993	1994	1995
Broad money	23.0	20.2	20.8	19.6[b]
Consumer price index	11.1	20.8[a]	10.0	9.1

Sources: Annual Report 1995; Czech National Bank, 1996.
Notes: [a]8 percentage points of inflation rate in 1993 could be attributed to the introduction of VAT at the beginning of the year.
[b]Net of Telecom; 22.8 percent respectively, including Telecom.

16.9 percent of GDP in 1993, 1994, and 1995, respectively, the ratio of incremental net foreign assets to broad money reached 64 percent in 1995 (see Tables 4.4, 4.5, 4.6).

The CNB, which targets M2, was faced with higher-than-projected growth of money stock. For example, in both 1994 and 1995, the CNB declared an interval of 14–17 percent in the growth rate of M2 as consistent with the targeted rate of inflation, but the actual growth was 20.8 and 19.6

percent, respectively. A similar trend reemerged in the second quarter of 1995. This higher-than-targeted growth of M2, fueled in large part by the capital inflows, seems to correlate with the inflation rate, which did not decline despite a balanced or even surplus public budget.

Policy Response and the Management of Capital Flows

Theoretical Background for Policy Reactions

The standard open economy IS-LM model with capital flows, as formalized by Mundell and Fleming, is an appropriate framework to highlight in the simplest way the effects on a small open economy (see Frankel 1994, and Calvo, Leiderman, and Reinhart 1993). Indeed, the improvement in the capital account of the balance of payments generated by such a fall leads to a downward shift of the external balance schedule. Assuming imperfect capital mobility, and the economy will have a lower interest rate, the interest rate will be pushed downward even though it will remain higher than abroad. Two polar cases are important in this respect. Under a regime of fixed exchange rates, reserve inflows translate into increases in the money supply leading to the fall in the domestic interest rate and stimulating aggregate demand. The LM curve thus shifts endogenously to the right and the economy moves northeastward along the IS schedule and settles at a point of equilibrium. The other polar case is the one where the monetary authorities target money supply. In such a case, they have to sterilize the reserve inflows by reducing domestic credit, keeping the LM curve at the initial position, and the economy remains in the same point of equilibrium as before.

However, this is an unstable situation. Indeed, the accumulation of reserve inflows through a capital account surplus should translate into an appreciation of the domestic currency and a trade balance deficit. But the authorities may not be willing to allow an appreciation of the exchange rate. If they continue targeting the money supply, they may run into serious difficulties. As shown by Calvo (1991), this difficulty stems from the fact that the reduction in domestic credit has to be engineered through a direct or indirect increase in the stock of public debt. On the one hand, the debt service can become a burden for the government through a mounting budget deficit. On the other hand, the monetization or repudiation of the debt can spark capital outflows and ultimately a currency crisis (as happened in Mexico at the turn of 1994–95). The resulting depreciation is linked to the part of the interest differential between the country and the rest of the world that is expected to emerge due to domestic inflation expectations.

At a practical level, governments faced with very large capital inflows have a variety of alternative policy instruments that they can deploy. The right mix for a particular country will depend on domestic country circumstances, on a perception of what proportion of the flows are likely to be permanent, and on policy objectives.

The Policy Options in Managing Capital Flows

As Williamson (1999) clearly shows, governments faced with very large capital inflows have a variety of alternative policy instruments that can be deployed. Policy options and responses are also discussed in greater detail by Griffith-Jones later in this volume.

Sterilization Policies in the Czech Republic

Sterilization is a suitable policy response in order to curb inflationary pressures due to capital inflows. Especially in those countries where a fixed exchange rate regime is adopted, a surge in capital inflows can jeopardize control of monetary targets. Therefore in the case of the Czech Republic, where authorities give priority to price stabilization, the policy response to capital inflows plays a substantial role. The basic options for a central bank, which are not mutually exclusive, are the following:

(i) open market operations
(ii) a change in reserve requirements
(iii) the transfer of government deposits from commercial banks into a central bank
(iv) discouragement of foreign investors[3]

However, it should be stressed that sterilization goes hand in hand with costs being borne by central banks as well as commercial banks. Broadly speaking, the volume of costs is dependent on the interest rate differential and also on monetary policy instruments applied by a central bank (e.g., reserve requirements). At the same time, a further factor that cannot be neglected in this analysis is the time structure of capital inflows.

Sterilization policies were started in 1994. They consisted of a combination of all four options. Due to either a balanced or a surplus public budget, open market operations by the central bank had to rely on the bank's own issues of securities, the CNB bills, most of them of three and six months' maturity. Therefore, emissions of the CNB bills throughout 1994–95 had to be increased threefold (see Figure 4.2).

Figure 4.2 **Emissions of CNB Bills**

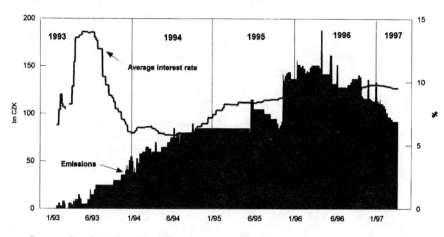

Source: Czech National Bank

The problem with the CNB bills is that the interest they bear is higher than the interest rate on foreign exchange reserves, and the quasi-fiscal deficit this implies represents the cost of this type of sterilization policy. Yet the sterilization has not reduced the rise of the money stock. Also, the rate of minimum reserves of commercial banks deposited with the central bank was changed several times. Regarding the change in compulsory reserve requirements, the CNB estimated in 1994 that about 30 billion koruna should be removed from the banking system by such a measure. On the other hand, one must be aware of the fact that reserve requirement policy, if it were applied over time, could both cause disintermediation—because of the rise in interest rates—and weaken the stability of the financial system as a whole. Thus, the policy of reserve requirements can be an effective measure only in the short term.

Reserve Requirements

Period	Demand Deposits	Time Deposits
January 1993–July 1994	9%	3%
August 1994–July 1995	12%	3%
August 1995	8.5%	8.5%
August 1996	11.5%	11.5%

Source: Czech National Bank

Therefore, the CNB decided to introduce an exchange rate risk via widening the fluctuation band from 0.7 to 7.5 percent around parity, effective 1 March 1996. After that, the capital inflow slowed down and more than US

Figure 4.3 **Effective Exchange Rates of Czech Koruna**

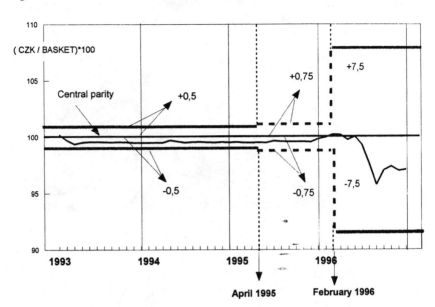

Source: Czech National Bank

$1 billion of short-term capital flew out of the country in the first half of 1996. The exchange rate remained at or below the parity level to the basket with the exception of January 1996. The trend toward appreciation of the koruna, which has prevailed (see Figure 4.3) since the wider fluctuation band was introduced, contradicts both the rising current account deficit and the decline in foreign exchange reserves.

The size of the capital inflow to the Czech Republic in 1995 reached the absorptive capacity, which is determined, inter alia, by the stage of restructuring processes at the company level. The microeconomic aspects are nowadays therefore as decisive in managing massive capital inflows as a consistent macroeconomic policy.

Empirical Evidence on the Degree of Sterilization

The extent of sterilization is usually measured by a policy reaction function as follows:

$$\Delta D = \alpha + \beta + \mu \Delta NFA \tag{1}$$

$$\Delta(D/Y) = a + bZ + c\Delta(NFA/Y) \tag{2}$$

where ΔNFA is the change in net foreign assets, Y is output, and Z a vector

Table 4.7

General Autoregressive Distributed Lag Model

Dependent Variable: DC
Czech Republic Dec. 1992–Dec. 1995

	Lags				
	0	1	2	F	Unit root t-test
DC	−1	0.231 (2.84)		8.06 [0.00]**	−9.44**
NFA			0.189 (8.69)	75.6 [0.00]**	
Cst	4.16 (9.58)			91.9 [0.00]**	

R^2 = 0.986; F(2, 34) = L 248.6 [0.00]; $\hat{\sigma}$ = 0.015; DW = 1.34; RSS = 0.008 for
3 variables and 37 observations. t statistic between brackets.

Long-run solution

$(DC)^*$ = 5.41 ÷ 0.246 NFA
(SE) (0.03) (0.006)

Wald test $\chi^2(1)$ = L361.7 [0.00]**

Error Correction Mechanism Mar. 1993–Dec. 1995

ΔDC = 0.005 ÷ 0.09ΔNFA ÷ 0.05ΔQ_{-1} − L24ΔP −0.386 (DC − DC*)$_{-1}$
    (0.90)   (2.20)   (3.55)   (−3.12) (−3.73)

R^2 = 0.550; F(4, 29) = 8.87 [0.00]; $\hat{\sigma}$ = 0.009; DW = 2.03; RSS = 0.002 for
5 variables and 34 observations.
Variance instability test: 0.110; Joint instability test: 1.27
Information criteria: SC = −8.95; HQ = −9.09; FPE = 0.001; AR 1–3; F(3, 26) = 0.08
    [0.97]; ARCH3 F(3, 23) = 0.51 [0.67];
Normality $\chi(2)$ = 0.60 [0.74]; RESET F(1, 28) = 1.61 [0.21]

of other variables (such as inflation, output growth, etc.) that determine the response of monetary authorities (see Argy 1981). In case one considers only the balance sheet of the central bank, ΔD is the change in net domestic assets of this bank and ΔNFA the change in its net foreign assets. However, one can also use a broader approach and, in terms of the monetary survey, including net assets of the banking sector, consider that D is domestic credit and NFA the net foreign assets of the central bank and commercial banks combined. In both cases, μ is the sterilization coefficient.

Old evidence on the extent of sterilization for industrial countries, surveyed by Kreinin and Officer (1978), indicated a significant negative μ coefficient. More recent evidence, also on industrial countries, is summarized by Fry (1995), with the common conclusion that such countries are able to sterilize capital flows substantially or even completely.

In the case of developing countries, Fry's estimates imply a rather low sterilization coefficient (c = –0.18 with pooling of twenty-seven countries over the 1960–88 period). This may be rationalized by the fact that some of these countries (such as Mexico, Turkey, or Venezuela) responded to the growth in net foreign assets by expanding domestic credit rather than by restricting it, in order to stimulate investment and growth by financing imports of capital equipment and raw materials. By contrast, sterilization seems to be substantial in Pacific basin countries such as Indonesia, Korea, Malaysia, the Philippines, Taiwan, and Thailand. Overall they sterilized more than 40 percent of increases in the net foreign assets of their banking systems (Fry 1995). Moreover, when one considers only the period starting in the late seventies or early eighties, the sterilization coefficient reaches at least 75 percent in all Pacific basin countries, except the Philippines.

Monetary Policy Reaction Functions and Sterilization

Our data cover the period December 1992 through December 1995. The main source is the monetary survey data of the Czech Republic, which come from revised series by the Czech National Bank. We work with monthly data, given the short sample at our disposal. We consider the domestic credit of the banking system and its net foreign assets, as reported in the monetary survey. The tests implemented start with a general autoregressive distributed lag model from which a long-run solution is derived. We test for cointegration, and when this test is positive, we examine the associated error correction mechanism. In a second stage, we check the robustness of these results by testing for cointegration in a vector autoregressive model, and by using a vector error correction model.

General Autorepressive Distributed Lag Model

We will examine in turn an equation with the level of domestic credit and another for the ratio of domestic credit to economic activity.

Variables in level

The estimated equation is as follows:

$$DC = a + \sum_i b_i DC_{t-i} + \sum_j c_j NFA_{t-j} + \sum_k f_k Q_{t-k}$$

where *DC* is domestic credit granted by the banking system, *NFA* is net foreign assets of the banking system, and *Q* is industrial output. (Variables and their source are presented in Table 4.4.)

Net foreign assets have an unambiguous positive effect on domestic credit with a two-month lag. The long-run effect is again positive, slightly higher and highly significant. In the error correction mechanism associated with this cointegrating relationship, the change in net foreign assets has a positive though small contribution, implying that far from contributing to the sterilization of reserve inflows, the change in domestic credit amplified their impact on the broad money supply. The coefficient of the error correction term is around −0.4, implying (when account is taken of the sign of their coefficient in the long-run relationship) that net foreign assets of a given month lead to an increase in domestic credit the following month with a proportion close to 0.1.

Normalized Variables

The estimated equation is as follows:

$$\frac{DC}{Y} = \alpha + \sum_i \beta_\iota \left(\frac{DC}{Y}\right)_{t-i} + \sum_j \gamma_j \left(\frac{NFA}{Y}\right)_{t-j} + \sum_k \theta_\kappa P_{t-k} + \sum_l \omega\lambda\, Q_{t-l}$$

where *DC* is domestic credit granted by the banking system, *Y* is retail sales in value, *NFA* is net foreign assets of the banking system, *P* is the retail price index, and *Q* is industrial production at constant prices.

The impact of the net foreign assets ratio on the domestic credit ratio is very sizable (Table 4.7) and positive with no lag, while its negative contribution with a one-month lag mitigates somewhat this effect, but not enough to prevent the long-run impact from being very high (around 0.5). This long-run solution does correspond to a cointegrating relationship. In the error correction mechanism, where we add a seasonal dummy (for January), when account is taken of the coefficient of the error correction term, the spillover from the net foreign assets ratio to the next month increase in the domestic credit ratio is 0.13.

The Dynamics of Capital Inflows and Monetary Policy with a VECM

We implement cointegration tests with the Johansen method and then examine VECMs.

We consider first the following system:

System A: $\left(\dfrac{DC}{Y}, \dfrac{NFA}{Y}, Q, P\right)$

At both the 5 percent and 1 percent levels, there is no ambiguity as to the existence of a single cointegrating vector in the Czech case (Table 4.8). In the vector error correction model estimated by full-information maximum likelihood, the variables in first differences have a nonsignificant contribution (and were thus omitted), except in the inflation equation (Table 4.9). The growth in industrial production and in the net foreign asset ratio depends on the level of the same variable in the previous month. We conclude that the net foreign asset ratio and industrial production are exogenous. Prices are only weakly exogenous. The domestic credit ratio and prices are not Granger-caused by any of the other three variables, while domestic credit is the only variable that is not weakly exogenous. The positive coefficient of $\left(\frac{NFA}{Y}\right)_{-1}$ in the equation for the dynamics of the domestic credit ratio implies that a high ratio of net foreign assets during a given month induces a rise in domestic credit the following month. This spillover of 0.17 is similar to what we obtained earlier in single equation error correction models.

Conclusion

After the surge of capital flows in Latin America, transitional economies in Central Europe were also hit by a wave of capital inflows. This chapter provides evidence on the degree of sterilization of such capital inflows in the Czech Republic.

The sterilization policies were deployed early enough and consisted of open-market operations, increases in minimum reserve requirements, and depositing revenues from privatization with the central bank. The degree of sterilization was, however, just a partial one. The main instrument of sterilization—issues of the CNB bills on a mass scale—resulted in an increase in interest rates, which in turn widened the interest rate differential and attracted more capital inflow. The sterilization policies were not accompanied by a budget surplus, and, given the size of capital inflow, the monetary policy alone perhaps could not do more.

Using first an unrestricted autoregressive general model, we estimate monetary policy reaction functions over the 1993–95 period with monthly data. In the long-run relationship, net foreign assets of the banking system have a positive impact on domestic credit. In the ECM for domestic credit, the change in net foreign assets has a positive impact while the error correction is highly significant.

Cointegration tests in a VAR enable us to show the robustness of these results. In the VECM, only error correction variables matter. This shows that regressions of the change on domestic credit on the change in net foreign assets, ignoring the error correcting term, may lead to a misleading conclusion.

Table 4.8

General Autoregressive Distributed Lag Model*

Czech Republic Dec. 1992–Dec. 1995

	0	1	2	Lag F	Unit root t-test
$\left(\dfrac{DC}{Y}\right)$	−1	0.398 (4.21)		17.8 [0.00]**	6.36**
$\left(\dfrac{NFA}{Y}\right)$	0.620 (10.0)	−0.309 (−5.19)		61.3 [0.00]**	
P			−1.23 (−8.02)	64.4 [0.00]**	
Q		0.123 (3.27)	[0.00]**	10.69	
Cst	8.67 (8.44)			71.2 [0.00]**	

$R^2 = 0.852$; $F(5,31) = 35.9$ [0.00]; $\hat{\sigma} = 0.02$; DW = 1.57; RSS = 0.01 for 6 variables and 37 observations.
t statistic between brackets.

Long-run solution

$$\left(\frac{DC}{Y}\right)^* = 14.4 \ \div \ 0.517 \ \left(\frac{NFA}{Y}\right) \ -2.06P \ \div 0.204Q$$

(SE)   (0.08)   (−0.35)   (0.07)
(1.46)

Wald test $\chi^2(2) - 51.6$ [0.00]**

Error Correction Mechanism

$$\Delta\frac{DC}{Y} = 0.016 \ \div \ 0.273 \ \Delta\frac{NFA}{Y} \ -0.318 \ \left[\left(\frac{DC}{Y}\right)_{-1} - \left(\frac{DC}{Y}\right)_{-1}\right] \ -0.095 \ DUQ1$$

(2.79) (3.78)   (−4.23)   (−4.89)

$R^2 = 0.843$; $F(3,32) = 57.3$ [0.00]; $\hat{\sigma} = 0.02$; DW = 2.04; RSS = 0.013 for 4 variables and 36 observations.
Variance instability tests: 0.088; Joint instability test: 0.78; SC = −7.46; HQ = −7.58; EPE = 0.005; AR L-4; $F(4,28) = 0.121$ [0.97]; ARCH 4 $F(4,24) = 0.43$ [0.78]; Normality $\chi^2(2) = 4.33$ [0.00]**; RESET $F(1,31) = 0.06$ [0.81].

Table 4.9

Cointegration Test (Johansen's method)

Czech Republic Dec. 1992–Dec. 1995

$$\text{System:} \left(\frac{DC}{Y}, \frac{NFA}{Y}, Q, P \right)$$

	Number of cointegrating vectors			
	0	1	2	3
(95%)	55.3**	15.7	4.97	0.26
	(47.2)	(29.7)	(15.4)	(3.8)

Constant and 3 seasonals for January, February, and July.

The empirical estimates of the monetary policy reaction function indicate that despite sizable open-market operations by the central bank, the massive capital inflow to the Czech Republic had a positive impact on the level of domestic credit. The sterilization efforts did not contain the inflationary impact of capital inflow on money stock. One can, however, argue that without sterilization, the impact of capital inflow would have been even larger.

The period of a strong foreign capital inflow up to 1995 was followed by a slowdown and even outflow of short-term capital in 1996 after the exchange rate band had been widened. The financial sector thus had to cope with the volatility of short-term capital.

Notes

1. That part draws on the econometric analysis conducted by Girardin and Klacek (1996).
2. The Czech Statistical Office provides data for the companies employing less than 100 employees.
3. Discouraging foreign investors is an appropriate way of influencing particularly the inflows of short-term capital.

Bibliography

Argy, V. (1981). *The Postwar International Money Crisis: An Analysis*. George Allen and Unwin.
Calvo, G., R. Sahay, and C. Vegh (1995). Capital Flows in Central and Eastern Europe: Evidence and Policy Options. IMF Working Paper.
Fry, M.J. (1995). *Money, Interest and Banking in Economic Development,* second edition. Johns Hopkins University Press.
Girardin, E., and J. Klacek (1996). Sterilization of Capital Inflows in Transition Econo-

mies: Econometric Investigation of the Czech and Polish Cases. Paper for the European Economic Association Conference in Istanbul.

Griffith-Jones, S. (1995). *Capital Flows to Latin America and Asia: Lessons for Central and Eastern Europe.* Institute of Development Studies, University of Sussex.

Grosfeld, I. (1994). Financial Systems in Transition: Is There a Case for a Bank Based System? Czech National Bank Annual Report.

Hrnčíř, M., and J. Klacek (1991). Link Between Fiscal and Monetary Policies in Transition: The Case of Czechoslovakia. Paper at the London Workshop, Institute for Fiscal Studies.

——— (1991). Stabilization Policies and Currency Convertibility in Czechoslovakia. Special issue of *European Economy.*

Klacek, J., and K. Kouba (1995). Macroeconomic Trends and Monetary Development in the Czech Republic. Paper at the symposium Re-evaluation of Economic Reforms in Central and Eastern Europe Since 1989, KOPINT-DATORG, Budapest.

Kouba, K. (1993). "Systemic Changes in the Czech Economy." In *Eastern Europe in Crises and the Way Out,* ed. C.T. Saunders. Macmillan.

Krainin, Mordechai E., and Officer, Lawrence H. (1978). The Monetary Approach to the Balance of Payments: A Survey. Princeton University, International Finance Section, Department of Economics.

Williamson, J. (1994). *The Management of Capital Inflows.* Chapter 2 in this volume.

Zemplinerova, A., Y. Katsoulacos, R. Lastovicka, and A. Marcincin (1995). Restructuring of Firms in Czech Manufacturing. Working Paper no. 73, CERGE-EI, Prague.

F32
P33 079

5

Capital Account Liberalization in the Czech Republic

Oldřich Dědek

Behavioral patterns of economic agents are always dressed in a plethora of legal norms. These norms express the preferences of policy makers about important events in the economy, shape the regulatory framework for those events, and give a push (or trigger brakes) if the course of events does not correspond to desired outcomes.

In reality, however, it may not be so easy to decide who leads and who follows—whether an institutional framework paves the way for events or whether this framework only acknowledges with a delay the spontaneous course of events. In many cases, this dual interrelationship may be hard to decode, but it seems crucial for a better understanding of the discretionary powers available to policy makers in a respective area.

The history of "external convertibility," or more specifically the liberalization of capital account in the Czech Republic, seems to possess all the attributes of the above mixture of top-down institutional reforms and bottom-up pressures of independent market forces. This paper tries to distill both ingredients of the mixture and assess their respective roles in promoting external deregulation.

The following section starts with current account liberalization, which is important for understanding the speed with which capital account deregulation was approached as part of "shock therapy." Then the chapter outlines the principles of sequencing the opening of capital account in the Czech Republic, and these are compared in the following section with the actual evolution of policy changes. Next I deal with regulatory responses to the growing demands for further relaxation of capital controls, and address some of the major issues arising from the obligations under IMF Article VIII. Finally, I evaluate various controls that have been introduced or were about to be introduced in the face of growing difficulties in managing the surge of capital inflows.

Sweeping Current Account Liberalization

After the collapse of Communist rule in the former Czechoslovakia the economy was subject to all sorts of distortions created by the command planning system. Administrative price controls supported by vast redistributions through a budgetary mechanism created a "Chinese wall" between domestic and world relative prices. There was only a weak correspondence between export performance in competitive foreign markets and the allocation of domestic resources, and the export performance itself was distorted by CMEA trade practices, which were frequently guided by political considerations rather than by criteria of market efficiency. Only a limited number of state-owned monopolies were licensed to conduct foreign trade. The household enterprise sector was further insulated from foreign markets through a cumbersome and politically abused rationing system of foreign currencies. The general shortage of Western consumer goods combined with the existence of a specialized shop network for convertible currency holders resulted in thriving corruption and a black market for foreign exchange.

One can therefore be hardly surprised that measures aimed at remedying the acute trade distortions constituted the core of the economic reform. A dispute emerged between proponents of a radical shake-up, on the one hand, and a more gradual approach, on the other.[1] The critics of "shock therapy" were concerned about the adverse consequences of sweeping trade liberalization, such as soaring unemployment brought about by poor adaptability of domestic producers, price hikes triggered by currency devaluations, and a deterioration of the trade balance due to strong import demand and weak export competitiveness.

In the end, it was the program of radical liberalization and deregulation that won majority support in the government. The monopoly position of specialized foreign trade companies was dismantled, and for all those interested in conducting foreign trade the government launched the policy of so-called internal convertibility.[2] The key feature of internal convertibility consisted of freeing up resident businesses' access to convertible currencies for trade-related transactions. In paying for imported goods and services, business firms were constrained only by their balances of domestic currency, while monetary authorities guaranteed the conversion—at the prevailing exchange rate—of those balances into a foreign currency without any limit.

The unlimited availability of foreign currency on the demand side was, however, combined with the surrender clause on the supply side. More specifically, all export earnings of convertible currency had to be sold—at the prevailing exchange rate—to authorized domestic banks. Holding foreign exchange accounts was not in general permitted.

At first, it was only the so-called legal subjects (i.e., incorporated businesses) that were subject to the rules of internal convertibility. Later on, the scope of eligible subjects was broadened to cover physical persons—entrepreneurs—as well.[3] The reason for the delay was the fear that, due to the links between small businesses and households, which are typically difficult to separate, scarce currencies might be diverted into private consumption. At the same time, subsuming small businesses under the regime of internal convertibility implied their compliance with the surrender clause and the obligation to give up their previous privilege of holding foreign exchange in their own bank accounts. The regulatory authorities, however, did not embark on a thorough process of monitoring the extent to which the accounts of small businesses and households were separated. Instead, the underlying idea was that the economy had reached a stable state in which they could afford to tolerate this sort of practice.

With respect to the household sector itself, the policy of internal convertibility allowed citizens to buy a limited but guaranteed amount of convertible currencies for foreign travel.[4] Undrawn quota in one year passed over to the next year. Keeping foreign accounts was allowed; no restrictions governed the private use of these balances except that the accounts had to be kept in domestic banks.

The Need to Attract Foreign Capital

Besides the efforts to liberalize external trade and to restore confidence in the domestic currency, the authorities had another major concern—how to attract foreign capital to restructure the Czechoslovak economy. The priority of opening the door for foreign capital was sound in many respects: from the central planning period, the economy inherited an obsolete stock of capital equipment, which had to be replaced and modernized; the business sector faced an unprecedented scale of privatization; the level of domestic savings was substantially smaller than the investment requirements needed for industrial modernization and restructuring; the underdeveloped banking and nonbanking financial sectors could not be expected to manage an efficient intermediation between lenders and borrowers.

Therefore, attention was paid to the need for creating a conducive environment for foreign investors. This, in turn, called for the establishment of a regulatory framework that would make investing in Czechoslovak assets an attractive and safe proposition. It should be noted that there was at that time fierce competition for foreign capital among many transition countries of similar country risk. It may be also interesting to note that the government was far less concerned about devising safeguards against the contingency of excessive capital inflows. Rather, the legislation was designed to attract foreign capital.

As a starting point, the former Czechoslovakia ensured constitutional protection for foreign investment. This principle was fully reflected in the Foreign Exchange Act, which established the freedom to repatriate profits, dividends, and interest as well as principal and equity stakes resulting from business activities of foreign investors. Only short-term investment (maturing in less than one year) continued to be subject to restrictions. The law stipulated the right of monetary authorities to control the outflow of short-term capital in order to maintain macroeconomic stability.

The Foreign Exchange Act also opened the way for foreign investors to use the domestic banking sector. Resident commercial banks were obliged to manage accounts denominated in the domestic currency on behalf of foreigners. The domestic currency was, therefore, allowed to be used as a transaction currency between residents and nonresidents as well as between nonresidents (in the accounts of resident banks only). In order to control transfers to and from abroad, a system of dual accounts was envisaged. Foreigners had to keep two accounts, one for payments associated with liberalized transactions and another for the remaining transactions, which continued to be regulated.

The Success Rate in Achieving the Desired Priorities

Despite the strong commitment to creating a favorable environment for foreign investors, the process of capital account liberalization was driven by conventional wisdom based on a cautious and piecemeal approach. As a result, the official strategy implied the following priorities:[5]

1. Capital inflows should take precedence over capital outflows, thus ensuring that scarce domestic savings are used to finance domestic investment rather than to acquire foreign assets.
2. Long-term capital inflows should take precedence over short-term capital inflows, thus protecting macroeconomic stability against disruptive speculation.

3. A major component of capital inflow should be foreign direct investment, which was seen as the most productive and stable utilization of foreign savings.

4. The number of agents licensed to conduct regulated capital transactions should be enlarged only gradually, starting with those institutions whose activities are easier to oversee and regulate.

In this way, policy makers in the Czech Republic intended to minimize capital controls and, at the same time, ensure that the economy was not exposed to the vagaries of excessive capital movements and to a drain of domestic savings. These stated priorities were to guarantee that the exposure to risks from the opening of the capital account was maintained within safe limits.

However, several events led to an erosion of these protective measures and pushed toward a deeper and faster deregulation than originally anticipated. The first was due to a loophole that arose from the agreements about investment protection and promotion that the Czechoslovak government and, subsequently, the Czech government have signed since 1991. The key deregulatory impulse of these agreements came from a broad definition of the term *investment,* which implicitly indicated that both long-term and short-term investment should enjoy the same degree of protection. Since international agreements take precedence over domestic legislation in the Czech legal system, the provisions of the Foreign Exchange Act through which the government retained some discretion over short-term flows became virtually meaningless.[6]

Another push came from the privatization process. Following the introduction of the voucher scheme, about 1,700 enterprises were transformed into publicly traded companies, and the list of these publicly traded issues was augmented by the establishment of some 500 mutual funds. One of the arguments that were raised in support of vouchers was that the domestic economy was short of private capital to finance privatization of state assets. But once shares, in the initial stage of the voucher privatization denominated in artificial units called "investment points," were ready to be traded for real money, the same argument applied: sales of shares would have led to a deep recession in the secondary market. The stock of traded issues was far in excess of money balances on the demand side. The only way out from such a gloomy predicament was to invite foreign portfolio investors to take part in trade sessions.

At the same time, secondary trading markets, which were mainly the Prague stock exchange and, to a lesser extent, the over-the-counter RM system, were exposed to competitive deregulation from neighboring emerging markets in Warsaw and Budapest, as well as from the mature Austrian and German markets. If foreign portfolio investors were to find in Prague substantially more impediments to moving in and out than in the competing markets next door, the capital market in former Czechoslovakia would soon have become of only peripheral interest in their eyes.

In principle, the voucher scheme created a unique opportunity for acquiring corporate control through bidding for shares in secondary markets. However, foreign direct investors were initially reluctant to use this route. They relied more on straight deals with incumbent management or government privatization agencies. In that way they could, for example, influence the composition of co-owners, avoid any responsibility for previous environmental damages, specify commitments to new injections of capital, and so on.

Notwithstanding the initial caution of foreign investors, the voucher privatization became a major vehicle for attracting portfolio investment, rocketing from scratch in 1992 to a level not far below that of FDI by 1994.[7] There is no dispute that the growing presence of foreign portfolio investors was beneficial for the Czech capital market. Besides supplying the desired liquidity, foreign portfolio investors exerted permanent pressure toward transparency, fair treatment of minority shareholders, higher disclosure discipline, and faster settlement procedures. In contrast with the original expectations, however, the composition of capital inflows acquired a somewhat riskier profile.

A major challenge for policy makers emanated from the domestic business sector's rising demand for foreign credits. The combination of tight monetary and fiscal policies, the burden of bad debts in banks' portfolios, the excessive risks involved in extending new credits, and, notably, the persistence of high inflation resulted in higher lending interest rates charged by domestic banks in comparison with those abroad.[8] In many cases, the sheer unavailability of long-term credits or the laxity of prudential limits constraining credit exposure to one client was why business firms, typically those with the highest creditworthiness, started to borrow abroad. The biggest Czech commercial banks also found it cheaper to raise funds in foreign financial markets. As a result, foreign direct borrowing (FDB) quickly became the most important item of capital inflows.[9]

To some extent, FDB is a less advantageous form of capital inflows than FDI. The reason is, of course, that the former has to be repaid during a fixed term irrespective of the commercial success or failure of the underlying business concern, while with the latter investors take up the commercial risk in exchange for the expectation of high returns and are, therefore, much more committed to the project through both good and bad times.

A boom in FDB can be partly explained by the failure of many borrowers to take proper account of exchange rate risks in calculating their costs of funds. Some firms seemed to forget that the exchange rate had not been fixed irrevocably, and that the apparent advantage of raising funds abroad might look different in the case of adverse exchange rate movements. The fixed exchange rate thus provided a sort of "greenhouse effect" that would prove dangerous for macroeconomic stability if the size of FDB reached a point where monetary authorities could no longer guarantee exchange rate stability.

The issue of "hot money" was another element that pushed the composition of foreign capital into a riskier profile. This type of volatile capital inflow was strongly encouraged by interest rate differentials, by the fixed exchange rate arrangement, and by growing capital mobility. Branches of foreign banks served as a major channel through which short-term foreign exchange deposits provided the basis for lending on the domestic interbank market or for buying government and central bank short-dated securities. The true extent of the "hot money" issue has been difficult to estimate due to the poor quality of available data. In any case, even the incomplete and inaccurate evidence pointed to the disturbing trend in which "hot money" was growing at a faster pace than the other components of capital inflows.[10]

Leaning with the Wind

Faced with growing pressures from the business sector to further liberalize the capital account transactions, the first reaction of the regulatory authorities was to succumb to those pressures. There were several reasons why further liberalization promised clear and rewarding benefits. The exposure of the domestic financial sector to foreign competition increased, the access to cheaper and longer-term credits improved, and the capital market enjoyed more liquidity. Easing some capital controls also had an important signaling effect, announcing that Czech policy makers were committed to a credible deregulatory program.

At the same time, some of the existing policies became questionable under the new circumstances. For example, once inward capital flows reached a point at which their volume became a matter of concern to monetary authorities, the existing policy of restricting capital outflows and discouraging the demand for foreign exchange might have been seen as irrational at a time when the inflows of foreign capital was threatening the internal price stability. Moreover, the prevailing restrictions were binding mainly for domestic businesses, rendering them less competitive vis-à-vis foreign competitors.

The regulatory bodies thus faced the dilemma of reconciling the existing regulatory framework with the rising demands for higher capital mobility. Fortunately, the legislation proved to be sufficiently flexible in this respect, and for some time there was no need to legislate changes.

The instrument that was targeted to accomplish deregulation was the prerogative of the authorities to grant permission for executing non-liberalized capital transactions. The law distinguished three types of trans-actions: (1) those that were liberalized, (2) those that were forbidden, and (3) those that could be pursued only with official permission. The stringency with which the permissions were granted became the major deregula-tory vehicle at that time. The approval process was, however, a one-way street in the sense that once a transaction was given a more benevolent treatment, it became difficult to revise the opinion at a later stage without damaging the credibility of the whole deregulation program.

Several important developments can be mentioned in this respect. In March 1994 one of the key attributes of internal convertibility—the surren-der clause—was phased out. Since then, requests to open foreign currency accounts submitted by domestic businesses were more or less automatically approved (provided the businesses were earners of foreign exchange). The business sector was thus allowed to manage its own balances of convertible currencies. The only requirement was to do so on their accounts with resi-dent banks only.

Private FDB was initially also subject to the compulsory approval of the monetary authorities. However, the stringency in screening the submitted applications was relaxed dramatically. The authorities soon realized that a credible assessment of requests to borrow on the basis of any precise efficiency criteria (for instance, by distinguishing between trade-related financing and that for speculative purposes) was beyond their capacity. Thus, except for a handful of evident cases that were supposed to mask money laundering or other criminal activities, the job of the regulators was limited to registering credits and to reminding less disciplined borrowers to comply with their duties.[11]

Regulation through granting permits became a highly informal procedure with respect to Czech direct investment abroad. This category of capital flows had to be fully liberalized under the association treaty between the Czech Republic and the European Union which came into effect on Febru-ary 1, 1995. FDI outflows to non-EU countries were also treated liberally as well, based on the argument that FDI tends to promote future export expansion. In either case, however, this kind of capital outflow occupied a marginal share in total capital movement.

Regarding the household sector, the annual tourist quota was increased from CZK 12,000 to CZK 100,000 at the beginning of 1995. The new limit substantially exceeded expenditures that the average Czech citizen devoted to travel purposes.

With the benefit of hindsight one could thus observe a remarkable dynamic of external sector liberalization despite the fact that the relevant legislation experienced only minor amendments. The accelerated speed of deregulation resulted from the combined effect of the growing pressures from the enterprise and household sectors, on the one hand, and the deliberately weak resistance to these pressures on the part of the regulatory authorities, on the other hand. The latter originated in the government policy of attracting foreign capital and integrating the Czech economy into the family of developed market economies.

IMF Article VIII Convertibility

The deregulation process noted in the previous section, which consisted of relaxing the vigor with which compulsory controls were exercised, started to lose momentum by the end of 1994, when the approach seemed to reach its limits. Further deregulation required a new legislative jacket.

Formally, the discussions centered around the effort to "upgrade" the Czech currency to a higher status of convertibility—the so-called convertibility under Article VIII of the IMF. The former Czechoslovakia rejoined the IMF in September 1990 under Article XIV, which allows a country to maintain and modify controls implemented at the time of the accession with regard to balance-of-payments considerations. The article assumes that the country will take steps to facilitate international payment relations once these controls are no longer necessary for maintaining the balance-of-payment equilibrium.

Article VIII represents a higher status of convertibility, which binds a country to remove all restrictions or bans on current account transactions. In this way, the country manifests a relatively high degree of internal stability by affording a fairly liberal (but not yet completely liberal) environment for foreign exchange transactions.

It should be noted, however, that the problems that had to be addressed in the process went far beyond the requirements posed by Article VIII regulating current transactions. As the ensuing discussions revealed, the core of the problem rested in reconciling the law with the already granted freedoms of capital movement.

The first task the new legislation was expected to accomplish was to catch up with the status quo in the economy. This meant rectifying the cases that needed to be regulated de jure but were liberalized de facto. For this reason, the philosophy of the new Foreign Exchange Act was changed, and instead of distinguishing between regulated and liberalized transactions, it was limited to a list of activities subject to a regulatory regime. All other transactions were treated as free.[12]

In this way, the act sanctioned the abolition of the surrender obligation, so everybody (i.e., not only earners of foreign exchange) was allowed to open foreign currency accounts and switch between different currency holdings (but still on the accounts of resident banks only). A similar kind of catching-up liberalization affected the outflow of foreign direct investment even outside the European Union countries, private borrowing from abroad, or purchases of real estate abroad by residents. In contrast to the previous ruling whereby an agent was required to ask a regulatory body for permission to execute any of the above activities, now the agent was required only to inform the authorities about the execution or intention to do so. In this way, the duty to apply was replaced by the duty to announce.

Another consequence of adopting Article VIII convertibility was the creation of a level playing field for all categories of residents regarding their access to current account transactions. To comply with this objective in practice, some controls on unilateral transfers as well as tourist limits for the household sector were abolished. The monetary impact of these measures was negligible because the already existing quotas (CZK 100,000) were more than enough to cover the average household demand for convertible currencies.[13]

There were some issues with a more profound impact on the degree of deregulation. A particular debate concerned whether to introduce the external circulation of domestic currency; that is, whether or not the Czech currency should be allowed to serve as a payment currency abroad provided that foreign counterparts agree to accept it. In terms of Article VIII, which is related to the removal of barriers to trade-related transactions, one should be inclined to allow the external circulation of domestic currency since its ban increases transaction costs and exposes traders to extra exchange rate risks. On the other hand, some policy makers were concerned about the fact that the external circulation might lead to a substantial loss of control over the money supply and to the formation of competing offshore markets for the Czech currency outside the Czech jurisdiction.

A detailed analysis carried out at the time revealed that the exclusion of external circulation from the new policy package would do more harm than good. First, the external circulation of banknotes and coins had already become a reality. For example, some Austrian and German banks were prepared to buy and sell the Czech currency as a part of their retail activities. Interestingly enough, the so-called Vienna parallel exchange rate was frequently exploited by the Czech monetary authorities as supporting evidence for the credibility of domestic monetary policies. The Czech currency was also increasingly used as reserve money in Polish areas close to the Czech border and in Slovakia.

As far as wire transfers are concerned, the concept of external circulation was misunderstood because, technically speaking, domestic currency never leaves a resident country. A Czech koruna deposit in a foreign bank is simultaneously a claim (that is, a deposit denominated in Czech currency) by the foreign bank on a Czech resident bank. The real question was whether foreign banks could use the Czech currency for settlement purposes in transactions between domestic businesses and foreign trade partners. At the same time, however, this kind of transaction was legal for foreign banks residing in the Czech Republic. In such a case, the foreign resident bank could serve as intermediary for payments denominated in Czech currency even between nonresidents. Under the circumstances, the payment system was already endowed with elements of external circulation of the currency. From this perspective, the external convertibility only brought more symmetry into the treatment of foreign resident banks, on the one hand, and foreign nonresident banks, on the other.

Potential dangers associated with the external circulation of currency stem from the obligation of monetary authorities to repurchase, on demand, nonresidents' holdings of domestic currency. Strictly speaking, Article VIII imposes on a country the obligation of unlimited conversion of only those balances that resulted from current account transactions or are intended for such transactions. This requirement, however, raises the question of how to earmark all other nonresident balances in order to shield the economy against the vagaries of volatile capital flows.

The previous system operated under the regime of dual nonresident accounts, one for liberalized and the other for regulated transactions. But the arrangement of two separate accounts is workable only as long as the monetary authorities can prevent leakages between the two accounts. If this protective capacity becomes questionable, which may be the case in turbulent periods, incentives will mount to use the account with the underlying commitment to unconstrained conversion for transactions that should not, in compliance with the law, enjoy such a treatment. The system of dual accounts also makes practical sense only for balances under the jurisdiction of domestic monetary authorities. This precondition, however, was not fully valid for the Czech currency, which had been allowed to circulate externally, as already noted.

As a result, the new Foreign Exchange Act did not take over the provisions for dual accounts due to their questionable ability to track the current or noncurrent origin of nonresident holdings of the Czech currency.[14] As a by-product, the Czech monetary authorities assumed, therefore, a much larger obligation for unlimited conversion than Article VIII convertibility itself would suggest.

In order to complete the description of the new regulatory environment, it should be noted that the updated foreign exchange legislation maintained several important capital controls. None of them, however, proved to be a significant constraint on capital mobility. These restrictions are as follows:

- credit extension by residents to nonresidents (exceptions are government credits, long-run credits associated with direct investment, and loans between individuals)[15]
- accounts of residents (denominated both in domestic and foreign currencies) held in a foreign bank abroad[16]
- access of foreign securities to the domestic primary and secondary financial markets[17]
- purchases of domestic real estate by nonresidents (exceptions are enumerated by the law)[18]
- extension of residents' guarantees to the liability of a nonresident to another nonresident

The above restrictions do not take the form of a strict ban but remain within the discretionary powers of the monetary authorities, which may grant or reject permission for conducting the transaction that is subject to regulation. In some cases, the law even authorizes the regulators to approve special licenses. A licensed agent is, therefore, allowed to conduct such a regulated activity on a permanent basis without the need to apply for the approval for every individual transaction (licensing is particularly relevant for securities dealers and portfolio managers). Moreover, the remaining regulations are mainly applicable to nonbanking financial institutions because the licenses of commercial banks are wide enough to cover a majority of regulated activities.

Be this as it may, much depends on the stringency with which the authorities exercise their regulatory powers. In this respect, one might expect that the previously benevolent approach will continue under the influence of two pressures. First, it has proved difficult for regulators to go against the demands of economic agents for greater capital mobility if they can back up these demands with sound arguments (one of them is the creation of a level playing field for domestic and foreign entities). Second is the determination to integrate the Czech economy into the family of developed market economies. This will call for the adoption of norms of behavior that are common in these economies.[19] The unfettered mobility that capital flows may at present enjoy is surely one of them.

Putting on the Brakes and Designing Safeguards

Until the beginning of 1995 one could observe only a one-way process toward capital account deregulation. This trend, in combination with prudent macroeconomic policies, the fixed exchange rate arrangement, and the steadily improving country risk, resulted in an unprecedented surge of capital inflow.[20] The surge started to raise questions about the capacity of the system to absorb the capital inflows, the coverage of risk exposure of firms borrowing abroad, the inflationary consequences generated by excess money supply, the high cost of sterilization, and so on. In other words, monetary authorities realized that the trend toward attracting foreign capital must be in one way or another accompanied by measures aimed at repelling "unwanted" forms of capital and maintaining the capital inflows within manageable limits.

In April 1995 the Czech National Bank introduced a 0.5 percent bid-ask spread for foreign exchange transactions between the bank and other commercial banks. This measure was partly intended as a repellent against short-term speculative capital on the basis of the following logic: If the price of buying the domestic currency is higher by 0.5 percent than the selling price, the foreign speculator loses 0.5 percent on every completed conversion (after switching back to the convertible currency). So, for example, the annualized investment into a one-month security entails twelve completed conversions, thus a 6 percent yield loss. This should be just enough to wipe out the 5 to 7 percent interest rate differential.[21]

In June 1995 the Czech National Bank threw more "sand into the wheels" of capital flows in the form of imposing limits on the so-called short-term open positions vis-à-vis nonresidents. The idea behind this measure was that a typical short-term speculation creates a currency mismatch on the commercial bank's balance sheet: The bank's liability (money deposited by a foreign speculator) is attached to a nonresident, while the bank's ultimate asset (credit extended to a domestic firm or investment into a money marked instrument), which was made possible by the speculator's liability, is marked as a resident one. In order to curtail such a speculative pattern, banks were required to keep the daily mismatch (i.e., the difference between short-term nonresident assets and short-term nonresident liabilities) below 30 percent of total short-term nonresident assets, at the very most CZK 500 million.

However, the practical impact of the above measure seemed limited.

Frankly speaking, few would have expected a different outcome given the ease with which such controls could be circumvented.[22] On the other hand, one should not play down their signaling effect, announcing for the first time that the central bank is prepared to take stronger steps if necessary.[23]

In fact, the new Foreign Exchange Act paved the way for more forcible measures in case of unfavorable development in the external sector. The most important step was that the central bank is now authorized to impose interest-free deposit requirements on foreign exchange balances (having their origin, for example, in credits extended by nonresidents to residents, interbank deposits, or deposits of foreigners held in domestic banks). The measure received a mixed reaction, as views about the importance of deposit requirements differed. On the one hand, there was a positive experience with limited capital controls in some Latin American countries (Chile, Colombia). On the other hand, there was a growing sentiment that deposit requirements might damage a liberal track record and the credibility of the Czech external sector deregulation. The consensus was reached that the imposition of the measure would be warranted in case all other market-type solutions, including a change in exchange rate management, failed.

Last but not least, the act also provides for extraordinary measures under emergency conditions due to the balance-of-payments disequilibrium. Under such conditions (accompanied by a threat to the country's ability to honor its external obligations or by a disruptive attack on internal monetary stability), the government is authorized to suspend, for up to three months, many of the liberalized foreign exchange transactions. This sort of nonmarket defense against capital flight was backed by the argument that capital markets tend to "overshoot" in their reaction to fundamental imbalances. From this perspective, the state of emergency might be seen as a temporary respite during which economic agents should reconsider their judgments and cool down jittery emotions. No doubt, however, the best thing policy makers can do is to avoid testing whether the above logic can be put into practice.

Conclusion

In contrast to the radical approach to foreign trade liberalization, the deregulation of capital flows in the Czech Republic was envisaged, in accordance with the general consensus about reform sequencing, as a more gradual process. There was only one major amendment to the foreign exchange legislation after the introduction of so-called internal convertibility in January 1991. This occurred in October 1995 in connection with the adoption of the convertibility obligations under IMF Article VIII. Nevertheless, the standstill on the legal front was accompanied in real life by a strong trend toward relaxing the stringency with which regulatory authorities exercised their powers.

It is difficult to decide how important individual factors were in pushing for more extensive deregulation. With the benefit of hindsight it seems evident that one of the most influential factors was the proximity of the European Union and the desire to quickly integrate the Czech economy into the world economy and with developed market economies. From this point of view, any scenario of lifting capital controls that would have tried to copy the piecemeal and protracted route adopted by Western Europe in the 1960s and 1970s would have clashed with the completely different external environment and conditions of the 1990s. At the same time, the benefits from a liberalization of capital inflows were clear and large.

Although the Czech regulators had in mind certain priorities about the speed of liberalization and the composition of foreign capital inflows, these priorities were partly overridden by growing pressures from the business sector for more capital mobility. This development confirmed that the capacity of the liberally minded government was limited to choose an optimal mix of inflows once the financial markets grew out of their infancy.

As far as the "techniques" of deregulation are concerned, it made a difference whether a regulation was effective through a legal ban or through the prerogative of the authorities to grant permission for executing non-liberalized capital transactions. While the former approach created relatively rigid boundaries that could be moved by a new legislation only, the latter approach proved to be much more flexible, offering room for deregulation by changing the stringency with which the regulation was enforced.

Within a relatively short period of time the Czech Republic reached a high degree of deregulation of the external sector. This process was not marked by visible setbacks, even though the outside and inside economic pressures made it faster than originally envisaged. The most crucial outcome of the external deregulation is the new environment for policy making, which can no longer count on rigidities prevailing in a transition economy but must seriously take into account all the challenges pertaining to a liberal market economy.

Notes

1. The clash of the two opposing views came into the open in 1990 in the course of discussion about two competing scenarios: The first one, which supported a radical treatment, was elaborated by the Czechoslovak federal government, while a more gradualistic approach was advocated by the government of the Czech Republic.

2. The regime of internal convertibility came into effect at the beginning of 1991, on the basis of the Foreign Exchange Act, no. 528/1990.

3. This was provided for in the Amendment to the Foreign Exchange Act as of April 1992 (act no. 228/1992).

4. The limit periodically adjusted depending on overall economic conditions. The U.S. dollar equivalent of the limit per person and per year changed in the following way: $70 in 1990, $180 in 1991, $270 in 1992, $430 in 1994, $3,570 in 1995.

5. Rather than being expressed in an official document, the following priorities represented the philosophy of regulatory authorities that guided sequencing of the capital account liberalization.

6. Up to the end of 1994 the Czech Republic signed investment protection and promotion agreements with more than thirty countries. According to estimates at the time, as much as 80 percent of foreign investments were expected to receive preferential treatment on the basis of those agreements.

7. While FDI dropped from USD 983 million in 1992 to USD 842 million in 1994, portfolio investment increased from zero in 1992 to USD 819 million in 1994. See also chapter 3 by Drábek in this volume.

8. In terms of Maastricht criteria, the rate of inflation in 1995 and thereafter has remained three times higher than the EU benchmark, despite successful disinflation in the early 1990s.

9. In 1994 foreign direct borrowing was 1.4 times higher than foreign direct investment, while in 1992 the FDB/FDI ratio was only 0.3.

10. According to the Czech National Bank estimates, more than a third of capital inflows in 1995 were of the short-term speculative variety.

11. As an example of suspicious activities, a borrower with equity of USD 15,000 filed for credit of USD 120 million, with Costa Rica being the lender's country of residence. Another example: A private individual intended to borrow USD 18 million from a Nigerian lender at a cost of 8 percent and 20 years' maturity (source: CNB).

12. The new Foreign Exchange Act was enacted by the parliament on 26 September 1995 and came into effect several days later, on 1 October 1995.

13. The tourist limit might have been, however, binding for those wealthy people who could afford to pay for medical treatment abroad, study at foreign universities, etc. See also the relevant discussion in the previous section.

14. The experience gathered from the clearing arrangement between the Czech and Slovak Republics spurs skepticism about the efficiency of managing a system of dual accounts if the incentives to breach the rules are strong enough. The system also operated with two accounts—one for payments originated before the currency split and the other for payments originated after the currency split. When exchange rates used in these two accounts differed, speculative tactics emerged to exploit profit opportunities. The response of the regulators was weak, however, mainly due to the high cost of continuously verifying whether payment titles were declared correctly. For a detailed discussion see Dědek et al. 1996.

15. It seems that this regulation has had only a limited effect, considering that commercial banks, as the decisive providers of domestic credit to nonresidents, are beyond the reach of regulators in this respect, since banking licenses allow them to do this kind of business.

16. Securities firms diversifying their portfolios internationally are expected to become a major applicant for exemption from this control. As far as the household sector is concerned, no effective mechanism has been devised to monitor compliance with this so-called transfer duty.

17. This control soon proved counterproductive because nonresident issuers of a paper denominated in the Czech currency could easily use offshore markets that came into existence after the Czech currency was allowed to circulate externally.

18. The continuation of this restriction was primarily motivated by political reasons rather than by balance-of-payments considerations.

19. A commitment toward capital account deregulation stems particularly from membership in the OECD. According to well-informed sources, the prestigious achievement of being the first among the post-Communist countries to do this was a major factor that accelerated the adoption of the new Foreign Exchange Act.

20. In 1995 the share of net capital inflow in GDP reached 18.4 percent. For more details, see the chapter written by Drábek in this volume.

21. The above logic is, however, to some extent flawed. Why should a speculator undergo the currency conversion every time he or she rolls over the short-term speculative position in a Czech asset? A more reasonable strategy would be to renew a short-term position from the proceeds of already matured assets and thus avoid the loss from paying the bid-ask spread. Merits of the above measure should be seen, therefore, in other areas: as a source of revenue for the central bank that partly offsets the high cost of sterilization, and as an incentive for commercial banks to trade foreign exchange among themselves rather than relying on the central bank facility.

22. With respect to limits on short-term open nonresident positions, banks tended to rearrange short-term liabilities (with maturities of less than one year) as long-term liabilities that were not subject to the control. To give some figures, while the shares of short-term and medium-term deposits of foreign banks in the domestic banking sector (which is an important source of capital for branches and subsidiaries of foreign banks operating in the Czech Republic) were 80.4 and 16.1 percent, respectively, at the end of June 1995, within two months after the regulation came into effect these shares changed to 47.8 and 50.0 percent, respectively. Another escape channel was to interpose a domestic nonbank financial institution between a foreign speculator and a domestic bank. In this way, the bank's nonresident liability is transformed into a resident liability.

23. A proper role of capital controls should be viewed in conjunction with other measures used to cope with capital inflows: limiting central bank refinancing facilities, shifting government deposits from commercial banks to the central bank, increasing reserve requirements, and particularly sterilizing open market operations. On this point see J. Klacek's chapter in this book.

Bibliography

Artis, M.J. 1998. "Exchange Controls and the EMS." *European Economy,* no. 36 (May), 163–81.

Basevi, G. 1988. "Liberalization of Capital Movements in the European Community: A Proposal, with Special Reference to the Case of Italy." *European Economy,* no. 36 (May), 71–84.

Bercuson, K.B., and L.M. Koeinig. 1993. "The Recent Surge in Capital Inflows to Asia: Cause and Macroeconomic Impact." SEACEN/IMF Seminar, Seoul, May.

Boissieu, Christian de. 1988. "Financial Liberalization and the Evolution of the EMS." *European Economy,* no. 36 (May), 53–70.

Calvo, G.A. 1990. "The Perils of Sterilization." IMF Working Paper (March).

Calvo, G.A., L. Leiderman, and C.M. Reinhart. 1993. "Capital Inflows and Real Exchange Rate Appreciation in Latin America." *IMF Staff Papers* 40, no. 1 (March), 108–51.

Dědek, O. 1995. "Currency Convertibility and Exchange Rate Policies in the Czech Republic." Czech National Bank, Institute of Economics, Working Paper no. 38, Praha.

Dědek, O. et al. 1996. *The Break-up of Czechoslovakia: An In-Depth Economic Analysis* (Avebury: Aldershot).

Devlin, R., R. Ffrench-Davis, and S. Griffith-Jones. 1995. "Surges in Capital Flows and Development." In *Coping with Capital Surges,* ed. R. Ffrench-Davis and S. Griffith-Jones (Boulder, CO: Lynne Rienner).

Dufey, G., and J. Giddy. 1994. *The International Money Market* (Englewood, NJ: Prentice-Hall).

Eichengreen, Barry, James Tobin, and Charles Wyplosz. 1995. "Two Cases for Sand in the Wheels of International Finance." *Economic Journal,* 105, no. 428 (January), 162–72.

Fleming, John M. 1974. "Dual Exchange Markets and Other Remedies for Disruptive Capital Flows." *IMF Staff Papers,* 21, no. 1 (March), 1–27.

Folkerts-Landau, D., and T. Ito. 1995. *International Capital Markets* (Washington, DC: IMF).

Garber, P.B., and M.P. Taylor. 1995. "Sand in the Wheels of Foreign Exchange Markets: A Sceptical Note." *Economic Journal,* 105, no. 428 (January), 173–81.

Gowland, D. 1991. *Money, Inflation and Unemployment* (Brighton: Harvester Wheatsheaf).

Gros, D., and N. Thygesen. 1992. *European Monetary Integration* (London: Longman).

Hrnčíř, Miroslav. 1993. "Foreign Exchange Rate Regime and Economic Recovery." *Prague Economic Papers* 2, no. 1.

Hrnčíř, Miroslav, and Jan Klacek. 1991. "Stabilization Policies and Currency Convertibility in Czechoslovakia." *European Economy,* special edition, no. 2, 17–39.

Janáčková, Stanislava. 1994. "Transforming the Czech Economy: Role of Convertibility and Exchange Rate Anchor." Czech National Bank, Institute of Economics, Working Paper no. 24, Praha.

Kenen, Peter B. 1988. *Managing Exchange Rates* (London and New York: Routledge).

———. 1995. "Capital Controls, the EMS and EMU." *Economic Journal,* 105, no. 428 (January), 181–220.

Lanyi, A. 1975. "Separate Exchange Markets for Capital and Current Transactions." *IMF Staff Papers,* 22, no. 3 (November), 714–19.

Martinez, C.C.A. 1988. "Financial Liberalization: The Spanish Perspective." *European Economy,* no. 36 (May), 105–14.

Mathieson, Donald J., and L. Rojas-Suarez. 1993. "Liberalization of the Capital Account." IMF Occasional Paper no. 103 (March).

McKinnon, Ronald J. 1991. *The Order of Economic Liberalization: Financial Control in the Transition to a Market Economy* (Baltimore: Johns Hopkins University Press).

Quirk, P.J. 1994. "Recent Experience with Floating Exchange Rates in Developing Countries." In *Approaches to Exchange Rate Policy* (IMF Institute).

Reisen, Helmut. 1993. "Capital Flows and Their Effect on the Monetary Base." *OECD Review,* no. 51 (December), 113–22.

Soros, George. 1994. *The Alchemy of Finance* (New York: John Wiley and Sons).

Schadler, George S., M. Carkovic, A. Bennett, and R. Kahn. 1993. "Recent Experiences with Surges in Capital Inflows." IMF Occasional Paper no. 108 (December).

Steinherr, A., and G. de Schrevel. 1998. "Liberalization of Financial Transactions in the Community with Particular Reference to Belgium, Denmark and Netherlands." *European Economy,* no. 36 (May), 115–47.

Williamson, John. 1992. "Exchange Rate Management." *Economic Journal* 103, no. 416 (January), 188–97.

———. 1999. "The Management of Capital Flows." Chapter 2 in this volume.

Wyplosz, Charles. 1988. "Capital Flow Liberalization and the EMS: A French Perspective." *European Economy,* no. 36 (May), 85–103.

079
F32 P33

6

Capital Inflows and
Their Management in Hungary,
1995–1997

Pál Gáspár

The increased net inflows of foreign capital have been an increasingly important factor in explaining the recent changes in macroeconomic performance and structural reforms. While these inflows reflected increased confidence in the domestic economy and economic policies after the almost complete loss of credibility in 1994, they have also created serious problems for policy makers and required significant macroeconomic adjustment. This paper tries to capture some of these benefits and costs of inflows and deals with causes and consequences of capital inflows to Hungary between 1995 and 1997.

The first section briefly summarizes the major developments on the capital account between 1990 and 1994 and some of the special structural features of capital inflows to Hungary. The next section provides a brief description of the factors leading to the surge of capital inflows between 1995 and 1997, and evaluates the major macroeconomic consequences of these inflows. We shall then describe the policy adjustments and evaluate the efficiency of policy measures applied. The chapter ends with a section that offers conclusions and some policy lessons.

Structural Features of Capital Inflows to Hungary

Capital inflows to Hungary in the first half of the 1990s had three distinct features, described in detail in Oblath 1997. First, the inflows were charac-

Table 6.1

Distribution of Hungary's Debt Between Public and Private Sectors
(percentage distribution)

	1990	1991	1992	1993	1994	1995	1996	1997
Gross debt	100	100	100	100	100	100	100	100
Public	*85.6*	*85.8*	*82.9*	*84.2*	*80.4*	*75.5*	*70.3*	*61.8*
NBH	83.4	79.1	75.2	75.9	72.3	68.9	62.4	54.3
Government	2.2	6.7	7.7	8.3	8.1	6.6	7.9	7.5
Private	*14.4*	*14.2*	*17.1*	*15.8*	*19.6*	*24.5*	*29.7*	*38.2*
Banks	8.6	8.8	8.4	7.4	8.5	9.4	11.8	20.9
Enterprises	5.8	5.4	8.7	8.4	11.1	15.1	17.9	17.2
Net debt	100	100	100	100	100	100	100	100
Public	—	—	—	*92.1*	*83*	*69.1*	*61.4*	*47*
NBH	102.4	94.5	87.8	79.5	71.6	59.3	51.4	35.8
Government	1.5	8.9	11	12.6	11.4	9.8	10.1	11.2
Private	—	—	—	*7.9*	*17*	*30.9*	*38.6*	*53*
Banks	4.3	4.1	2.4	3.1	7.4	12.7	11	22.1
Enterprises	−8.2	−7.5	−1.2	4.8	9.6	18.2	27.6	30.9

Source: National Bank of Hungary (1998).
Note: NBH stands for National Bank of Hungary.

terized by public portfolio flows reflecting large public sector borrowing requirements and, from 1993, the financing requirements of the rising current account deficits. Second, private portfolio inflows were by that time minor due to institutional deficiencies (weak capital markets with a low supply of assets, etc.), uncertainties surrounding the macroeconomic policy mix, and a poor corporate performance. Finally, the private capital flows consisted mostly of foreign direct investment.

The composition of inflows has changed considerably since the second quarter of 1995. While the importance of private foreign direct investment remained large due to the increased absorptive capacity of the economy and to further privatization measures, private portfolio investments have been growing most rapidly. Three major factors have contributed to this growth. First, further liberalization of the capital account has increased the turnover in the domestic capital markets and increased demand for investment instruments. Second, the ongoing stabilization program resulted in a level of interest rates that led to a large premium on domestic investments and hence to a strong interest from international institutional investors. Third, these differences in real returns have stimulated foreign direct borrowing by domestic banks and enterprises.

In contrast to the period 1990–94, the increased net private inflows were accompanied by large public capital outflows that exceeded the gross public capital inflows. The latter mainly represented privatization revenues. The proceeds from privatization (amounting in 1995–97 to almost U.S. $7 billion) were mostly used to retire the existing foreign public debt and/or to refinance the old debt that carried high interest rates with new debt but with a better interest rate and maturity conditions. This resulted in a large deficit on the public capital account in 1996 and 1997. In 1996 the deficit was almost equal to private capital inflows, leading to an overall balance on the capital account. As a result of these developments, the composition of the gross and net private and public sector foreign debt has been changed.

Causes of Increased Capital Inflows

The rapid increase of capital inflows and their changing composition were driven by several factors. Most of them can be attributed to the exchange-rate-based stabilization program adopted in Hungary in the second quarter of 1995. As shown by Begg (1996), Calvo (1994), Calvo and Végh (1992), Edwards (1996), and others, exchange rate stabilization programs have generally been followed by large increases in net capital inflows. The major reasons behind this phenomenon have been as follows:

1. Exchange rate stability provided by the exchange rate anchor
2. Appreciation of the real exchange rate, typically reflecting inflation differences driven by the relatively slow disinflation in the non-tradables sector and, in some cases, an appreciation in the nominal exchange rate
3. A significant interest rate premium brought about by large domestic public debt and public sector borrowing requirements, plus tight monetary policies combined with a decline in domestic savings
4. Liberalization of capital account
5. Absence of a major recession due to a rapid revival of consumption or investment expenditures, financed by external savings

Most of the stylized facts associated in the literature with the exchange-rate-based stabilization programs have been present in Hungary. The stabilization package and the devaluation-cum-changes in the exchange rate regime were followed by short inflation bursts, after which inflation declined but remained at moderate levels, reflecting a significant inflation inertia. The interest rate premium on assets denominated in the domestic currency increased rapidly, reaching 10 percentage points between the third quarter of 1995 and the second quarter of 1996; it declined but remained significant thereafter.

The credibility problems of the exchange rate regime were overcome by the end of 1995, as the improvements in the current account and in fiscal balances, and the increased competitiveness of the tradables sector, weakened devaluation expectations. In the existing crawling peg regime the gradual decline of the crawl was credible, and provided the exchange rate with stability.

Finally, the exchange-rate-based stabilization program was not followed by a recession; while output declined in the second and third quarters, GDP stagnated in 1995 as a whole, increasing by 1.3 percent in 1996 and 4.4 percent in 1997. The cuts in public and private consumption were offset by rapid increases in exports and private investments, which have become the driving forces of the recovery.

In addition to the stabilization program, the net inflow of foreign capital has been stimulated by structural reforms, especially the privatization of publicly owned enterprises and banks. The privatization process has been extended from the competitive sectors to the public utilities, and the privatization of the banking sector has been completed. Privatization also contributed indirectly to the inflow of portfolio and foreign direct investments, and the increased share of private sector in domestic economic activities and enhanced competitiveness of the economy have stimulated further inflows.

Finally, capital inflows have increased due to the rapid liberalization of capital account. Most of the exchange rate restrictions have been abolished, and the full current account convertibility of the currency was established by 1996. Besides that, capital inflows and outflows were liberalized, and the capital account can now be regarded as an open one with the exception of continued restrictions on short-term capital movements.

Managing Capital Inflows in Hungary

Capital inflows may have to be accompanied in certain situations by policy adjustments aimed at reducing the adverse macroeconomic consequences of capital surges. Looking at the experience of the middle-income countries in the major recipient regions (Latin America and Southeast Asia), five major sets of policy instruments can be identified.[1]

The first line of defense consists mainly of restricting and regulating the gross inflow of foreign capital by imposing administrative reporting requirements, setting nonremunerated reserve requirements, and maintaining selective restrictions for different inflows. The second set of instruments consists of measures regulating the net inflow of foreign capital by either

Table 6.2

Hungary: Interventions by the Central Bank (in million U.S. $)

	Q1	Q2	Q3	Q4
1995	−500	1,009	1,789	1,079
1996	1,271	547	1,316	852
1997	471	1,236	1,435	322

Source: National Bank of Hungary 1998.

increasing the costs of inflows or reducing restrictions in the goods and assets markets on capital outflows.

The third set of instruments includes interventions in the foreign exchange market to affect the supply of and demand for foreign and domestic currency. These interventions may take sterilized or nonsterilized form and have been widely used by central banks. The aim of these measures is to avoid the adverse monetary effects of currency conversion and, as in the former case, the appreciation of the domestic currency. The next set of measures consists of adjustments in major macroeconomic policies, including the exchange rate regime, fiscal policies, and the use of incomes policy. Their major objective is to weaken the growth of aggregate demand and thus to reduce internal sources of inflation. The final set of policy instruments includes structural reforms aimed at reducing the existing microeconomic distortions. This may include measures to increase competition in the banking sector, to improve the quality of banking supervision, or to privatize domestic banks. Looking at the recent experience of Hungary, we shall show that the weight given to these instruments was different than in other economies facing large capital inflows.

Sterilization Measures

The scope of foreign capital inflows in Hungary has required the active use of sterilized intervention by the central bank in order to prevent the growth of the money supply. Since the money supply has two components—net foreign assets and net domestic assets—the increase in net foreign assets due to increased conversion of external real balances into domestic ones must be offset by a corresponding reduction in net domestic assets in order to maintain a given monetary target. This constitutes the essence of sterilized interventions carried out by central banks in the capital-importing countries.

Figure 6.1 shows that the money supply was driven in 1995 and 1996 by the rapid accumulation of net foreign assets by the central bank due to the

Figure 6.1 Changes in Monetary Base and Its Composition

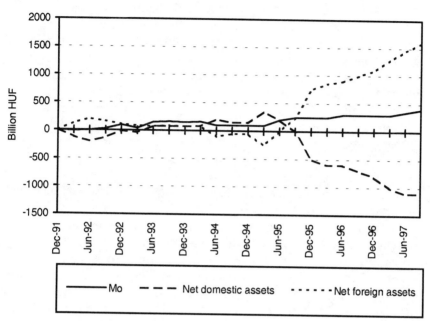

Source: Barabas-Hamecz 1997.

conversion of foreign real balances. But the dynamics and structure of this conversion reveal many features of the capital inflows specific to Hungary.

Conversion of foreign real balances into domestic assets—after actually reaching a negative level in the first quarter of 1995 due to capital flight associated with the expected devaluation and currency crisis—became significant only beginning in the third quarter of 1995, when the credibility of the stabilization program was established. Conversion was extremely rapid in the remaining part of 1995 and in the first quarter of 1996. As the interest premium declined and the scope for short-term speculative inflows decreased, net conversion was stabilized in the second quarter of 1996. Nevertheless, net capital inflows remained significant throughout the whole year and exceeded the 1995 level.

Another source of conversion for domestic real balances at that time was the change in the currency composition of private (household and enterprise) savings, reflected as changes in the structure of deposits. In 1995 the household sector increased its foreign currency savings in the first quarter, when the expected devaluation wiped out savings denominated in domestic currency, and in the last quarter of the year, when the uncertainties regarding the future of the crawling peg regime increased. This was, however, followed in 1996 by a steady decline of foreign currency saving by the private sector as the interest premium on the domestic deposits increased the relative returns on domestic deposits. Altogether the central bank faced a conversion of more than U.S. $1.1 billion due to the differences in foreign currency and domestic currency returns. This was another source of the increase in both net foreign assets and sterilization requirements.

In 1997 the major source of conversion stemmed from the increase of portfolio investments driven by the increased capitalization of the stock exchange, the increase in the supply of assets, and the improving macroeconomic and corporate sector performance. Besides portfolio investments, large privatization revenues were realized in 1997. Thus, privatization proved to be a power factor of capital inflows in the second and third quarters of the year.

In order to sterilize the monetary consequences of the increased net foreign assets, the central bank used four different instruments. In 1995 the main sources of sterilization were the decline of net credits to the banking sector and the decline in net demand against the government. The latter involved the use of two different instruments: the sale of government securities from the central bank's portfolio and the requirement that large privatization revenues be deposited at the central bank at the end of 1995.

The central bank increased its holdings of government securities in the first half of 1995 when the high public sector borrowing requirement forced it to step in as the lender of last resort. However, by the second half of the year the central bank had almost fully cleared its portfolio, as it had to sell most of the government securities for sterilization purposes. The sterilization was especially significant in the third and last quarters, as the uncertainties regarding the future exchange rate regime weakened the speculative inflows. On the other hand, the decline in the net demand against the government in the last quarter of 1995 was caused by the inflow of privatization revenues deposited at the central bank. As these revenues were used in the first quarter of 1996 to repay a part of the existing net foreign debt, they did not have any monetary impact.

The other tool of sterilization policy was the decline of net credits extended to the banking sector. The central bank tried to close down the existing channels of liquidity by hardening the conditions for foreign exchange swap operations (which were an important source of liquidity growth in 1993–94) by increasing the statutory reserve requirements on banks' deposits, and also by changing the way the reserve requirements were calculated. All these measures have decreased the amount of net credits extended by the central bank to the banking sector.

The instruments of sterilization also changed somewhat in 1996 com-

Table 6.3

Hungary: Changes in the Instruments of Sterilization (billion HUF)

	1995	1996
Change in passive repurchase agreements	50	164
Decline of NBH credits to banks	105	24
Sale of government bonds held by NBH	64	71
Change in the treasury's account at the NBH	26	72
Other	94	117
Total	339	448

Sources: Oblath 1997, National Bank of Hungary 1998, and author's calculations.

pared with the previous year. The reduction of the net credits extended to the banking sector was no longer used for sterilization purposes. The central bank continued to sell government securities from its portfolio, especially after the introduction of the provision that allowed banks the conversion of interest-free devaluation losses for interest-bearing government securities. This practice gained new momentum in 1996. These conversion measures allowed the central bank to replenish its depleted portfolio and use government securities for sterilization in 1996.

Notwithstanding these conversions, the sterilization requirements exceeded the amount of government securities available in the portfolio of the central bank, and the central bank, therefore, had to rely on the passive repurchase agreements. Repurchase agreements with different maturities had already been used by the central bank in 1994 and 1995. However, the amount of transactions was relatively insignificant, and as these measures were an important source of liquidity of the banking sector, the monetary authorities primarily relied on the active repurchase agreements. The picture changed in mid-1995, when the passive repurchase agreements became dominant. In 1996 the passive repurchase agreements in the portfolio of the central bank increased by almost U.S. $1 billion, allowing the central bank to use them for sterilization purposes.

In 1996 another instrument was used for sterilization: sales of government securities. The debt management center of the treasury issued in that year more government securities than would have been required by the public sector borrowing requirement. These additional securities were then deposited in the account of the central government, kept at the central bank. This account paid a market return to the treasury and forced the central bank to reduce its net domestic assets; thus it constituted a sterilization instrument. The use of this instrument required a very tight coordination of fiscal and monetary policies.

Table 6.4

Intervention and Sterilization in Hungary (billion HUF)

	1995	1996
Intervention	452	589
Change in base money	113	141
Sterilization	339	448
Degree of sterilization	0.75	0.76

Sources: Oblath 1997 and National Bank of Hungary 1998.

The sterilization policy of the central bank experienced a new turn in 1997 when the emphasis of the monetary authorities was shifted to two major instruments. While the use of repurchase agreements remained significant, the central bank lengthened the maturity of these instruments (primarily to six- and twelve-month maturities). The second instrument was the new policy of sales of central bank bonds. The use of central bank bonds was the result of the government-sponsored debt restructuring program through which the central government fully assumed the costs of debt service by replacing the credits extended by the central bank for foreign-currency-denominated central bank loans.

While this change brought higher interest revenues to the central bank to service external debt and reduced its losses, it left the bank without government bonds in its portfolio. It also forced it to look for new methods of sterilization. In addition, the maturity and returns of these bonds were determined by the need to stop the fall in domestic interest rates, which was seen as detrimental to the effort of containing inflation and of stimulating domestic savings. The latter were two important objectives besides the aim of stabilizing of stimulating capital inflows. Thus the central bank bonds constituted direct competition to the treasury bonds, complicating the public debt management, and they have taken over a significant burden of the sterilization from other instruments.

The sterilization of capital inflows was significant in 1995 and 1996. Between the third quarter of 1995 and the last quarter of 1996 the central bank sterilized about 75 percent of all capital inflows, including the conversion of deposits by the private sector from foreign to domestic currency (Table 6.4).

The high degree of sterilization could be initially explained by the fear that a substantial portion of these inflows was short-term and speculative, and later by the explicit exchange rate and inflation targets and by the rather limited scope for the use of other instruments in managing capital inflows.

Figure 6.2 **Changes in Real Money Supply, 1992–1997** (in percent)

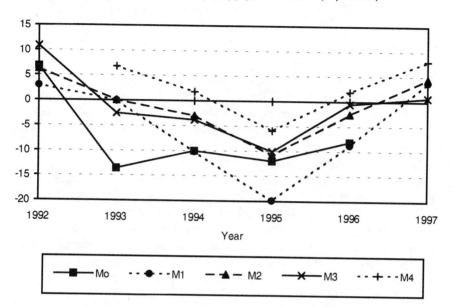

As the current account and foreign debt positions still warranted some concern, the central bank felt that current account improvements could not be maintained without these sterilization measures. By adopting the sterilized interventions the central bank could pursue its policy of maintaining a neutral or restrictive monetary policy, preventing the rapid decline of interest rates and maintaining incentives for savers in the private sector.

However, the sterilization of capital inflows has been very costly by international standards. The sterilization weakened the declining trend of interest rates, but this has meant increased debt service payments by the central government, as the average and marginal interest rates on its debt remained high. Moreover, apart from affecting the interest balance of the general government, the central bank incurred losses due to the difference on the returns on its assets and liabilities that have been covered by transfers from the central government.

In addition to the fiscal costs, the heavy sterilization of capital inflows pushed the exchange rate down to the lower end of the exchange rate band, weakening the flexibility of the exchange rate policy and practically eliminating any autonomy of the monetary policy. This is because the sterilization helped maintain an interest premium on domestic-currency-denominated assets, which increased demand for domestic currency, keeping the exchange rate at the lower end of the band. As a result, the crawling band regime, although relatively narrow by international standards, functioned as a crawling peg regime, creating the difficulties for monetary authorities noted above.

Fiscal Adjustment

As capital inflows reflect the increased demand for domestic assets, they are accompanied by a growth of domestic aggregate demand. Thus, another policy response to stem the expansionary impact of capital inflows is the adjustment of fiscal balances, which has three targets.

The first target is to reduce the fiscal deficit in order to offset the impact of rising domestic private investment and consumption. The second channel of influence is through the impact of fiscal correction on interest rates. Fiscal adjustment reduces the public sector borrowing requirement, and this gradually leads to the decline of public debt, reducing the interest premium on domestic debt. The decline in fiscal deficit could therefore reduce the pressure on domestic interest rates to rise, thus weakening the incentives for capital inflows. Finally, fiscal correction is also needed to allow for the possibility of rising interest payments following the sterilization of capital inflows by monetary authorities.

Fiscal developments in Hungary, especially the asymmetry between the timing of the adjustments in the flow and stock positions of the general government accounts, have influenced capital inflows. While the greater restrictiveness of fiscal policy, decline in cash balances, and operational deficits helped the adjustments, the large public debt, debt service payments, and the high interest premium generated by public sector borrowing requirements stimulated capital inflows during 1995 and 1996.

The fiscal adjustment was at the centerpiece of the stabilization package introduced in March 1995, aimed at reversing the growth of both public debt and general government borrowing requirements. The dynamics and the structure of fiscal adjustment have had a very strong impact on macroeconomic developments.

In 1995 the correction came from the shift in the primary balance of the central government from a deficit of 2.4 percent in 1994 to a surplus equal to 1.6 percent of GDP in 1995. The adjustment mostly came from the drastic reduction of primary expenditures coupled with some extraordinary primary revenues (from the introduction of a temporary import surcharge). While the adjustment in the primary balance reduced the public sector borrowing requirement, the rapid increase of inflation and the temporary growth of the interest premium on domestic public debt resulted in high interest rates and thus increased the interest payments of the general government.

The second source of fiscal correction was revenues from privatization, reaching in 1995 almost 7 percent of GDP. While privatization revenues decreased the total deficit of the general government, they did not reduce public sector borrowing requirements in 1995, as they were mostly collected in December 1995. The pressure exerted by the public sector on the financial markets and interest rates continued, therefore, throughout 1995. As a consequence, the correction in the primary balance in 1995 appeared to be insufficient due to increasing interest payments on public debt. In addition, the lags in collecting privatization revenues maintained real interest rate differences and contributed to the growth of short-term capital inflows.

The growth of privatization revenues was a very important factor in fiscal correction and debt management in 1996. The privatization revenues were partly used to retire foreign public debt, thus bringing the required reversal in foreign debt/GDP and total public debt/GDP ratios. On the other hand, a part of the privatization receipts was used to finance current expenditures, and as the revenues were deposited by the central government at the central bank account at almost market interest rates, the primary and overall fiscal balance improved.

The inflow of privatization revenues and its use to retire public debt has signaled the sustainability of fiscal adjustment and of the crawling peg regime. As the dangers of inflationary deficit financing and the possible default on public debt declined, this has both increased the credibility of the preannounced exchange rate regime and reduced inflation expectations. This was followed by a significant decline in domestic nominal returns and the interest premium on domestic debt. While the interest premium was about 8 to 10 percent at the end of 1995 and early 1996, the corresponding margin has declined to less than 2 to 3 percent by the end of 1996.

The positive developments created by capital inflow and the use of privatization revenues were reinforced by continuing fiscal adjustment. The primary surplus increased more than expected, reaching 4.2 percent of GDP in 1996. At the same time, the gradual decline in actual and expected inflation reduced interest rate levels, and this led to a decline in interest payments from 8.3 percent of GDP in 1995 to 6.9 percent in 1996. The decline was very significant if measured in terms of cash balances, but it was less pronounced if measured on the accrual basis. This mainly reflected longer maturities of public debt and of newly issued debt instruments. While the average maturity of newly issued government securities in 1995 was less than nine months, the corresponding maturity doubled in 1996.

While this further increased the confidence in public debt management and fiscal policy, it also widened the gap between interest payments defined on accrual and cash bases, postponing the repayment of several public debt instruments to 1997.[2] Therefore, one could see a general worsening of fiscal bal-

Figure 6.3 **Premium on 3-month T-Bills** (in percent)

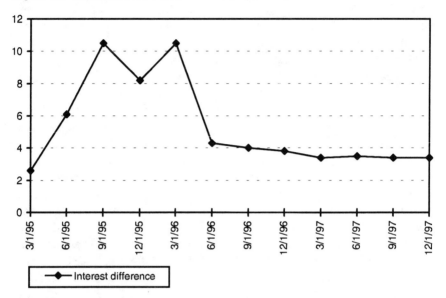

Source: Central Bank of Hungary

ances in 1997; the smaller primary surplus reflected the easing of the fiscal stance, a decline in earlier (temporary) revenues, the growth of interest payments and of the borrowing requirements of the general government, and the inclusion of the full costs of foreign debt service in the current expenditures.

Declining fiscal deficits and public debt ratios helped reverse the inflow of speculative capital due to the decreasing interest premium on domestic public debt. On the other hand, the gradual shift from short-term to longer-term maturities in the case of new issues, and the substantial lengthening of the average maturity of the public debt, also contributed to the change in the nature of inflows, as investors with a buy-and-hold strategy increased their investments, while short-term speculators lost their previous interest.

Apart from the improvement in the flow and stock positions of the consolidated central government, fiscal policy played a direct role in sterilizing capital inflows. While this has put an additional burden on the central government, it has also been a rather efficient way of sterilizing the monetary consequences of capital inflows.

Exchange Rate Policies

As they represent an increase in foreigners' demand for domestic assets, capital inflows should bring about a gradual appreciation in the domestic

Table 6.5

Hungary: Changes in the General Government Balances (percent of GDP)

	1994	1995	1996	1997
Cash balance	−8.4	−6.7	−3.1	−4.9
Primary balance	−2.7	1.6	4.2	3.2
Interest expenditures	−6.5	−8.4	−6.5	−7.9
NBH revenues (+) or losses (−)	0.5	0	−0.8	−0.3
Operational balance	−5.5	−2.1	0.6	−0.1
Changes in general government debt	−2.1	−1.2	−13.7	−8.1
Total revenues	50.3	46.4	45.7	43.5
Total expenditures	59.1	52.6	48.7	48.5

Source: National Bank of Hungary 1997.

currency. However, as international experience amply demonstrates, governments were generally reluctant to allow the appreciation of their exchange rates.

One of the reasons for resisting the appreciation of currency is that policy makers are generally unaware whether the observed appreciation represents a movement toward equilibrium due to rising productivity or simply a misalignment that should be corrected.

Another reason for resisting currency appreciation is related to the impact on the balance of payments, which may lead to abrupt changes in government policy and currency collapses. This would be the case in situations when the real exchange rate appreciation would not result in the so-called hysteresis effect in the tradables sector, representing long-term losses in competitiveness. Finally, it is generally unclear whether capital inflows are of permanent or temporary nature. The policy makers fear that allowing an appreciation in the real exchange rate would be followed by a reversal on capital flows, and this would create serious macroeconomic imbalances.

On the other hand, appreciation of the real exchange rate may also weaken the growth of domestic aggregate demand, and this will counter the impact of the growth of domestic liquidity from capital inflows. The currency appreciation is likely to increase the demand for imports and the current account deficit if the competitiveness of the tradables sector is not increasing at the same rate.

In Hungary, the use of exchange rate policy was determined in the period of rapid capital inflows simultaneously by the developments on the current account and by inflation expectations. The rate of devaluation was set in 1995 in accordance with the steep depreciation of the forint and the expected increase in domestic inflation. The rate of crawl was primarily determined in 1995 by the need to reduce the current account deficit at the cost of higher inflation. The real depreciation had to increase the competitiveness of the tradable sector. The nominal exchange rate appeared overvalued—the overvaluation was especially large if measured in terms of unit labor costs due to the decline in real wages. But rapid decline in the crawl was seen as threatening the current account position and thus the credibility of the adjustment program. Those sentiments were especially strong in 1995, when the possibility of financial crisis was real, insofar as the net foreign debt and interest payments remained high and the credibility of the economic policy package was still low.

The priority given to the current account objective and to the competitiveness of the tradables sector was also reflected in 1996, when the crawl was reduced from 1.3 percent per month to 1.2 percent per month and maintained for more than a year, while the rate of inflation declined from 28 to 19 percent annually. The rate of the crawl was maintained throughout 1996, and it was reduced further by an additional 0.1 percentage point in April 1997 and again in August 1997.

How can the changes in the rate of devaluation be evaluated? The cautious approach of the central bank was justified by the currency crisis following the increase in the current account deficit to unsustainable levels in the Czech Republic, Mexico, and other crisis-prone economies. Another factor justifying the policy of the central bank was that the monetary impact of the foreign capital inflows was difficult to assess *ex ante,* and there was a well-founded fear that inflation might increase, the sterilization measures notwithstanding. This could have resulted in an unexpected appreciation of the real exchange rate and the adverse consequences noted above.

Another reason for the cautious approach in 1995 was that the macroeconomic indicators only improved in the last quarter, and the outcome of the program was still uncertain at that time. The central bank feared that too rapid a decline in the rate of crawl would create adverse expectations and would not be consistent with fiscal and disinflation developments, thus threatening the credibility of the exchange rate regime.

The rate of the crawl could have been decreased in 1996, when the macroeconomic indicators improved, the credit rating of Hungary improved, the competitiveness of the tradables sector increased, and the current account deficit was shrinking rapidly. Moreover, the interest premium on Hungarian securities declined, reflecting increased confidence and improved economic performance. This would have sent a signal to the markets that the central bank had a very firm anti-inflationary stance and was willing to commit itself to the policy of disinflation. At the same time, this

Figure 6.4 **Changes in Real Exchange Rate Indices, 1990–1997**
(Previous year = 100)

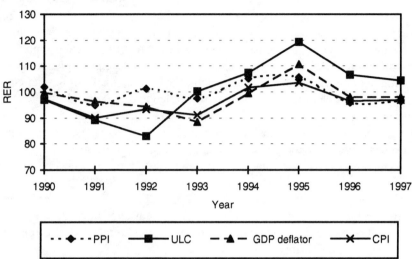

Source: National Bank of Hungary

Notes: PPI stands for producer price index, ULC for unit labor costs, CPI for consumer price index, and GDP for gross domestic product.

change would have directly increased the inflationary pressures, which persisted in 1996.

The crawling peg regime stabilized the backward-looking exchange rate expectations and maintained the inflation inertia. On the other hand, the rate of the crawl had a direct and strong impact on the prices of tradables. The reduction in the crawl would have positively affected these two sources of inflation.

Another question of the exchange rate regime is related to the width of the band. The initially adopted band had a relatively narrow range of 2.25 percent around the central parity. An alternative would have been a wider band. This would have increased the risk to foreign investors, reduced the pressures on the monetary policy, increased the autonomy of the monetary authorities, and reduced the costs of sterilization measures.

The band was eventually widened, and the question is why it happened. The international experience from economies with fixed or adjustable exchange rate regimes shows that a widening of the band may bring the expected results, while its costs (such as the expected appreciation of the currency and the increasing flexibility and inflation expectations) are relatively small.

One of the reasons why the band was not initially widened is related to the actual position of the exchange rate in that period. During the whole period the exchange rate was at the lower end of the band, and constant pressures were pushing it into this position. During the first twenty-one months of the crawl there were only two occasions when the exchange rate moved from the lower end of the band, but the movement was less than 20 percent of the band width. There was, therefore, an expectation at the central bank that a widening of the band would have led to an immediate appreciation of the nominal exchange rate, as the inflow of foreign capital and the continuing conversion of savings by domestic households from foreign currency to forint-denominated deposits would have kept demand for the domestic currency increasing. This would have resulted in an appreciation of the real exchange rate, considerably worsened the competitiveness of the tradables sector, and complicated the current account adjustment.

The central bank also took the position at the time that a decline in the interest premium on Hungarian investments could only be gradual. The bank feared, therefore, that the appreciation of the domestic currency coupled with the interest premium would result in currency and interest gains for foreign investors. A widening of the band would have led to a further increase of capital inflows.

Notwithstanding these considerations, one may argue that the management of capital inflows could have been less costly and more efficient if the band had been adjusted and widened. A widening of the band would have resulted in greater exchange rate flexibility and this—notwithstanding the possibility of short-term appreciation immediately after the widening of the band—would have reduced the pressure on the domestic currency. In addition, the widening would have increased the flexibility of monetary management, as the interest rates were tied to the exchange rate, which was kept at the lower end of the band. Moreover, the increased flexibility would have also reduced the costs of sterilization.

In sum, the exchange rate policy was initially relatively successful, although the unresolved conflict between the current account objective, on the one hand, and the inflation target, on the other, was resolved at the cost of higher inflation. At that time, the major issue was to increase the competitiveness of the tradables sector and enhance the credibility of macroeconomic policies. Beginning in early 1997, however, it would have been much more effective to allow a more rapid decline in the rate of the crawl associated with a wider band. This would have produced better results in terms of both inflation performance and the management of capital inflows.

Restricting Capital Inflows

Restrictions on capital inflows are used by policy makers in the belief that they may have a strong and swift impact (e.g., Griffith-Jones 1994, Nunnenkamp

1993). Nevertheless, the limitations are well known, as these regulations can easily be circumvented, are inefficient, and create further distortions. The Eastern and Central European economies have used different restrictions in trying to reduce the inflows of foreign capital, including quantitative restrictions on short-term borrowing by banks, imposing interest-free deposit requirements by banks, increasing the conversion costs, and so on.

In contrast with the other advanced transition economies, new quantitative restrictions were not imposed in Hungary with the aim of regulating gross capital inflows. Even though there have been restrictions on capital movements, they were more related to the degree of the actual capital account convertibility. For example, banks have to apply for permission from the central bank for their foreign borrowings, while foreign investors were not allowed to purchase government bonds with maturities of less than one year. But these restrictions were not very serious and could be easily circumvented; the central bank has granted almost automatically permission for banks to borrow abroad, while foreigners could also obtain long-term bonds for short-term purposes, as explained further below.

Moreover, the central bank encouraged foreign borrowing by domestic banks in order to mitigate the high costs of public sector borrowing requirements. A clear sign of this policy was that the reserve requirements on banks' foreign liabilities were lower than those on domestic ones. While the interest paid on foreign-currency-denominated reserves was also lower, the costs of this financial repression were higher in the case of domestic currency in comparison to foreign-currency-denominated (and mostly external) deposits.

In sum, we may conclude that the quantitative restrictions have been gradually abolished during the last years in accordance with the increasing openness of the Hungarian financial sector and with the policy of reducing the deflationary impact of financial repression due to high public sector borrowing requirements. While most of the existing quantitative restrictions were gradually eliminated, new restrictions were not introduced to stem the inflow of foreign capital. Clearly, the adverse experiences of other countries with quantitative restrictions played a role, and so did the belief that the inflationary impact of inflows could be neutralized by other policy instruments. Last but not least, the period of time during which Hungary faced massive capital inflows has been relatively short, perhaps too short to consider many drastic measures.

Policies to Encourage Net Capital Inflows

Policies affecting net capital inflows may comprise measures aimed at increasing the outflow of capital. This, together with liberalization of imports,

Table 6.6

Hungary: Composition of the Current Account Balance (percent of GDP)

	1990	1991	1992	1993	1994	1995	1996	1997
Current account balance	0.3	0.8	0.9	−9.1	−9.4	−5.7	−3.9	−2.2
Primary balance	4.5	5.0	4.5	−5.9	−6.4	−1.6	−0.7	−0.1
Trade balance	0.9	0.6	−0.1	−8.6	−8.7	−5.5	−6.0	−3.8
Net interest and capital incomes	−4.2	−4.2	−3.6	−3.2	−3.0	−4.1	−3.2	−2.1

aimed at increasing the demand for foreign currency and thus mitigating the impact of inflows on domestic monetary aggregates. While all these measures were used in Hungary and had an impact on the net inflow of foreign capital, they were less related to the management of capital flows than designed as structural and institutional measures.

Import liberalization had mostly been completed before the recent surge of capital inflows. Concerns about the current account deficit also did not play any role in managing capital inflows except in 1993 and 1994, when capital inflows were driven by the widening current account deficits and the need for external financing. Before the adoption of the crawling peg regime, the large current account deficits were financed by rising capital inflows— albeit with worsening return and maturity conditions. Starting in the second quarter of 1995, the exchange-rate-based stabilization program simultaneously resulted in an improvement in current account balance and in a further growth of capital inflows. The initial current account deficit was dramatic, and an improvement in both the credibility of the program and the sustainability of the foreign debt position were, therefore, sine qua non.

As a result, a further increase in the current account deficit could not be used as an argument to introduce measures to reduce net demand for domestic currency; moreover, the improvements in the current account balance were required to maintain capital inflows and stabilize the credibility gains after the introduction of the crawling peg regime. In fact, the current account deficit was almost halved between 1994 and 1996 (declining from 9.4 percent of GDP in 1994 to 4 percent in 1996), while in 1997 it declined further, to about 2 percent of GDP (Table 6.6).

Furthermore, a detailed analysis of the structure of current account deficit reveals that the improvement has created further problems for the monetary authorities. Some part of the improvement was due to the growth of the recorded net tourism revenues, which increased the conversion of foreign currency revenues into forint.[3] These growing revenues further increased the demand for domestic currency, putting additional pressures on the central bank.

The current account target was, therefore, determined by the immediate need to reduce the deficit and later to increase the credibility of the exchange rate regime. It did not provide any room for a more relaxed policy to stem inflows. In contrast, the liberalization of capital outflows got a new impetus from mid-1995 onward. When Hungary became a member of OECD, further capital-account-related measures had to be adopted in order to meet the OECD membership requirements. These measures included the relaxation of restrictions on financial market and credit operations, as well as more liberal treatment of short-term capital inflows (including, among others, the de facto opportunity given to foreign investors to purchase domestic securities with maturities of less than one year).[4]

At the same time, capital outflows were considerably eased. The most important changes were related to allowing residents to buy, with the permission of the central bank, real estate abroad, shares in foreign enterprises not exceeding 10 percent of their base capital, and triple-A-rated enterprise and government securities in OECD member states. In addition, rules concerning the conversion of forint-denominated assets of nonresidents were eased, as the latter could open convertible forint accounts, allowing them to deposit their revenues from forint operations and convert them without limit.

In sum, while the capital outflow liberalization was not directly intended as a measure to stem the net capital inflows and their monetary consequences, it had some impact. But this impact may have increased the credibility of domestic macroeconomic policies, and this, in turn, may have stimulated further inflows. The outflows so far have been relatively small, although a reversal in this trend may be expected in the future.

Institutional Reforms

Adverse consequences of rapid capital inflows will be multiplied in the presence of a weak and inefficient financial system (e.g., Schadler et al. 1993). The increase of foreign exposure of commercial banks may lead to boom-and-bust cycles, increase their currency risk, and weaken the quality of their portfolios. A successful management of capital inflows requires, therefore, the strengthening of the banking sector, which should imply four concurrent measures. The capital base of banks should be increased by establishing capital asset ratios at least in accordance with the Basel Rules.[5] In addition, the banks' portfolios should be sound, public involvement minimized, and competition increased.

While the first set of measures refers to banks' financial indicators, the second set of instruments is more closely associated with the regulation and supervision of the financial sector. Supervision must be strengthened, competitive structures should be enhanced, and measures are needed to strengthen the resilience of the banking sector to potential adverse shocks.

In Hungary, the measures related to the first set were implemented before and during the episode of least capital inflow. But, again, the measures were not directly related to the management of inflows but coincided with structural reforms and with privatization in the banking sector. Due to the banking consolidation programs and privatization of banks in 1995 and 1996, the capital-asset ratios of all banks exceeded the required 8 percent, and the average for the whole Hungarian banking sector was around 15 percent in 1996.

The profitability of banks also improved substantially; while in 1993 the whole banking sector recorded an after-tax loss of 150 billion forint, or 4 percent of GDP, in 1996 the total profits equaled 68.2 billion forint, or 1 percent of GDP. The share of nonperforming assets in the portfolios of banks declined from 12.5 percent in 1994 to around 5 percent in 1996. These changes in the banking sector have improved the competitive position of Hungarian banks, increased the prudence of their lending, weakened the chances of a possible boom-and-bust cycle, and reduced the likelihood of a banking crisis in case of a rapid reversal of capital flows.

Lessons for Other Countries

There are a few lessons that could be tentatively drawn from the Hungarian experience with managing capital inflows.

Large capital inflows have mixed macroeconomic consequences. On the positive side, they increase the pool of savings to finance increasing investments, tend to reduce the level of high domestic interest rates, result in all the standard gains associated with inflows of foreign direct investment, and increase the discipline of macroeconomic policies. On the other hand, the management of capital inflows creates significant fiscal and quasi-fiscal costs, leads to the loss of monetary autonomy, and increases the costs of disinflation (cf., for example, Zahler 1992).

The Hungarian experience also points to the questionable efficiency and high costs of sterilized interventions. While the uncertainties concerning the nature of capital inflows and the differences in time preferences of policy makers and investors may justify sterilization, excessive reliance on these measures is not welcome due to their fiscal costs and to problems caused for the conduct of exchange rate and monetary policies.

Exchange rate flexibility plays an important role in the management of capital flows. While there are several arguments in favor of using the fixed exchange rate regime as a nominal anchor against inflation, exchange rate flexibility increases monetary autonomy and reduces the costs of managing inflows.

Fiscal adjustment and tight incomes policies constitute an essential element of the macroeconomic adjustment in economies facing continuous inflows of foreign capital. They are needed to weaken the adverse impact of inflows on inflation and on the money supply and to avoid speculative attacks. Fiscal adjustments also help in changing the structure of expenditures from private and public consumption to investments.

The brief history of capital inflows into Hungary also demonstrates how important structural reforms are in both stimulating and managing capital inflows. Privatization of the state-owned enterprises, opening of the banking sector, reduction in the government involvement in the distribution of goods and services, and reforms of the pension system all could increase the absorptive capacity of recipient economies.

Some of the common trends in Central and East European economies suggest that these countries will face further significant capital inflows. These economies should, therefore, accelerate structural reforms (especially in the banking sector and in public redistribution) and maintain very tight macroeconomic policies.

Notes

1. The experiences of the Latin American economies are discussed in detail in Ffrench-Davies and Griffith-Jones 1995, Calvo, Leiderman, and Reinhardt 1993, Nunnenkamp 1993, and Frankel and Okongwu 1995, while the experiences of the Southeast Asian countries can be found in Reisen 1993b and Khan and Reinhardt 1996.

2. This is one of the reasons why the fiscal deficit, measured on a cash basis, increased in 1997, even though interest expenditures were higher in 1997 on a cash basis in comparison to those defined on an accrual basis. The other reason for the worsening in the fiscal balance and for the increase in interest expenditures was technical—a switch in the accounting of public debt from the books of the central bank to the general government. Until 1996, the central bank was the ultimate "owner" of foreign public debt, and it re-lent the domestic currency equivalent of this debt to the government. In order to reduce the actual interest expenditures of the central government, it paid to the central bank only the international return, while the losses due to the devaluation of the domestic currency were assumed by the central bank. This has led to increasing central bank losses. It was, therefore, decided that from 1 January 1997 these debts would become central government foreign-currency-denominated debts and the government would pay the full interest and the actual principal as well as the foreign exchange losses to the central bank, which continued to provide the direct service of their debt. While this increased in 1997, the interest expenditures of the central government did not, of course, change the balances of the consolidated (i.e., central bank and central government) public sector.

3. The actual revenues from tourism may not have increased, but the reported figures did. This was due to the fact that the households started to convert their foreign-cur-

rency-denominated revenues from tourism into forint as the credibility of the announced exchange rate crawl improved and in order to gain from the interest premium.

4. According to the current regulations, foreigners are allowed to directly purchase only medium- and long-term securities (with maturities over one year). But the regulations also allow investors to buy longer-term paper independently of the actual maturity of the paper. If the paper is long-term but matures within one year, investors can buy it. It means, for example, that foreigners can buy in the secondary market twelve-month treasury bills maturing in one day, one week, or one month without any restriction.

5. Strictly speaking, the capital base of banks in developing (and, equally, in transition) economies should exceed the ones laid down in the Basel Rules in order to provide for greater security and stability of the banking sectors.

References

Begg, David. 1996. "Monetary Policy in Transition Economies." IMF Working Paper no. 108 (September).

Calvo, Guillermo. 1990. "The Perils of Sterilization." IMF Working Paper no. 90/13 (March).

Calvo, Guillermo, L. Leiderman, and Carmen Reinhardt. 1993. "Capital Inflows to Latin America: The Role of External Factors." *IMF Staff Papers* 40, pp. 108–51.

Calvo, Guillermo. 1994. "Inflows of Capital to Developing Countries in the 1990s: Causes and Effects." *Journal of Economic Perspectives*, no. 3.

Calvo, Guillermo, Richard Sahay, and Carlos Végh. 1995. "Capital Flows in Central and Eastern Europe." IMF Working Paper no. 95/57.

Calvo, Guillermo, and Carlos Végh. 1993. "Exchange Rate Based Stabilisation Under Imperfect Credibility." In *Open-Economy Macroeconomics,* ed. Helmut Frisch and Andreas Worgotter (London: Macmillan).

Edwards, Sebastian, ed. 1996. *Capital Controls, Exchange Rates and Monetary Policy in the World Economy* (New York: Cambridge University Press).

Ffrench-Davis, Ricardo, and Stephany Griffith-Jones. 1995. *Coping with Capital Surges* (Boulder, CO: Lynne Rienner).

Frankel, Jacob, and C. Okongwu. 1995. "Liberalised Portfolio Capital Inflows in Emerging Markets: Sterilisation, Expectations and the Incompleteness of Interest Rate Convergence." National Bureau for Economic Research, Cambridge, MA Working Paper no. 5156.

Khan, Mohsin, and Carmen Reinhardt. 1996. "Capital Flows in the APEC Region." IMF Occasional Papers, no. 122.

Griffith-Jones, Stephany. 1994. "Coping with Capital Surges." In *Latin American Capital Flows: Living with Volatility,* ed. S. Griffith-Jones and R. Ffrench-Davies (Washington, D.C.: Group of Thirty).

Nunnenkamp, Peter. 1993. "The Return of Foreign Capital to Latin America." Kiel Working Paper no. 574, Kiel IWE.

Oblath, Gustav. 1997. "Capital Inflows to Hungary in 1995–1996: Composition, Effects and Policy Responses." KOPINT-DATORG Discussion Papers no. 49, Budapest (December).

Reisen, Helmut. 1993a. "The Case for Sterilized Intervention." *CEPAL Review* (August).

Reisen, Helmut. 1993b. "The Impossible Trinity in South-East Asia." In *International Economic Insights* (Washington, DC: Institute for International Economics).

Schadler, S., M. Carkovic, A. Benett, and R. Kahn. 1993. "Recent Experiences with Surges in Capital Inflows." IMF Occasional Paper no. 108.

Zahler, R. 1992. "Monetary Policy and an Open Capital Account." *CEPAL Review,* no. 48.

7

Managing Capital Flows in Poland, 1995–1998

Stanislaw Gomulka

The OECD countries have liberalized capital markets during the last two decades or so. Most of these countries maintained considerable capital controls in the 1950s and 1960s, when they were the world's emerging economies in relation to U.S. capital (Shafer 1995). Today, the postsocialist transition economies are the emerging economies in Europe. They are joining the liberalized OECD, and the question is whether they should follow the policy adopted by the OECD countries at their earlier, similar level of development or whether they should liberalize their financial markets faster. Poland has been encouraging foreign direct investment, including the purchase of company shares, but it has also been attempting to limit the inflow of speculative short-term capital. The policy has so far been successful without the use of any capital controls.

The primary purpose of this paper is to explain the policy and the reasons for its apparent success. The following section gives the basic facts and discusses the reasons why these inflows started to be sizable only recently. Afterward, we shall report the results of an econometric test designed to explain large changes in portfolio capital inflows in the years 1995–97 and give the motivations behind the policy responses adopted to manage these inflows. The last two analytical sections evaluate the effectiveness of these policy responses, note their negative side effects and the threats to macroeconomic stability that emerged in the years 1997–98, and list policy responses to these threats. In the concluding section we shall attempt to identify the policy implications that can be drawn from the recent experience.

Table 7.1

Capital Inflows and Their Components in Poland, 1990–1997 (convertible currencies only, in billion U.S. dollars)

	1989	1990	1991	1992	1993	1994	1995	1996	1997
1. Gross official reserves, end of year	2.5	4.7	3.8	4.3	4.3	6.0	15.0	18.0	20.6
2. Change in R	—	2.2	−0.9	0.5	0	1.7	8.9	3.1	2.6
3. Current account[a]	−1.4	0.6	−2.0	0.9	0.6	2.2	5.5	−1.4	−4.3
4. Capital account (Δ-CA) of which:	—	1.6	1.1	−0.4	0.6	−0.5	3.4	4.5	6.9
Portfolio investment	na	na	na	na	na	−0.6	1.2	0.2	—
Direct foreign investment	—	0	0.1	0.3	0.6	0.5	1.1	2.2	—
IMF credit	0	0.5	0.3	0	−0.1	0.6	−1.4	0	0
Other long-term credits	—	0.4	−0.8	0.6	0.9	0.9	0.7	0.4	—
Other capital inflows[b]	—	0.7	−1.5	−1.3	−2.0	−1.9	1.8	1.7	—
5. NIR, end of year	1.6	7.8	6.5	8.1	8.8	11.3	20.4	21.8	23.6
6. Δ NIR	—	6.2	−1.3	1.6	0.6	2.5	9.1	1.4	2.8

Abbreviations and symbols:
R = Gross official reserves. CA = Current account. na = not available. NIR = Net international reserves. IMF = International Monetary Fund. Δ = Change.

Source: National Bank of Poland.

Notes: [a]Includes unclassified (cross-border and other) trade. [b]Includes portfolio investment in years 1990–1993, errors and omissions and valuation adjustments in all years, may also include some direct foreign investment.

Capital Inflows: How Large and What Causes?

The basic facts are given in Table 7.1. Here, net capital inflows are defined as the difference between the changes in gross official reserves of the central bank, the National Bank of Poland (NBP), and the current account balance. The table also gives the net international reserves (NIR) of the banking system.[1] The system includes, in addition to the NBP, all commercial banks. The NIR, expressed in local currency at current exchange rates, and net domestic assets of the banking system represent the total stock of money, known as "broad money" or M2.

The Balcerowicz package of liberalization and stabilization measures of January 2, 1990, included the suspension of servicing of most of the foreign debt to private creditors. The foreign debt to official creditors had not been serviced since February 1981. Thus, in the early 1990s, Poland had the credit rating of a country in default of international payments obligations. A debt reduction agreement with official creditors, represented by the Paris Club, was reached in March 1991 (signed April 1991). However, negotiations with private creditors, represented by the London Club, were prolonged. An outline agreement was reached only in March 1994 and signed in October 1994. The consequence of these prolonged negotiations was that only at the end of 1994 was Poland given an investment grade status by international rating agencies. By that time, apart from the resumption of debt servicing, all key macroeconomic indicators had improved significantly. This improvement continued in the years 1995–97. Given these developments, especially the external debt "problem," it should not be surprising that foreign direct investment and other private capital inflows were small during the first five years of transition (1990–94) and that they began to be sizable only in 1995.

A key indicator of external creditworthiness is the level of net international reserves (NIR). Poland's reserves increased in the years 1990–97 about tenfold, by some USD 20 billion. This increase took place predominantly in the years 1990 and 1995. It is interesting that in 1990 the gross official reserves of the central bank increased by only USD 2.2 billion, compared with the USD 7.8 billion increase in total NIR. In that year, the increase of international reserves was thus concentrated in commercial banks. Given the small inflows of foreign private capital, the increase must have mainly been due to the sale of foreign exchange to commercial banks by domestic residents.

In 1995 the main buyer of foreign exchange became the NBP, with commercial banks acting as intermediaries. The primary source of the exchange was the current account surplus. Moreover, for the first time since 1989, portfolio investment also became significant. At USD 1.2 billion, the cumulative portfolio investment in 1995 amounted to about 0.8 percent of GDP and 6 percent of NIR. The investment continued to increase rapidly in the first five months of 1996 (Table 7.2). It was this increase from the middle of 1995 to the middle of 1996 that alarmed the central bank and led to the adoption of "defensive" measures (discussed below). Further measures were adopted in early 1998.

An Econometric Test

Portfolio investments have three components.[2] One represents the purchase of enterprise shares, usually on the stock exchange. The second is the purchase of bonds issued or guaranteed by the central government. The third is the purchase of paper issued by enterprises and municipalities without government guarantee. These types of investments tend to be short-term and

Table 7.2

The Data Set Used for the Estimation of Equation 1 and the Estimated Levels of Cumulative Foreign Portfolio Inflows, February 1995 to June 1997

t	NIR_{t-1}	r_t	Actual I_t	Predicted I_t
9502	11,914	2.8	33	−395
9503	12,846	4.9	−112	220
9504	13,080	4.4	137	182
9505	14,536	2.8	66	204
9506	15,307	2.8	240	372
9507	15,912	2.9	556	529
9508	17,029	2.9	629	788
9509	17,433	2.7	972	840
9510	18,551	2.2	1,026	999
9511	18,894	2.4	1,133	1,108
9512	19,397	2.5	1,171	1,239
9601	20,436	4.3	1,640	1,813
9602	20,572	3.2	1,883	1,640
9603	21,749	3.1	1,802	1,881
9604	22,035	3.1	1,479	1,944
9605	21,591	2.9	1,836	1,800
9606	22,011	2.7	1,618	1,860
9607	21,542	1.9	1,191	1,614
9608	21,960	1.2	1,195	1,577
9609	21,834	0.7	1,298	1,453
9610	21,433	0.7	1,243	1,361
9611	21,443	0.8	1,339	1,367
9612	21,619	0.8	1,362	1,420
9701	21,667	1.4	1,566	1,535
9702	21,473	1.7	1,918	1,562
9703	21,546	2.6	1,618	1,750
9704	21,094	3.1	2,032	1,743
9705	21,072	2.5	2,345	1,612
9706	21,713	2.7	2,601	1,801

Sources: National Bank of Poland for NIR_t and I_t, the Warsaw IMF office for r_t, and Equation (1) in the text for predicted I_t.

Notes: The figures in the first column ('t') refer to the year (the first two digits) and to the relevant month (the last two digits). The figures in the second column refer to the level of Net International Reserves ('NIR') in the preceding month ('t–1') and the figures in the third column ('r_t') refer to the current expected rate of return. The figures in the fourth column ('Actual I_t') refer to the current actual values of foreign portfolio inflows while those in the sixth column ('Predicted I_t') refer to the current values of foreign portfolio inflows estimated with the help of Equation 1 in the text.

speculative, designed to exploit international differences in yields. All three types have some well-known macroeconomic causes and effects.

These differences in yields depend crucially on expectations concerning exchange rates and risks. In 1994–95 Poland's strong current account balance led to a large increase in NIR. This increase led to expectations that the real exchange rate would appreciate. Both factors increased the expected net yields and, therefore, induced portfolio investment.

The monthly data for the years 1995–97 may be used to estimate the relationship between cumulative portfolio investment up to period t, the level of NIR at the end of period t-1(NIR_{t-1}) and the current expected rate of return (r_t). The relationship is as follows (t ratios in parentheses),

$$I_t = -3609 + 0.255NIR_{t-1} = 190r_t = error\ term_t \qquad (1)$$
$$\quad\ \ (6.7) \qquad (10.3) \qquad (2.9)$$

where t numbers the months from February 1995 until June 1997. There are twenty-nine observations, and the test statistics are: $R^2 = 0.82$, $SE = 312$, and $DW = 0.96$. In this equation I and NIR are expressed in millions of U.S. dollars and r in percents. The variable r is the annualized yield pickup rate on three-month treasury bills minus the three-month LIBOR rate for basket currencies, minus rate of crawl. Both R^2 and t ratios are high, but the DW statistic indicates a significant autocorrelation of the error term. This autocorrelation may reflect sudden but infrequent shifts of the "climate" in the international capital market, in response to unexpected shocks.

A high level of NIR reduces the country risk of default and therefore encourages portfolio investments. Moreover, an increasing level of reserves may also create expectations of an appreciation of the exchange rate, either through a reduction in the rate of crawl or in the movement within the band, thus encouraging portfolio investments further.

During the twenty-nine months covered by this test, portfolio investment was initially increasing rapidly, parallel to, and apparently in response to, a fast rise in NIR. Later in the period, the level of NIR stabilized and a fall in the dollar rate of return induced a capital outflow. The dominant form of portfolio investment during that period was the purchase by foreigners of government bonds (T-bonds). Some of these purchases were made in the secondary market, where the sellers were Polish financial institutions, mainly commercial banks and insurance companies. These institutions were reducing their positions in T-bonds in order to invest in the more profitable NBP paper. During the period in question, the NBP paper was offered at a premium compared to T-bonds. This reflected the fact that the NBP was conducting large-scale open market operations in response to large increases in NIR, while the Ministry of Finance

Figure 7.1 **Poland: Portfolio Investment, Actual and Estimated, Cumulative 1995–97** (in million U.S. $)

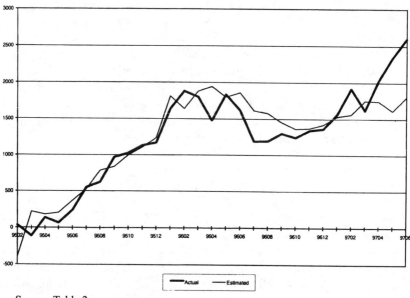

Source: Table 2

was successfully reducing the bank financing of the budget deficit. An additional factor causing the gap between the two yields was the legal restriction forbidding foreign investors to buy any NBP paper.

The two key features of the Polish cumulative portfolio investment have been, first, a remarkable regularity (Equation 1, Figure 7.1) and, second, their relatively modest level. The very substantial increases in reserves, both official and NIR, in 1995 were mainly related to the current account surplus. Foreign portfolio investments were simply an additional factor, accounting for about one-eighth of the increases. Moreover, if the estimated Equation 1 is to be believed, portfolio investments do not yet react strongly to changes in the yield pickup rate, their stock increasing by USD 190 million only in response to the increase in the yield by 1 percentage point. Furthermore, this equation implies that individual foreign institutions undertake portfolio investments as if there were an agreement between them not to breach a ceiling level, equal to about a quarter of the NIR, for the entire stock of such investments. An investment rule of this type would reflect caution and, if it continued to operate, would give the central bank considerable space for controlling the demand for credit with an interest rate policy.

Borrowing abroad by Polish residents has recently become easier, but its volume is still very low. It is therefore too early to assess whether this type of borrowing will prove more responsive to interest rate differentials.

International capital mobility between Poland and other countries is likely to increase. However, the country risks for all transition economies, including those that perform well, are still high compared to developed economies or to the most successful emerging economies. Mobility may, therefore, increase only slowly.

Policy Responses

The Polish exchange rate policy of a preannounced crawling peg, adopted in October 1991, was intended to stabilize the real exchange rate and, in this way, to protect exporters. One of its implications was that any large external shock, such as a sudden change in the demand for Polish exports, would be transmitted to the domestic economy through an impact on the money supply, with further implications for inflation, credit expansion, interest rates and the level of economic activity. The modifications in exchange rate policy that Poland undertook in 1995 were motivated primary by the desire to strike a better balance between overall economic stability and protection of the export sector. This concern for overall stability also included a desire to develop some protection against excessive portfolio movements, inward and outward.

The large current account surplus that emerged at the end of 1994 and at the beginning of 1995 meant that an appreciation of the real exchange rate was required. The rate of crawl at that time (since August 27, 1993) was 1.6 percent per month. This was reduced first to 1.5 percent (September 13, 1993) and, soon afterward, to 1.4 percent (November 30, 1994). However, it was realized that small reductions in the rate of crawl would have little overall effect and that therefore the buildup of appreciation expectations would continue. This, in turn, would fuel speculative capital inflows. A more decisive policy action was required.

Such an action was proposed in the spring of 1995 and implemented on May 16, 1995. The new policy had three components:

(a) An immediate up-front appreciation by 3 percent
(b) The introduction of a band ±7 percent around central parity
(c) Holding down the rate of crawl at 1.2 percent per month for the central parity

Component (a) was intended to reduce appreciation expectations immediately. A larger appreciation may have been required, but this was resisted by the authorities in order to protect the export-led recovery. The total nominal appreciation of the zloty against the U.S. dollar between the end of January 1995 and the end of May 1995 was 4.5 percent, implying that the real effective appreciation of the zloty/dollar rate during that time amounted to about 10 percent. About half of this was a direct result of the new exchange rate policy (the remaining half reflected changes in cross rates). The reasons for retaining the crawling peg, component (b) of the policy, were twofold: to continue to provide exporters and importers with some stability of the real exchange rate and to reduce the pickup yield for portfolio investors. The main motivation behind the introduction of the 14 percent band was also standard: to allow the market some influence over the exchange rates, and in this way to somewhat increase the exchange rate risk for portfolio investors.[3] This partial marketization of the exchange rate also had the advantage, for the NBP and the government, of reducing the political cost of any future appreciation or devaluation. However, the modest size of the band was intended to reassure exporters and importers that the costs stemming from fluctuations in the real exchange rate would remain limited.

A large continuing buildup of reserves in the second half of 1995 forced the authorities to appreciate the zloty within the band by an additional 3 percent. On December 22, 1995, the band itself had to be enlarged by 6 percent to provide room for a further step appreciation (initially by 2.5 percent).

An alternative policy of restricting the growth of reserves was suggested by certain top officials of the Ministry of Finance. They proposed to reduce market rates of interest substantially in order to stimulate domestic demand. The intention of such a measure would be to stimulate imports and to arrest, in this way rather than through an exchange rate appreciation, the growth of international reserves. A reduction of interest rates would have also protected the country against excessive portfolio capital inflows. However, the policy was rejected by the NBP, although in practice market interest rates were later allowed to decline gradually. This decline indeed led to a rapid increase of domestic demand and imports in 1996 (see next section). The refusal by the NBP to substantially reduce interest rates was motivated by the desire to retain attractive real rates on zloty deposits. This, in turn, was needed in view of the fact that total deposits in 1995 continued to be a small proportion of GDP. Moreover, foreign currency deposits increased substantially in the period 1991–95, both in absolute terms and as a proportion of broad money. By the beginning of 1995, these dollar deposits already represented nearly 30 percent of broad money. The flight from the zloty indicated the mistrust of the population regarding the conduct of monetary policy and was a key reason for raising interest rates in early 1995.

The policy that was actually adopted—a combination of a measured real zloty appreciation and the continuation of moderately high real interest rates— corrected the earlier alarming trends, and has, therefore, proved effective.

Responses to New Policies and Negative Side Effects

In the period 1995–97, imports were also stimulated by the gradual phasing out of the 6 percent import surcharge (introduced on December 17, 1992) and significant reductions of import tariffs. Falling inflation led to a substantial reduction of nominal interest rates, and this stimulated the demand for credit and, therefore, also for imports. Increased profitability of enterprises and recapitalization of banks reduced underperforming assets and therefore increased the ability of commercial banks to supply new credit (NBP 1996). Imports were also stimulated by an exceptionally rapid growth of investment and a fairly rapid growth of real income. On the other hand, the real exchange rate appreciation, the rapid growth of domestic demand, and the slow economic growth in Western Europe kept the growth of exports low in 1996–97. All these developments in imports and exports led to an exceptionally swift change in current account position, from a surplus of 4 percent of GDP in 1995 to a deficit of 1 percent of GDP in 1996 and a deficit of 3.1 percent of GDP in 1997.

In the light of these facts, can the exchange rate and monetary policies in 1995–97 be considered to have been successful?

It is certain that a long list of important objectives has been met as a result of these policies, at least to some extent. These achievements are: the excessive growth of international reserves has been arrested; the level of international reserves has in the meantime increased to a (more or less) desirable level; the inflow of portfolio capital has been successfully controlled without the use of administrative measures; the dollarization of domestic savings has been reversed; the inflow of foreign direct investment has increased substantially; the rapid growth of GDP and investment has continued; and the downward trend for the rate of inflation has been maintained.

In the earlier sections of this paper I explained or indicated the links between the policies adopted and these clearly positive outcomes. However, apart from the positive results, there have also been some negative side effects. Three of these have been particularly important: (a) an excessive credit expansion, (b) a slower rate of disinflation than targeted, and (c) a high cost of sterilization of foreign money inflows.

The cost of sterilization increased rapidly in the course of 1995, amounting to 0.6 percent of GDP in that year and 0.8 percent of GDP in 1996. Consequently, the NBP operating profits declined sharply, from about 1 percent of GDP in 1994 to close to zero in 1996. The deterioration in profits was not provided for in the state budget and hence came under public criticism from the government. Moreover, an outdated pay system was still in operation at the NBP, whereby bonuses for a substantial number of employees were linked to profits. In early 1996, keeping operating profits positive became, therefore, a major policy concern for the NBP. This concern was one of the factors that led to a scaling down of open market operations in the second half of 1996, which, in turn, resulted in a fall of market interest rates. This fall was an important factor that sustained rapid credit expansion in 1996. At the same time, lower interest rates and rapid credit expansion helped to induce an outflow of portfolio capital and helped stabilize the level of international reserves in 1996.

The Evolving Threats to Macroeconomic Stability and Policy Responses

By 1994 the rate of economic growth was already high and the principal question for the designers of economic policy was how to sustain growth while keeping the risks to macroeconomic stability under control. Initially, in 1994–95, this risk came mainly from the excessive increase in international reserves, due to an unexpectedly large current account surplus in 1995 of some 4 percent of GDP. We have already discussed the policy responses. The required adjustment in the current account was a deterioration by some 7 to 8 percent of GDP. This was in part due to the fact that the inflow of foreign direct investment, suppressed during 1990–94, suddenly increased rapidly. Consequently, a surplus on capital account on the order of 4 to 5 percent of GDP could be assumed to be a stable and long-term feature of the Polish balance of payments. The adjustment achieved during the years 1996–97 was almost exactly as planned (Table 7.1). However, this final result masks the fact that by the end of 1996 a large credit expansion and a rapid growth of domestic demand increased the danger that the current account deficit could become, in the years 1997–98, much larger than the targeted level of between 3 and 5 percent of GDP. The specter of a macroeconomic instability of the Hungarian type (1995) or of the Czech type (1997) exercised the minds of policy makers during 1997. The policy responses involved first a monetary tightening and a relaxation of the exchange rate policy and, in the second half of 1997, a significant fiscal tightening. The monetary policy adjustment started early and, being preemptive, could be and was gradual. The measures taken by the NBP were two rounds of increases of reserve requirements for commercial banks (first half of 1997), followed by increases of NBP's headline interest rates (August 1997). These measures were supported by larger open money operations. They succeeded in raising nominal deposit and credit interest rates by 3 to 5 percentage points in a period when the inflation rate dropped by some 5 percentage points. The exchange rate policy adjustment took the form of keeping the rate of crawl above the rate of producer price inflation throughout 1997. The result was an effective real devaluation by some 5 percent against the basket. The fiscal tightening was also substantial, a reduction of the state budget balance (in cash terms) by some 4 percent of GDP as between the second half and the first half of 1997. This package of adjustments was substantial enough to succeed in keeping the current account outcome in the target zone, while being gradual enough to maintain the disinflation process and to sustain rapid growth of economic activity. The policy of high interest rates did produce the risk of renewed of pressure from speculative capital inflows. However, both external developments (the Czech mini-crisis in June 1997 and the Southeast Asian crisis in the autumn of 1997) and the internal developments (the parliamentary election in September 1997 and the election victory by AWS, a somewhat populist party) enhanced the country risk, thus providing the needed protection against such pressure.

The two concerns from 1997, an excessive credit expansion and a potentially excessive current account deficit, continued in 1998. However, three new threats to macroeconomic stability have emerged since then:

- Fiscal position: fears that the projected structural reforms (health, pensions, education and regional government) would be excessively costly
- Inflationary pressures: fears that the softer exchange rate policy may slow down the disinflation process
- Capital surge: fears that the high market interest rates and much improved macroeconomic fundamentals may begin to attract excessive volumes of short-term foreign capital

There was again a need to come up with the right policy responses. The threat of large short-term capital inflows was this time real enough to require immediate attention. A substantial reduction of interest rates would remove it, but the credit expansion was yet too fast, giving the NBP no room for such a move. Moreover, the government increased excise taxes and removed some subsidies at the beginning of 1998. Although these measures improved the prospects of a good fiscal outcome, their immediate effect was an increased rate of inflation. This also restricted the room for a reduction of interest rates.

The initial policy response, chosen in February 1998, was, therefore, a widening of the exchange rate band, from ± 7 percent to ± 10 percent, and a reduction in the rate of crawl, from 1 percent to 0.8 percent a month. Apart from the "visible" band, the NBP operated a narrower, "invisible" band. The latter was also much increased. The purposes of such a policy were twofold: once again, to increase the exchange rate risk for foreign speculators and to improve the prospect of meeting the inflation target. The downside risk was that the zloty would appreciate significantly within the band, thus posing a threat to the current account target. That threat was, however, mitigated by the contractionary effects of the continued fiscal and monetary tightening at home and the expansionary effect of improved business conditions abroad, particularly in the vital EU market. The second policy response was by the government, to reduce the short-term fiscal cost of structural reforms and to institute other measures that would eliminate the budget deficit of the entire public sector over the medium term. The purpose of this policy, apart from improving macroeconomic stability, was also to increase savings and thus to sustain growth.

The full effect of these measures is not yet known at the time of writing this essay. However, the immediate aim of substantially reducing the inflow of short-term foreign capital has been achieved.

Concluding Remarks

The case for controlling capital inflows to Poland is as yet weak. The Polish government still has other instruments at its disposal to deploy against large movements in short-term capital flows, such as the elimination of the budget deficit and a more flexible exchange rate. This paper suggests that foreign investors are guided to a large extent by long-term measures of creditworthiness, such as NIR or net foreign debt, and not simply or mainly by short-term interest rates. In these circumstances the central bank retains a degree of freedom in conducting the interest rate policy. Still, there is a case for having available standby measures, to be activated in the case of sudden changes that would otherwise force large shifts in the exchange rate and inflict costly real adjustments. A change of legislation that would give the NBP and the government powers to impose certain restrictions in emergency situations is under consideration.

The situation may change, however, with the arrival on the international debt market of Polish enterprises, commercial banks, municipalities, and local governments. These agents are likely to be guided above all by differentials in real interest rates and to be less sophisticated in estimating exchange rate risks than are foreign portfolio investors. There are several possible policy responses to such a change of circumstances. Any such response must take into account the well-known inability of the central bank to target simultaneously monetary aggregates, interest rates, and the exchange rate (a point stressed recently by Rosati 1996 and National Bank of Poland 1997). If and when Poland joins the European Monetary Union, the exchange rate flexibility for the central bank and the exchange rate risks for economic agents will both be removed. The burden of adjustment would then shift to fiscal policy and wage rates, with limited assistance provided by interest rates. However, the transition period to such a monetary union may well be of considerable duration. During that period, it may be necessary to keep real interest rates high to control credit expansion and inflation. A strong protection against speculative capital inflows would thus still be needed. The main burden of such policies may continue to fall on a more flexible exchange rate policy. But some tax-based measures, perhaps of the Tobin type against speculative capital and another type directed at domestic enterprises and institutions, may also be needed.

Notes

An early version of this paper was presented at a seminar on Managing Capital Flows in Central and Eastern Europe, Brighton, 26 March 1997. Comments by the seminar participants have been most helpful in writing the final version.

1. Net international reserves (NIR) of the banking system consist of reserve assets minus reserve liabilities. According to standard IMF definitions, reserve assets consist of monetary gold, holdings of SDRs, reserve position in the IMF, holdings of foreign exchange in convertible currencies, and claims on nonresident financial institutions denominated in convertible currencies (if any). Reserve liabilities are liabilities in convertible currencies to nonresidents with an original maturity of up to and including one year, as well as all liabilities arising from balance-of-payments support borrowing from foreign banks, institutions and governments, irrespective of their maturity.

2. Portfolio investments consist of portfolio assets minus portfolio liabilities. Liabilities consist of (a) sales by domestic residents to foreign residents of shares in banks, funds, enterprises and other economic units representing less than 10 percent of total share capital, (b) any debt instruments issued by municipalities and local and central governments, as well as banks and other domestic economic units, and (c) sales of financial derivatives by domestic banks and other domestic economic units. Portfolio assets cover the same categories, except that the buyers are domestic persons, legal or physical, while the sellers are foreign persons.

3. A large portfolio inflow (outflow) would strengthen (weaken) the zloty, thus reducing the pickup yield.

Bibliography

Durjasz, P., and R. Kokoszczynski, 1995. "From Fixed to Flexible Exchange Rate Regime: The Case of Poland 1985–1995." Warsaw, National Bank of Poland, presented at the CEPR conference on Convertibility and Exchange Rate Policy, Sofia, September 22–23, 1995.

Edwards, Sebastian, ed. 1995. *Capital Controls, Exchange Rates and Monetary Policy in the World Economy* (Cambridge: Cambridge University Press).

Gomulka, Stanislav. 1995. "The IMF-Supported Programs of Poland and Russia, 1990–1994: Principles, Errors and Results." *Journal of Comparative Economics* 20 (June), 316–46.

———. 1997. "Monetary Policies and Problems in Poland." London: London School of Economics, presented at the workshop on Monetary Problems of Economies in Transition, Budapest, 7–8 February, 1997.

Halpern, Laszlo, and Charles Wyplosz. 1995. "Equilibrium Real Exchange Rates in Transition." London CEPR Discussion Paper Series no. 1145 (April).

NBP (National Bank of Poland). 1996. "Raport o Inflacji" (Inflation Report). Warsaw (December).

Nuti, Mario D. 1996. "Inflation, Interest and Exchange Rates in the Transition." *Economics of Transition* 4 (1), 137–58.

Rodlauer, M. 1996. "Monetary Policy in Poland: Challenges and Options." IMF's Warsaw Office, October.

Rosati, Dariusz. 1996. "Exchange Rate Policies During Transition from Plan to Market." *Economics of Transition* 4 (1), 159–84.

Shafer, Jeffrey R. 1995. "Experience with Controls on International Capital Movements in OECD Countries: Solution of Problem for Monetary Policy?" In *Capital Controls, Exchange Rates and Monetary Policy in the World Economy,* ed. S. Edwards (Cambridge: Cambridge University Press).

Sheets, Nothan. 1995. "Capital Flight from the Countries in Transition: Some Empirical Evidence." *The Journal of Policy Reform* 1 (3), 259–78.

09
F32

8

Capital Flows to Latin America
Lessons for Central and Eastern Europe

Stephany Griffith-Jones

This chapter starts by examining briefly the main issues that both practice and theory have shown arise in relation to capital flows.

Second, it brings out—with a broad brush—the experience of Latin America. The experiences of Chile (positive) and Mexico (at present, unfortunately, negative) are highlighted.

Third, the paper extracts what are seen as the key issues and policy lessons for Central and Eastern Europe, and finishes by posing a number of questions the case studies should address.

Framework for Analyzing Capital Flows

External capital flows have long been assigned an important role in development. Even more, external capital clearly needs to play a particularly important role in sustaining the transition to the market.

Among the positive effects of external capital flows are: (a) they are seen as mobilizing external savings, which it is hoped will mainly supplement domestic savings, and thus raise investment, growth, and employment; (b) they are seen as helping to smooth out expenditure over time, for example if a country faces a sharp deterioration in its terms of trade; and (c) these flows are expected to increase the microefficiency of production, by causing lower intermediation spreads between lenders and borrowers. Perhaps more important—particularly in the case of transition economies—micro or sectoral efficiency can be expected to be boosted by the transfer of technology and management know-how, which often accompanies foreign direct investment (see Devlin, Ffrench-Davis, and Griffith-Jones 1995).

Therefore, we can conclude that private capital inflows have important beneficial effects particularly valuable for transitional economies, to help fund the high investment required for an acceleration of economic growth and for undertaking the necessary large economic restructuring.

However, external capital flows can also have very negative effects on domestic economies. Even though these are to a great extent the problems of success, nevertheless their negative effects can be seriously magnified if the flows are badly managed. The scale of potential problems that can arise from large capital inflows was dramatically illustrated by the Mexican crisis, which started in December 1994, and even more by the 1997–98 Asian crisis.

The first central issue is that of the potential temporary nature and volatility of capital flows, and of the high costs—both for domestic economies and, in cases such as the Mexican and Asian ones, also for the international system—that can be incurred by the volatility of such flows. As economic history and economic analysis have taught us, private capital markets (and especially international ones) are often characterized by successive periods of overlending (and overinvestment) followed by underlending (and underinvestment), often resulting in costly financial and/or debt crises.[1] It is interesting in this context that there have been five great debt crises—resulting from earlier lending booms—that occurred in Latin America since the region's independence. These debt crises occurred in the mid-1820s, mid-1870s, early 1880s, 1930s, and 1980s (Marichal 1989). However, though apparently more frequent in that region, debt crises have also occurred often in other areas, as Kindleberger (1978) describes.

Furthermore, the concern has been raised that having such a high proportion of capital flows to emerging markets now channeled via portfolio flows is an important additional source of volatility.[2] In this context, it is important to stress that the Latin American debt crisis of the 1980s was one of commercial bank flows; this implied that during the crisis the stock of bank loans previously made remained in the countries, as these loans had been made on average for around seven years. This is in contrast to mainly portfolio flows that came into Mexico in the early 1990s and left so quickly during and after December 1994. Indeed, the Mexican central bank is reported to have lost U.S. $6 billion of reserves in one single day. Thus, the issue in the 1990s seems to be not only of sustainability of new inflows, but of the risk of very rapid reversal. Furthermore, not only do these new portfolio flows seem more volatile; securitization has made investors face-

Table 8.1

Composition of Capital Flows,–Latin America (%)

	1978–82	1990–93
FDI	15.1	33.0
Portfolio	4.9	68.1
Other long-term	63.6	–32.1
Other short-term	16.4	30.5
Total	100.0	100.0

Sources: Reisen 1995 and *IMF World Economic Outlook,* October 1994.

less, thus making negotiations (e.g., for rescheduling) with them far more difficult or impossible.

In this context, it is important to examine not just the level but also the composition of external capital flowing into a country or region. An important distinction in this context is the extent to which capital flows are likely to be permanent or temporary (and thus volatile). It is difficult to judge *ex ante* the "temperature" of flows, that is, how "hot" or "cool" they are (see Claessens et al. 1995 and Reisen 1995). However, it seems valuable to follow Turner's (1991) ranking of capital flows ranging from the most permanent to the most temporary: (1) long-term bank lending; (2) foreign direct investment; (3) portfolio investment; (4) short-term bank flows. For the first two categories, additional flows or their servicing can vary but the existing stock remains for a long period. For the latter two, the stock can fairly easily flow out.

One of the important features of capital flows in the early 1990s to Latin America has been the potential reversibility of those flows (see Table 8.1). Thus in Latin America the more volatile portfolio flows reached 68 percent of total gross capital flows in the 1990–93 period.

A second central issue about foreign capital flows relates to their use in the recipient economy, and in particular to their impact on productive capacity. In this context, it is important to ascertain what proportion of these external flows goes to investment in the recipient country, how productive this investment is, and what part of it goes—directly or indirectly—to the production of tradables. If a large proportion of the capital flows goes to increase investment, if such investment is efficient, and if a high proportion of the output generated by the new investment goes into tradables, this improves both the long-term impact of external capital flows on the recipient country's growth and its shorter-term ability to cope better with changes in the volumes of external capital flows.

The Policy Experiences of Managing Capital Flows

As Williamson (1994) very clearly shows, governments faced with very large capital inflows have a variety of alternative policy instruments that can be deployed. The right mix for a particular country will depend on domestic country circumstances, on a perception of what proportion of the flows are likely to be permanent, and on policy objectives.

It would seem desirable that among the policy objectives countries should follow in this context are: (1) maintain international competitiveness, which is particularly crucial for very open economies; (2) avoid over-reliance on short-term capital flows, which may either decline or reverse themselves; (3) encourage more long-term capital flows; (4) avoid risk of future debt or foreign exchange crises; and (5) attempt to complement increased external savings with higher domestic savings, therefore avoiding displacement of domestic savings by external savings, as occurred in several Latin American countries in the early 1990s.

It seems useful to order in three levels the policy measures that can be pursued (see ECLAC 1994).

An initial level of intervention arises in the foreign exchange market. The purpose of intervention is to moderate trends toward excessive appreciation of the real exchange rate, since this rate has become one of the main instruments of export promotion. This point was well summarized by the president of the central bank of Chile (Zahler 1992): "If the exchange rate remains below equilibrium for too long, it will have at least two kinds of undesirable effects. First, the tradables sector of the economy may be hurt. It is a well known fact that many of the economies that have been successful in recent years (especially the small ones) have based their development on the growth of the export sector. . . . Second, . . . sooner or later the value of the currency will have to return to its level of long-term equilibrium (or even rise above it for a time), and this will put pressure on prices, thereby jeopardizing the goal of curbing inflation" (Zahler, p. 92).

At the first level of intervention, two very different situations can be observed, depending on how central banks respond to increases in capital inflows. One response is not to intervene at this first level (not to accumulate reserves). In this case, capital flows would not bring about any changes in the international assets held by central banks, and their entire increase would put pressure on the exchange market to revaluate. In this way, the international capital market is used for funding an increase in the current account deficit, which will lead to increased investment and/or consumption. The other situation occurs when the central bank intervenes at the first level by accumulating reserves. In this situation, a decision must be taken whether or not to sterilize the effects of the accumulation of reserves on the money supply. At this second level, intervention involves choosing between active and passive monetary policies (in terms of managing aggregate demand), which also determines its relationship with stabilization.

In the final instance, countries can always consider revising the nature of the capital account liberalization in order to regulate the composition of inflows. A third level of intervention then occurs. Some countries have chosen to open up to the inflow of capital and to establish only those intervention mechanisms that will prevent the entry of short-term speculative capital, which does not contribute to the investment process.

To sum up, policy options are available at three levels: (i) intervention in the foreign exchange market through an accumulation of reserves compatible with the various aspects of exchange rate policy; (ii) central bank sterilization of the monetary effect of the accumulation of reserves in order to influence the level and composition of aggregate demand; and (iii) regulation of capital movements in order to alter their level and composition in favor of long-term flows.

The possible combinations between the first and second levels of intervention yield different mixes of exchange rate policy and monetary policy, which make it possible to distinguish two major intervention alternatives. The first, favored by countries that have chosen to maintain a passive monetary policy, is known as nonsterilized intervention. It involves accumulating substantial international reserves, since the central bank buys the foreign currency brought in by capital flows in exchange for national currency, without sterilizing the monetary effect of these operations. However, if adjustment by way of an increase in imports does not occur fast enough, this alternative can expand the monetary base beyond desirable limits. This usually results in inflationary pressures, causing appreciations in the real exchange rate and tendencies toward excesses and changes in the composition of expenditure.

The second alternative, adopted by countries that, together with defending the exchange rate, have chosen to pursue active monetary policies, is known as sterilized intervention. Like nonsterilized intervention, it involves accumulating reserves, but systematically approaches the second level of intervention by applying a sterilization of the monetary effects of these operations. The purpose is to isolate the money stock from fluctuations stemming from the mobility of foreign capital. This type of sterilization, if effective, prevents domestic real interest rates from falling. In economies that are making full use of their productive capacity, this has the advantage of helping control aggregate spending and preventing further appreciation of the real exchange rate. However, with this option, if interest rate differentials persist, capital inflows continue to be stimulated, generating further needs for sterilization; at the same time, the intervention may be a source of quasi-fiscal deficits, since the central bank is placing commercial paper in the domestic market at higher interest rates than those it obtains on its international reserves. These quasi-fiscal losses may be partly offset by a subsequent capital gain derived from the appreciation of foreign exchange reserves.

These two reasons imply that the alternative of sterilized intervention has been combined with other policy measures: (i) at the first level of intervention, to influence the exchange market; (ii) at the second level of intervention, to regulate aggregate demand through mechanisms other than the interest rate; and (iii) at the third level of intervention, to modify the level and composition of capital flows, either directly, through restrictions and charges aimed particularly at short-term capital, or indirectly, by generating exchange rate uncertainty. Among the possible measures, the following are noteworthy (see also Table 8.2, for measures applied in Argentina, Colombia, Costa Rica, Chile, and Mexico):

At the first level, measures can include: (i) increasing the demand for foreign exchange through incentives for the outflow of capital during periods of surplus funds (this can be done by relaxing the rules governing investment by nationals abroad and the repatriation of foreign direct investment, and by authorizing institutional investors to invest abroad and various debtors to make advance payments abroad); (ii) applying foreign trade measures, to liberalize; (iii) promoting the introduction of mechanisms that encourage productivity increases.

At the second level of intervention, the purpose of which is to control the impact on aggregate demand, measures include: (i) introducing mechanisms for regulating financial systems in order to avoid distortions in the sector and remedy weaknesses in the prudential financial regulation of the banking system; (ii) imposing fiscal discipline in order to reduce the additional pressure on demand; (iii) supplementing exchange rate policy with social contracts on prices and wages.

At the third level of intervention, designed to alter the composition of capital inflows, measures include: (i) applying indirect exchange rate measures aimed at reducing the entry of short-term capital by introducing an element of uncertainty as to the evolution of the exchange rate, through intervention by the respective central bank in the determination of this rate over the short term; (ii) adoption of direct measures imposing restrictions on capital inflows, which can take the form of adjustments of the reserve requirements, often without interest, on bank deposits or other credits from abroad, and various kinds of quantitative controls (requirements as to minimum maturity periods, minimum volumes for bond issues, caps on interest rates on foreign capital, and regulations on the participation of foreign capital in the stock market).

Latin American Experiences

Experiences of Nonsterilized Intervention

This alternative has often been adopted by countries that favor price stability as a key objective of economic policy. This is based on the expectation that national interest and inflation rates will rapidly converge with international rates. Much of the success of this strategy ultimately depends on the confidence of economic agents in the monetary authority's ability to maintain the nominal exchange rate.

While, in practice, countries can be seen to have used different policy mixes, Argentina is one of the countries that have come closest to this alternative, starting from high levels of inflation. In terms of combating inflation, the policies instituted in the 1990s in Argentina have drastically reduced the inflation rate.

Though the Argentine alternative—based on fixing of the nominal exchange rate, the adoption of monetary rules that do not sterilize the effects of capital flows on the monetary supply, and the implementation of a set of structural reforms—has resulted in important achievements in the area of stabilization, it was accompanied by an appreciation of the real exchange rate. This has led to a sharp increase in its current account deficit. As a result, Argentina was the country most strongly affected by the "tequila effect." Though it has not been forced to devalue, it had to impose a very strong deflationary package and shore up its increasingly fragile banking system, hit by large withdrawals after December 1994.

Experiences of Sterilized Intervention

This alternative has been preferred by countries that have maintained an active monetary policy and, at the same time, a more cautious position as regards the nature of capital flows. It reflects a concern for competitiveness and the continued development of the tradables sector.

Among the Latin American countries that have opted for active intervention, Chile has done so most persistently. In 1990, the Chilean authorities started to take measures to regulate capital inflows and sterilize the monetary effects of the accumulation of reserves, through interventions in the foreign exchange and money markets. Chile used basically three instruments for these purposes: an exchange rate policy based on "dirty" floating

Table 8.2

Latin America and Central America: Summary of Intervention Measures Adopted with Regard to Capital Inflows, Selected Countries

	Argentina	Colombia	Costa Rica	Chile	Mexico
First Level (Moderation of the impact of capital inflows on exchange rate appreciation—accumulation of reserves)	March 1991: Convertibility Act, designed to fix the nominal exchange rate and deregulate the foreign exchange market. Liberalization and trade opening.	June 1991: Introduction of float band (*certicambios*). January 1992: All exporters allowed to keep part of their returns abroad, and residents allowed to keep up to U.S. $500,000 in assets abroad without prior permission. February 1992: Reduction of the minimum maturity period for external loans to finance working capital and fixed investment. Liberalization of trade.	Early 1992: Introduction of floating with intervention.	1991: Float band introduced. March 1992: "Dirty" float allowed within the band. July 1992: Exchange rate pegged to a basket of currencies of trading partners. 1991: Increase in the percentage of foreign currency deposits that banks can use for foreign trade. Investment by nationals and pension funds abroad made more flexible. Reduction of the time limit for remitting capital brought in through debt conversion operations.	Floating band with fixed floor. November 1991: Band ceiling devalued by 20 centavos a day. October 1992: Daily devaluation extended to 40 centavos of new pesos.

Second Level (Sterilization of the monetary effect of exchange operations)	Strengthening of public finances and introduction of a passive monetary policy.	Strengthening of public finances. January-October 1991: Active monetary policy. October 1991: Interest rates freed and sterilization abandoned.	Strengthening of public finances. Monetary policy uses open market operations and reserve requirements on deposits for foreign and national currency.	Strengthening of public finances. Active monetary policy through open market operations.	Strengthening of public finances. Moderate sterilization.
Third Level (Moderation of capital inflows).	June 1991: 3% tax on transactions in foreign currency generated by personal services abroad. February 1992: Increase in the commission on purchases of foreign currency by the Central Bank from 1.5% to 5%. June 1992: Regulation of the entry of foreign currency as payment for services.			June 1991: Reserve requirement of 20% without interest must be paid on credit obtained abroad. July 1991: This requirement is extended to all credit with terms of under six months. January 1992: Requirement extended to all deposits in foreign currency in commercial banks. Marginal requirements with respect to interbank deposits. Reserve requirement increased from 20% to 30%.	The amount of liabilities in foreign currency is limited to the equivalent of 10% of total liabilities.

of the exchange rate around a benchmark value determined on the basis of a basket of currencies, sterilization of the monetary effects of the accumulation of reserves through open market operations, and the application of charges and reserve requirements in order to regulate the entry of capital and discourage excessive, short-term flows.

The Chilean authorities opted for intervention in order to influence determination of the real exchange rate in the short term, on the basis of two assumptions: (i) the monetary authority has a better idea of future trends in the balance of payments and their effects on the economy, and (ii) its planning horizon is longer-term than that of agents operating in short-term markets (Zahler 1992).

Chile's exchange rate policy has undergone important changes in recent years. In 1983 it adopted a crawling peg policy, which involved determining a benchmark price for the dollar. This was devalued daily by the central bank on the basis of domestic and external inflation differentials. At the same time, in order to allow the market to play a role, the price for the purchase and sale of foreign exchange was allowed to float within a band around the benchmark value of the dollar. In mid-1989 this band was fixed at 5 percent of this value (see Ffrench-Davis, Agosin, and Uttoff 1985).

Since capital inflows intensified as of 1990, the official exchange rate repeatedly settled around the lower limit of the band, forcing the central bank to intervene. As a result, the central bank had to buy up U.S. $1.5 billion in 1990 and U.S. $3 billion in 1991 and also had to carry out numerous open market operations to sterilize the monetary effect of foreign exchange operations.

Apart from this large inflow of capital, in Chile there was an improvement in the current account. The authorities viewed some of the factors that were contributing to the positive evolution of the current and capital accounts as more permanent, and proceeded to accommodate these tendencies through two additional measures: (i) a 2 percent revaluation in June 1991, supplemented by a reduction in customs tariffs from 15 percent to 11 percent; (ii) a further revaluation of 5 percent in January 1992. The foreign exchange market exerted persistent pressure toward a higher appreciation. Convinced they were dealing largely with transitory factors, the Chilean authorities adopted a series of measures to moderate the revaluation pressures.

Some of the main measures were: (i) establishment in 1991 of a reserve requirement of 20 percent and a tax of 1.2 percent on short-term external credits; (ii) widening in 1992 of the float band from 5 to 10 percent of the dollar benchmark value, to create more uncertainty in the formation of short-term expectations; (iii) supplementation of this measure in March 1992 when the central bank decided to intervene on a discretionary basis within the limits of the band ("dirty" float); (iv) raising of the reserve requirement in May 1992 to 30 percent; and (v) amendment of exchange rate regulations in July 1992 in order to reduce the linkage of Chile's monetary policy with that of the United States and to link it more closely with that of Chile's other main trading partners; to do this, the benchmark exchange rate was pegged to a basket of currencies, made up of the United States dollar (50 percent), the German mark (30 percent), and the Japanese yen (20 percent).

Chile has also adopted a number of important measures to encourage selective, gradual capital outflows. In 1991 it increased the percentage of deposits in foreign currency that commercial banks could use for financing external trade; it made the process of investment abroad by national enterprises more flexible; it reduced the period for remitting capital brought in through debt conversion operations; and it authorized private pension funds (AFPs) to invest part of their portfolio abroad, in low-risk instruments.

Another important characteristic of the Chilean experience has been the central bank's access to the domestic financial market in order to counter the liquidity created by the accumulation of reserves, which tripled between 1989 and 1993. The national financial market has developed substantially, because of the reform of the pension system. In fact, the pension funds' rate of accumulation of resources has been greater than the increase in the supply of authorized financial assets, and they now have a majority share in the market for some specific instruments. This development of the capital market has allowed the central bank to place very large volumes of relatively long-term notes, mainly with the object of sterilizing the increased liquidity resulting from purchases of foreign exchange.

On the whole, recent events following the Mexican crisis have confirmed the success of the Chilean strategy; however, it should be stressed that it has had its costs. Ffrench-Davis, Agosin, and Uthoff (1995) estimated that the immediate cost of monetary sterilization in Chile reached 0.5 percent of GDP in 1992. Williamson (1994) reports similar costs of sterilization for Colombia, a country that followed a strategy fairly similar to that of Chile.

It is interesting that the Chilean economic authorities based their macromanagement of capital flows on the assumption that these were—to a large extent—temporary. As a consequence, they adopted a policy package (which included discouragement of short-term capital flows and sterilization of capital inflows) consistent with this assumption. Paradoxically, the success of these policies has implied that a rather large part of the capital inflows have been permanent, at least in the medium term (1990–95).

This is in sharp contrast with Mexico, where the economic authorities assumed that a large part of the capital inflows would be, at least in the medium term, permanent (sustained by factors such as Mexico's entry into NAFTA and the OECD). As a result, the Mexican authorities followed policies consistent with this assumption; they allowed a level of exchange rate that implied a very large increase of the current account deficit, they were somewhat ambivalent on attempting to control short-term capital flows, and—even worse—allowed foreigners to buy up a very high proportion of very short-term treasury securities. Indeed, a very high proportion of Mexico's external debt financing raised in the 1990s was very short-term debt, denominated initially in local currency and—in 1994—converted into dollar-denominated securities. Again, paradoxically, the large imbalances created by the policies pursued, the short-term nature of a large proportion of the inflows, as well as other factors (such as serious political problems in Mexico in 1994), meant that a large part of the external capital flows not only became temporary, but were very rapidly reversed.

The Mexican authorities seem to have made two types of mistakes. During the first stage of heavy capital inflows (1990–93), they allowed the exchange rate to become overvalued, and the current account deficit to grow very rapidly, to 8 percent of GDP in 1993. Though they adopted several measures to curb overvaluation of the peso and to sterilize inflows (Gurría 1995), these measures were not as comprehensive as they should have been. Some *ex ante* justification for these Mexican policies could be found in the fact that until 1993 foreign capital was pouring into Mexico at such levels that foreign exchange reserves were still rising, even though the current account deficit had grown to such a large magnitude.

During 1994, two very important changes occurred simultaneously that had a major impact on capital flows to Mexico. First, U.S. interest rates started to rise from their previously very low level, thus sharply diminishing the relative attractiveness of Mexican paper—and that of other emerging markets—to U.S. investors. Second, a number of serious political events—the revolt in Chiapas, the murder of the presidential candidate and of the president of the ruling party—seriously undermined the perception that Mexico had low political risk. Both these factors combined to provoke a sharp change in the willingness of foreign investors, and especially U.S. ones, to continue channeling funds to Mexico. As a result, foreign exchange reserves fell quite sharply in early 1994 (see Figure 8.1). The problem was that for almost twelve months, the Mexican authorities did not recognize that this was a major (and permanent) change in investors' perception. As a result, most of the measures adopted (such as switching from peso-denominated treasury bills to dollar-denominated treasury bills) assumed that the problem was temporary. Measures such as an important acceleration of the crawling peg, a one-off devaluation (for example, in March 1994), and/or a

Figure 8.1 **Capital Account and Foreign Exchange Reserves**
(billions of dollars)

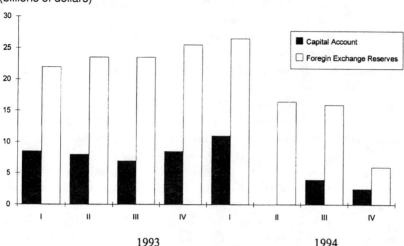

Source: El Indicador Economico, Serfin, Mexico, February 1995.

tightening of monetary policy, which would have been the automatic response to falling reserves, were not adopted. The failure to recognize the permanent change in foreign investors' attitude and to respond accordingly was a major mistake. It was based on a reluctance to recognize the fact that if investors and/or lenders are willing to finance at one moment a country's large current account deficit, this by no means implies they will continue doing so indefinitely, particularly if circumstances (both external and/or domestic) change. Mexican officials would have been far wiser to heed— both before 1994 and especially during 1994—Williamson's (1994) prudent rule "that positive shocks should be treated as temporary and negative shocks as permanent." The fact that they ignored it had a very high cost for the Mexican economy.

More generally, the issue of increased fragility and systemic risk in domestic financial markets that results from large surges in capital flows is an important source of concern, particularly if these capital flows are very volatile. Indeed, the large outflow of capital from Mexico and the large depreciation of the peso, for example, have significantly weakened the Mexican banking system. This problem was, of course, also extremely serious in the Asian crisis.

In the case of Central and Eastern Europe, domestic financial systems are already relatively fragile (see Griffith-Jones and Drabek 1995). As a result, one of the major sources of concern with very large capital inflows in the East European case is with their potential contribution to greater financial vulnerability (Calvo, Sahay, and Vegh 1995). This by itself may be an important argument for preferring sterilized to nonsterilized intervention, as the smaller expansion of liquidity in the financial system (and especially the banks) caused by the former reduces risks of banking crisis.

Conclusions and Questions for Case Study Research

A review of previous experience and of the literature seems to show us that no single policy is more appropriate for managing capital inflows, but that countries choosing a package of policies seem most successful.

It seems important to stress that—where necessary—such a package should include less orthodox measures, such as discouraging short-term capital flows when these become too large. The positive experience of Chile illustrates this. Though this statement would have been considered with great skepticism in more conservative circles before the Mexican crisis and before the Asian crisis, the need to curtail or discourage excessive short-term capital inflows in emerging markets has become widely accepted even in the most conservative circles and institutions.[3] This analysis also has some implications for the timing and speed of capital account liberalization, as once certain capital controls on inflows are removed, it becomes very difficult to get them back. In the case of Central and East European countries, any temporary measures to discourage or curtail excessive short-term capital inflows, as well as the timing and speed of capital account liberalization, must be made compatible in the near future with forthcoming negotiations with the EU on accession to membership by those countries.

However, less conventional measures, such as discouraging short-term flows and sterilized intervention, also have some problematic features. Therefore, they are most effective when complemented by more conventional measures, such as (where appropriate) some liberalization of capital outflows and tightening of fiscal policy. Furthermore, measures such as sterilized intervention are most effective when they are properly adapted to the development of local capital markets.

It seems valuable for countries' authorities to have a sense of the size of capital inflows that are desirable. Williamson (1994) provides us with a useful framework for determining a maximum for capital inflows, dependent on the existing debt/GDP ratio and on the rate of growth of the economy. According to Williamson's approach, a sustainable and therefore desirable steady state current account deficit level should not be more than 0.4 times the expected long-term growth rate of the economy. This would imply moving toward a debt/GDP ratio of 40 percent, traditionally considered to be a desirable maximum limit. Of course, a country that starts with a debt/GDP ratio lower than 40 percent can run a greater deficit for a while, but it should not let the current account deficit get too much larger, because it is difficult to adjust back when the debt limit approaches. Naturally, a country starting with a debt/GDP ratio higher than 40 percent should not have any (or as small as possible) current account deficit.

However, Williamson suggests that nondebt foreign claims, including foreign holdings of shares in domestic companies, should have a lower weighting than debt-creating flows. Particularly given the volatility of the former flows in the recent Mexican crisis, it would seem desirable to give equal (100 percent) weighting to both debt-creating and non-debt-creating flows, with the possible exception of foreign direct investment.

In this sense, it seems valuable to use an indicator that links sustainable level of total capital inflows (and not just debt-related ones) with level of exports. Dadush, Dhareshwar, and Johannes (1994) have developed such a ratio, based on the traditional rule of thumb that the debt/export ratio should not exceed 200 percent, and transformed it into a maximum limit of 200 percent for the ratio of a country's increased net liabilities divided by exports. Following this line of analysis, an indicator, which is very simple to calculate, is derived which is equivalent to:

$$\frac{\text{Current Account Deficit}}{\text{Exports}} \div \frac{\text{Change in Exports}}{\text{Exports}}$$

Dadush et al. then assume that the rule of thumb that can be applied is that this new indicator (which we can call LTE, liability increase to export increase ratio) should not be higher than 2, and that it should be calculated using averages for

$$\frac{\text{Current Account Deficit}}{\text{Exports}} + \text{export growth for the four years available}$$

It is interesting that in the preliminary calculations carried out by Dadush et al. in late 1994, Mexico was one of the few countries whose LTE was well above 2; it may be a source of concern that both Hungary and Poland were also among the countries with ratios above 2, though it needs to be pointed out that both countries were a special case, as exports fell in the early 1990s due to both the economic transition and the transition to Western export markets, linked to the breakdown first of Comecon and then of the FSU. However, this does indicate some preliminary reason for concern to reduce those countries' LTE, which can be achieved by expanding exports and/or by possibly discouraging inflows, especially of a short-term nature.

It should be stressed that the LTE does have one problem in that it refers to all net capital flows, thus including foreign direct investment, which seems to be less volatile than other capital flows.

For this the LTE indicator could also be complemented by another, which measures annual short-term flows (e.g., of flows of debt with maturity less than a year, or easily reversible equity flows) as proportion of total capital flows, and of GDP. If these latter ratios were high by international standards and/or rising fairly rapidly, this should encourage countries' authorities to act more decisively to curb such flows.

Finally, as discussed above, an important policy objective in managing capital flows will be to maintain medium-term external competitiveness for the economy, for which overvaluation of the exchange rate must be avoided.

The use of the exchange rate as an anchor to stabilize prices can in the medium term cause large real exchange rate appreciation and a change in the composition of output against tradables, which can lead to growing current account deficits. An extreme reliance on this approach to attack inflation is clearly a high-risk strategy. It is therefore more sensible to (a) be slightly less ambitious on reducing inflation, say, to one-digit levels, and (b), more important, rely on other means, such as fiscal, monetary, and incomes policy, to reduce inflation.

Questions for Case Studies

In the context of the above discussion it is suggested that the following questions and issues be examined in the country case studies.

1. What are the main features and scale of the flows coming into the country? What are the main categories of flows coming in relating to FDI, equity investment, bonds bank lending, and others? What are their financial conditions in terms of maturities, costs, and other? Did financial innovations take place that facilitated their inflow? Did these innovations carry different risks than more traditional instruments?

2. In what proportion do these different categories of flows seem to be permanent or transitory? What are the main reasons why different categories of flows are seen to enter the country? Are these reasons linked mainly to national or international developments? Are these factors likely to remain?

3. How are these external private flows being used in the country? What sectors are they going into? If possible, determine to what extent they are going into productive investment, especially in tradables. What other destinations do they have?

Is the government/private sector monitoring the microeconomic impact of these flows, in individual cases, at a sectoral level and in aggregate? If it is not, would it be desirable/feasible? How could this be done in the existing institutional and policy framework?

4. What has the policy response of the monetary and other financial authorities been? To what extent have they adopted an active policy response? What policy instruments have been used? Have all (some) inflows been discouraged, and how has this been done?

5. Has there been nonsterilized intervention? Or have flows been sterilized? What proportion? Through what mechanisms? What was the cost of such sterilization, as percent of GDP? Has the cost of sterilization become so large that it has become problematic? How have economic authorities reacted?

6. Have fiscal measures been taken to compensate for the effect of these flows?

7. Have measures been taken to relax controls on capital outflows or to liberalize imports?

8. Has the exchange rate policy been modified (for example, by creating or widening a band for exchange rate fluctuations)?

9. What effects have these different policy measures had? What lessons can be drawn from this experience?

10. In your opinion, what alternative policy measures could have been used? How and why would their effects have been more desirable?

11. What have been the main macroeconomic effects of different kinds of flows and of their management? What are the likely future macroeconomic effects of these flows? In particular, what are estimated effects on output, on investment, on domestic savings, on inflation levels? What are the estimated effects of recent flows and of the policies to manage them on levels of foreign exchange reserves, the level of money supply, the level of interest rates, and the level of both nominal and real exchange rates? What are the likely long-term growth effects if the level of flows is sustained, if it increases, and if it decreases? Are there risks that the flows could fall suddenly or be reversed? What macroeconomic impact would that have? What effects could it have on the financial system?

12. If you calculated indicators for your country, such as Williamson's sustainable steady state current account deficit and Dadush et al.'s LTE (for details see above), as well as the ratio of reversible capital inflows to total capital inflows (and their evolution), do you think the level and structure of capital flows coming into your country is a sustainable one? Why? Should any policy action be taken to make them more sustainable? Which ones?

Notes

This paper was first presented at the workshop on Managing Capital Flows in Central and Eastern Europe, held in Prague on 15–16 June, 1995. I would like to thank Jan Klacek, John Williamson, Helmut Reisen, Zdeněk Drábek, and the other workshop participants for their comments.

1. See, for example, Kindleberger 1978, Stiglitz and Weiss 1981, Guttentag and Herring 1984, and Mishkin 1991 for different—but related—analysis of capital market imperfections.

2. See, for example, Ffrench-Davis and Griffith-Jones 1995, Calvo, Leiderman, and Reinhart 1993, Reisen 1993, and *IMF Survey* 1995.

3. Interview material.

Bibliography

Calvo, G., L. Leiderman, and C. Reinhart. 1993. "Capital Inflows and Real Exchange Rate Appreciation in Latin America: The Role of External Factors." *IMF Staff Papers,* March.

Calvo, G., R. Sahay, and C. Vegh. 1995. "Capital Flows in Central and Eastern Europe: Evidence and Policy Options." IMF Working Paper, April.

Claessens, S., M. Dooley, and A. Warner. 1995. "Portfolio Capital Flows: Hot or Cold?" *The World Bank Economic Review,* vol. 9, no. 1.

Dadush, V., A. Dhareshwar, and R. Johannes. 1994. "Are Private Capital Flows to Developing Countries Sustainable?" World Bank International Economics Department.

Devlin, R., R. Ffrench-Davis, and S. Griffith-Jones. 1995. "Surges in Capital Flows and Development: An Overview of Policy Issues." In *Coping with Capital Surges,* ed. R. Ffrench-Davis and S. Griffith-Jones. Lynne Rienner.

ECLAS. 1994. *Policies to Improve Linkages with the Global Economy.* Santiago, Chile.

Ffrench-Davis, R., M. Agosin, and A. Uthoff. 1995. "Capital Movements and Macro-Economic Stability in Chile." In *Coping with Capital Surges,* ed. R. Ffrench-Davis and S. Griffith-Jones. Lynne Rienner.

Folkerts-Landau, D., J. Schinas, M. Cassard, V. Ng, M. Reinhart, and M. Spencer. 1995. "Effect of Capital Flows on Domestic Financial Sectors in APEC Countries." In *Capital Flows in the APEC Region,* ed. M. Khan and C. Reinhart. IMF Occasional Paper 122, IMF. Washington, DC, March, pp. 31–57.

Griffith-Jones, S. 1995. "European Private Flows to Latin America: The Facts and the Issues." In *Coping with Capital Surges,* ed. R. Ffrench-Davis and S. Griffith-Jones. Lynne Rienner.

Griffith-Jones, S., and Z. Drabek, eds. 1995. *Financial Sector Reform in Central and Eastern Europe.* Macmillan.

Gurría, A. 1995. "Capital Flows: The Mexican Case." In *Coping with Capital Surges,* ed. R. Ffrench-Davis and S. Griffith-Jones. Lynne Rienner.

Guttentag, J.M., and Herring, R.J. 1984. "Credit Rationing and Financial Disorder." *Journal of Finance* 39.

IMF Survey. 1995. "Living with the Reality of Integrated Global Capital Markets." April 3.

IMF. *World Economic Outlooks and International Financial Statistics.*

Kindleberger, C. 1978. *Manias, Panics and Crashes: A History of Financial Crises.* Basic Books.

Khan, M., and C. Reinhart. 1995. "Macro-economic management in APEC Economies: The Response to Capital Flows." In *Capital Flows in the APEC Region,* ed. M. Khan and C. Reinhart.

Marichal, Carlos. 1989. "A Century of Debt Crises in Latin America: From Independence to the Great Depression 1820–1930." Princeton University Press.

Mishkin, F.S. 1991. "Asymmetric Information and Financial Crises: A Historical Perspective." In *Financial Markets and Financial Crises,* ed. G. Hubbard. University of Chicago Press.

Reisen, H. 1993. "Capital Flows and Their Effect on the Monetary Base." *CEPAL Review* 51.

———. 1995. "Managing Temporary Capital Inflows: Lessons from Asia and Latin America." Distinguished Lecture, Pakistan Institute of Development Economics, Islamabad.

Stiglitz, J., and A. Weiss. 1981. "Credit Rationing in Markets with Imperfect Information." *American Economic Review* 72.

Turner, Philip. 1991. "Capital Flows in the 1980s: A Survey of Major Trends." *BIS Economic Papers* 30.

Williamson, J. 1994. "The Management of Capital Inflows." Institute for International Economics, December.

Zahler, R. 1992. "Monetary Policy and an Open Capital Account." *CEPAL Review* 48.

(Spain) F32
9
F21

International Capital Flows in the Spanish Economy

Lessons from the Experience of the Last Ten Years

José Garcia Solanes

International capital movements have increased remarkably since the mid-1980s in industrialized countries and since the beginning of the 1990s in some less developed economies as well. This is the financial side of the accelerating economic integration of the world economy. Three broad beneficial aspects of this phenomenon have been widely recognized in the literature. First, by reducing the foreign exchange constraint, capital inflows facilitate recovery and higher economic growth. Second, they provide the financing needed to continue the adjustment programs in countries more concerned with stabilization goals. Finally, they ease the transition to new institutional economic environments, such as full-fledged market economies or the accession to wider economic areas.

The first two groups of effects are easily found in recent years, in the new emergent Asian economies and in some countries of the South American cone as well, whereas the last one is clearly apparent in the experiences of the East European countries that have transformed their economies according to market-oriented rules and also the Southern European countries that entered the European Union.

Some authors (Devlin, Ffrench-Davis, and Griffith-Jones 1994) have also stressed that certain kinds of capital mobility created by rapid and deep financial deregulation, such as in some Latin American countries (mainly Mexico and Argentina), may have far less satisfactory effects, as a consequence of informational problems and systemic market failures that are inherent to the trade in financial instruments. In this case, prudential actions are needed in the process of financial liberalization.

The main objective of this chapter is to analyze the policy issues related to the increase of international capital movements in Spain since the accession of this country to the EC in 1986, and to draw some lessons for East European countries engaged in economic liberalization programs and market-oriented transformations. In particular, I want to investigate the likely macroeconomic effects of this phenomenon on the Spanish economy, and the extent to which it has constrained the achievement of both the foreign exchange objectives and the implementation of an independent domestic monetary policy by the Bank of Spain. The next section examines the most significant statistical trends of outflows and inflows, conveniently classified according to their maturity. The following section analyzes the causes and determinants of the inflows, and makes an effort to distinguish between the determinants that are more likely to produce unsustainable or destabilizing capital inflows and those that are deemed to cause sustainable and equilibrating flows. Next I investigate the policy responses by the Spanish authorities to the surge in capital inflows, paying special attention to the consequences of participating in the exchange rate mechanism (ERM) of the European Monetary System (EMS). The broad economic effects of capital inflows are examined in the subsequent section; they are derived from the results obtained in the preceding sections. The final section explains the most relevant conclusions and derives some policy recommendations for Central and Eastern Europe, based on the experience of Spain.

Statistical Trends

Tables 9.1 to 9.7 present the amounts of capital flows in the Spanish economy for the period 1987–96, grouped according to maturity criteria established by the International Monetary Fund. The first two tables refer to foreign direct investment (outflows and inflows, respectively). Tables 9.3 and 9.4 report similar information for portfolio investments, but include additional details in their columns two and three concerning the securities that are used as a vehicle in those movements. Tables 9.5 and 9.6 show the total amount of short-term flows (column one) and the participation of economic sectors in them (columns two to four). Table 9.7 shows the *net* flows (inflows minus outflows) of each group of movements and their proportion with respect to the GDP. Negative signs preceding the figures

Table 9.1

Direct Investment Abroad (millions of U.S. dollars)

	Direct Investment
1987	−745
1988	−1,235
1989	−1,473
1990	−3,522
1991	−4,442
1992	−2,192
1993	−2,652
1994	−3,831
1995	−3,574
1996	−4,633

Source: Balance-of-payments statistics, IMF, 1996.

Table 9.2

Direct Investment in Spain (millions of U.S. dollars)

	Direct Investment
1987	4,571
1988	7,021
1989	8,428
1990	13,984
1991	12,493
1992	13,276
1993	8,144
1994	9,359
1995	6,250
1996	6,409

Source: Balance-of-payments statistics, IMF, 1996.

Table 9.3

Portfolio Investment Assets (millions of U.S. dollars)

	Portfolio Investment	Equity Securities	Debt Securities
1987	29	29	0
1988	−136	−136	0
1989	−166	−166	0
1990	−1,367	−329	−1,308
1991	−2,410	−327	−2,083
1992	−2,811	−145	−2,666
1993	−6,772	−764	−6,008
1994	−1,837	−1,047	−790
1995	−619	−534	−85
1996	−3,772	−758	−3,014

Source: Balance-of-payments statistics, IMF, 1996.

Table 9.4

Portfolio Investment Liabilities (millions of U.S. dollars)

	Portfolio Investment	Equity Securities	Debt Securities
1987	3,770	3,434	336
1988	2,427	2,100	327
1989	8,155	6,387	1,768
1990	10,385	4,309	6,077
1991	22,489	2,772	19,717
1992	12,169	3,648	8,521
1993	56,125	6,491	49,633
1994	−19,310	1,154	−20,464
1995	21,307	43,466	16,961
1996	2,480	221	2,259

Source: Balance-of-payments statistics, IMF, 1996.

Table 9.5

Other Investment Assets (millions of U.S. dollars)

	Other inv. assets	General government	Banks	Other sectors
1987	−793	−271	1,140	−76
1988	−596	−785	1,315	−1,127
1989	−108	−737	1,336	−708
1990	−13,175	−532	−7,520	−47,044
1991	−7,740	−635	−3,215	−3,849
1992	−4,442	−823	−28,758	−10,786
1993	−75,295	−587	−66,388	−8,198
1994	9,149	−737	18,541	−6,019
1995	−37,515	−413	−27,043	−10,059
1996	1,408	−682	9,821	−7,731

Source: Balance-of-payments statistics, IMF, 1996.

Table 9.6

Other Investment Liabilities (millions of U.S. dollars)

	Other inv. liabilities	General government	Banks	Other sectors
1987	5,812	648	1,641	3,328
1988	7,134	670	2,643	4,125
1989	3,506	1,364	1,547	−47
1990	16,665	1,274	14,402	988
1991	11,624	−271	8,169	3,725
1992	25,958	3,418	13,609	8,932
1993	20,172	152	13,614	6,405
1994	11,940	1,376	17,427	−778
1995	6,798	1,949	4,144	705
1996	17,795	−296	19,128	−1,037

Source: Balance-of-payments statistics, IMF, 1996.

identify outflows. Figures 9.1 to 9.6 offer the evolution of the flows that correspond to each of the first six tables.

The following paragraphs present some comments about the amounts and economic meaning of the capital movements reported in the tables. Let me look first at investments in foreign assets by Spanish residents, which in general represent outflows of funds (Tables 9.1, 9.3, and 9.5, and Figures 9.1, 9.3, and 9.5). Direct investment abroad (Table 9.1 and Figure 9.1) seems clearly related to the nature of the two phases of the business cycle

Table 9.7

Net Flows (Inflows Minus Outflows) (millions of U.S. dollars)

Year	Direct investment	% Over GDP	Portfolio investment	% Over GDP	Other investment	% Over GPD
1987	3,826	1.30	3,799	1.29	6,605	2.25
1988	5,786	1.68	2,291	0.66	6,538	1.89
1989	6,955	1.83	7,989	2.10	3,398	0.89
1990	10,462	2.12	9,018	1.83	3,490	0.71
1991	8,051	1.52	20,079	3.79	3,884	0.73
1992	11,084	1.92	9,358	1.62	−14,484	2.50
1993	5,782	1.15	49,353	10.32	−55,123	11.52
1994	5,528	1.14	−21,147	4.37	21,089	4.36
1995	2,676	0.48	20,688	3.70	−30,717	5.49
1996	1,776	0.32	−1,292	0.23	19,203	3.45

Source: Obtained from Tables 9.1–9.6.

that is embedded in the period of the sample. During the expansionary phase that extended up to 1991, direct investment abroad by Spanish residents increased steadily. The biggest annual amount was achieved in 1991, and represented 0.8 percent of the GDP of that year. During the recessive years 1992 and 1993, direct investment abroad declined considerably, but gained new stimulus beginning in 1994, with the help of the expansionary phase that started in that year.

Portfolio and short-term outflows (Tables 9.3 and 9.5 and Figures 9.3 and 9.5, respectively) were not significant during the first three years, due to the strict official regulations and limits applied up to 1989, but increased vigorously and became more variable after 1990, when more permissive legislation, which especially favored movements of shorter maturity, entered in force.[1]

It is important to note that the high volatility of the short-term outflows during these years (which would obviously be more apparent with data of higher frequency) was very related to exchange rate expectations and, consequently, to speculative activities. Thus the impressive outward jumps of these flows in 1992, 1993, and 1995, which gave rise to a significant negative short-term balance (see Table 9.7), were narrowly linked to the weakness of the Spanish currency and provoked four devaluations of this currency in those years. In 1994 and 1996 speculators inverted their movements in order to reap the capital gains of their previous movements (after-devaluation speculative transactions). Consequently, the sale of short-term foreign assets exceeded the purchase of these securities, giving as a result a

Figure 9.1 **Direct Investment Abroad** (millions of U.S. dollars)

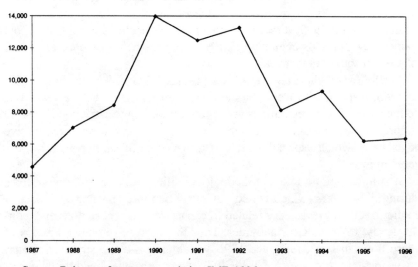

Source: Balance-of-payments statistics, IMF, 1996

Figure 9.2 **Direct Investment in Spain** (millions of U.S. dollars)

Source: Balance-of-payments statistics, IMF, 1996

net inflow in those years. The highest short-term outflow was achieved in 1993 and amounted to 15.7 percent of GDP. As seen in Tables 9.3 and 9.5, the most significant vehicles for portfolio and short-term flows were debt (mostly public) and bank deposits, respectively.

Figure 9.3 **Portfolio Investment Assets** (millions of U.S. dollars)

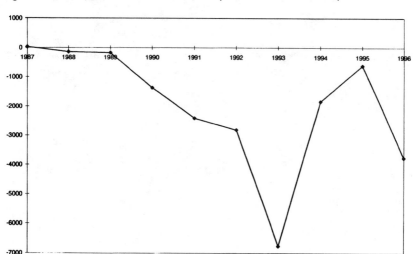

Source: Balance-of-payments statistics, IMF, 1996.

Figure 9.4 **Portfolio Investment Liabilities** (millions of U.S. dollars)

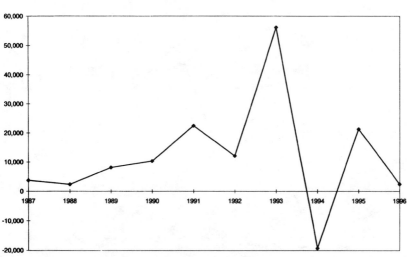

Source: Balance-of-payments statistics, IMF, 1996.

Let me now look at investments on domestic liabilities by examining the contents of Tables 9.2, 9.4, and 9.6, and Figures 9.2, 9.4, and 9.6. As in the case of outflows, foreign direct investments (Table 9.2 and Figure 9.2) show an inverted U shape, very closely related to the phases of the business

Figure 9.5 **Other Investment Assets** (millions of U.S. dollars)

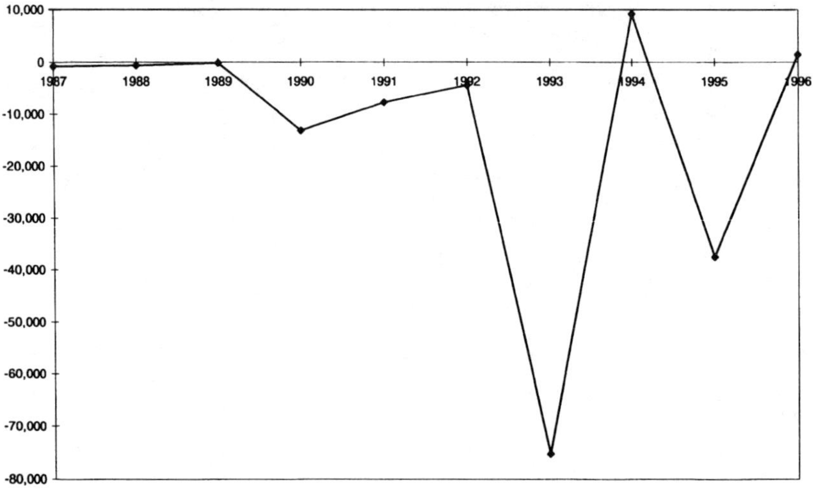

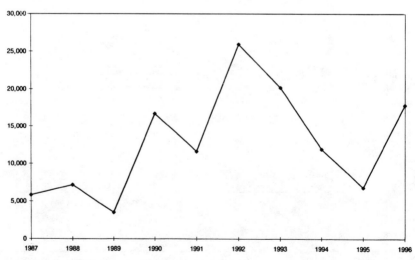

Source: Balance-of-payments statistics, IMF, 1996.

Figure 9.6 **Other Investment Liabilities** (millions of U.S. dollars)

Source: Balance-of-payments statistics, IMF, 1996.

cycle. During the subperiod of economic expansion these flows increased steadily until 1990, achieving then their maximum level, equal to 2.8 percent of GDP. This level remained more or less stable during the two following years, and jumped considerably down in the recessive year 1993.

Portfolio investments (Table 9.4 and Figure 9.4) show an increasing trend from 1989 to 1993, when portfolio inflows achieved 11.7 percent of GDP. This evolution is linked to two qualitative changes during the period. First, at the end of 1990 restrictions established in mid-1987 and in February 1989 on the purchases of Spanish public debt by foreigners were abolished.[2] This is the reason why the bond market became the most important recipient of capital inflows since 1990, to the point that the amounts channeled through private and government bonds more than quintupled the quantities entered via equities. Second, the public sector was a very active agent in those years, as shown by the fact that the funds it absorbed stood for 80.3 percent and 93 percent of total portfolio flows in 1991 and 1992, respectively.

Short-term capital inflows (Table 9.6 and Figure 9.6) also exhibited a positive trend beginning in 1987, although with higher variability than the flows with longer maturity. The peak was reached in 1992 and represented 4.5 percent of GDP. As for the case of portfolio investments, the inflows attracted by the public sector were by far more relevant than those of the private sector, especially since 1990 (see columns two to four of Table 9.6), as a consequence of the liberalizing measures adopted at the end of that year. The most important assets for these kinds of transactions were short-term deposits and treasury bills.

To summarize the characteristics and nature of the capital flows in the Spanish economy since the mid-eighties, it can be said that three main kinds of movements increased substantially since 1987. The financial balance is clearly positive, indicating that net inflows have contributed to fill the gap between the need for funds, on the one hand, and the availability of funds coming from the accumulated stocks (financial wealth) and savings, on the other hand. The biggest amounts of outflows and inflows correspond to 1992 and 1993. In those years the *net* balance of the movements with longer maturity (foreign direct investments and portfolio movements) considered together amounted to 3.6 and 11.5 percent of GDP, respectively. Foreign direct investments are the most stable movements. Since their main determinants are economic prospects and returns in a long horizon, they are closely related to the up and down stages of the business cycle of Spain and other industrialized countries.

Portfolio investments and short-term capital flows have been more volatile because they depend mainly on short-term expected returns and represent the biggest amounts on both the outflow and inflow sides. Although short-term inflows and outflows were volatile when observed separately, their net annual balance was remarkably stable except in the years of monetary turbulence in the EMS, when outflows clearly dominated. Once the international speculative turmoil subsided, short-term flows came back to normal levels. This leads me to think that a large part of the total financial balance is rather stable and that it is not likely to create problems of sustainability for the coming years. However, in order to make more accurate evaluations of the sustainable or stabilizing nature of capital inflows in Spain, we need to go into the causes of those movements. I do that in the following section of this chapter.

The Main Determinants of the Surge in Capital Inflows in Spain

Three groups of factors are candidates to explain the big increase of international capital inflows to Spain in recent years.

Domestic Structural Changes Prior to and During The Years of the Surge in Inflows

In the second half of the 1970s, the Spanish authorities initiated a process aimed at modernizing the domestic productive and financial systems, giving more scope for the play of market forces. The main objective was to eliminate gradually the structural rigidities inherited from the economic Franquist regime. Important actions were adopted in several areas. The most recent ones can be found in the Convergence Program, elaborated by the government in 1992 to adapt the real side of the Spanish economy to that of the more advanced countries of the European Union, and can be grouped into four categories.[3]

Measures to Reduce the Rigidities of the Spanish Labor Market

The first one concerns the downward rigidity of payments to workers. In 1977 the Moncloa Agreements, joint agreements by unions and entrepreneurs, were achieved under the initiative of the government to moderate the increase of real wages. More recently, additional measures have been adopted to make real wages more sensitive to cyclical real activity and employment: labor negotiations are promoted at lower and more decentralized (geographical and sector) levels, the clauses of pegging wages to prices have been suppressed, and public enterprises have adopted more rational behavior by proposing salary rewards that correspond more closely to productivity changes of the labor force.

A second point of public attention has been excessive protection of permanent workers and the low mobility of the labor force. To solve these problems, legal measures were adopted in 1984 and 1985 favoring fixed-term contracts and part-time employment, and promoting the training of workers. The third kind of measure aims at lowering the high wage reserve of Spanish workers. For this purpose, the amount of unemployment subsidies was reduced in 1992, and since then a less advantageous fiscal treatment has been accorded to wage rewards in the personal income tax.

A fourth group of actions have been designed to solve mismatch problems, such as the implementation of special professional training programs. Also, financial aids have been approved to overcome the housing problems that arise when workers search for a job in other regions. Finally, special budgetary efforts have been made to reduce nonwage labor costs, especially the social security contributions of the Spanish enterprises.

Measures to Deregulate and Liberalize Private and Public Production and Trade

In 1985–87, key public enterprises in industrial and services sectors were sold in order to strengthen the play of the market forces. In 1989 a law was passed to foster competition in all the economic sectors of the country, and in 1992 new dispositions were decreed to reactivate the privatization process of some state-owned companies and to eliminate the state monopolies. Furthermore, professional activities were completely liberalized. In 1996 and 1997 the government of the Popular Party has pursued privatization even in the field of profit-earning firms and sectors, such as banks, telephone companies, and oil companies.

Of special relevance was the program of gradual foreign trade liberalization that was put in motion in 1986 to conform to the rules of the European single market that was intended to be achieved in January 1993.[4] As a result, trade openness increased substantially in Spain.

Measures to Reorganize the Public Sector and Reduce the Government Deficit

The main objective of the law of reconversion and reindustrialization of 1984 was to modernize economic sectors that were inefficient, or to replace them by others that fitted better with the local economic advantages. Although the law imposed a reduction of employment by 26 percent during 1984–86 in shipbuilding, steel, and textiles, these firms operate now according to competition rules and do not need permanent public compensations or financial aids. Furthermore, the government has reduced the negative consequences of its economic activity on the budget by both selling to the private sector the public firms with systematic deficits, as mentioned above, and no longer buying private enterprises that cannot survive by themselves.

Despite the abovementioned transformations of the public enterprises, and the fact that Spain has had a very agile and progressive fiscal system since 1977–78, the public deficit as a proportion of GDP did not achieve a stable low level until very recently. Thus, the public deficit increased systematically in the first half of the 1980s and reached 6.9 percent in 1985. Although an almost continuous reduction was observed during the following years until 1989, when the lowest level was reached (2.8 percent), new and unexpected factors appeared in 1993 that put the deficit at the level of 7.2 percent in that year. Since then, special corrective actions, adopted mainly by the Popular government, have been designed to reduce the deficit to levels compatible with the Maastricht Treaty.

Transformation of the Domestic Financial System

The changes undertaken in this field are not uniform across the different financial markets, and respond to two specific needs of the public sector that appeared in the 1970s and the 1980s, respectively.[5] The first one was the desire of the Bank of Spain to implement an active monetary policy hinged upon the control of the liquid assets of the banking system. To this end, the interbank money market was developed quickly by permitting foreign banks to operate in Spain since 1978, and reserve requirements were unified for all kinds of banking intermediaries in the second half of the seventies. Furthermore, the creation of new banks and the opening of additional branches were liberalized.

The second need of the public sector was for mechanisms to finance the bulk of its deficit. Thus in 1977 the government made use, for the first time, of market-determined interest rates to sell its public debt. However, the fiscal advantages incorporated in these assets in favor of their holders precluded the development of secondary markets until 1983, when a new class of bonds without fiscal exemption rights was launched by the government.

The development of secondary markets contributed to intensify the disintermediation process that was present during the second half of the 1980s, as shown by the decreasing participation of the banking sector in the total financial assets and liabilities of the domestic nonfinancial sectors. Furthermore, substantial reductions in banks' mandatory reserve and investment coefficients took place in these years. Some of these changes reflected the move toward the conditions imposed by EC accession.

The most striking feature in this last period was the boom in the market for the government's fixed yield assets in 1986. The Spanish government was especially active in this respect: its debt represented 69 percent of total placements in that year. The budgets of 1986 and 1987 gave a new impulse to the issue of public debt, by creating a system of bookkeeping entries of purchases of this type of debt, centralized in the Bank of Spain.

Some institutional changes initiated in 1985 laid the basis for a stronger development of the market for private bonds. For instance, the elimination of the fiscal advantages of private securities constituted an additional impulse for the secondary market. Furthermore, the introduction of new financial tools, such as assets with variable interest rates, assets with the option to anticipate redemption, and bonds convertible into shares, made this market more attractive for domestic and foreign investors.

The stock market has undergone important transformations in the last years, partly inspired by the norms promulgated by the EC Commission. Despite this, the stock market is still smaller and narrower in Spain than in other European countries with a similar degree of industrialization. Only 24 percent of the largest three hundred Spanish companies are currently quoted in the stock exchange, and the bulk of transactions are concentrated in a reduced group of firms (services and banking sectors).

The entry of Spain into the EC imposed other gradual financial transformations. Three of them were put in the single-market horizon of January 1993: complete freedom of establishment for domestic and foreign banks, freedom of services activities, and liberalization of capital movements. This last goal was achieved in February 1992, ten months before the deadline established by the EC Commission and after the liberalization of foreign trade was completely achieved.[6] Thus, the Spanish authorities have broadly respected the order of liberalization advised by Edwards (1984) and McKinnon (1986): first, the real (flows of goods and services) side of the economy, and second, the financial sector and capital movements. Furthermore, the liberalization of the capital account has been sequenced simultaneously with the liberalization of the domestic financial system, as suggested by Johnston and Ryan (1994).

As a result of the structural changes analyzed in the preceding paragraphs, the supply conditions of the Spanish economy improved remarkably in the second half of the 1980s. There are some related indicators that give support to this idea. The first one is that, according to OECD estimates, factor productivity increased more in Spain than in the remaining European countries of this organization during this period: 1.8 percent per year, against 1.3 percent per year, respectively.

The second one is offered by the increasing share of the profits of the manufacturing sector in the total profits of the economy since 1983. The third one is provided by the index of unit labor costs: the Spanish economy as a whole performed remarkably better than nineteen other industrialized countries taken as a whole during the 1980s.[7] Fourth, Spain shows very high rates of economic growth compared with the remaining EU countries during the period 1985–90 (an annual average rate of 4.1 percent, compared to 3.6 percent for the EU 15 as a whole). Finally, econometric estimations by Dolado and Viñals (1991) of an intertemporal model of the foreign Spanish sector indicate that nearly 75 percent of the real appreciation of the Spanish peseta during the period from 1985 to mid-1992 was due to permanent and equilibrating forces, such as productivity increases in the tradables sector.

It is likely that the abovementioned structural and fiscal changes had created expectations of lower inflation and higher economic growth rates, at least during the period 1986–90. This, together with political stability, was probably an important determinant of the foreign direct investment inflows registered in those years. In fact, the amount of long-term capital inflows was enough to finance the current account deficit of the period. During the years of higher inflows, the amounts of longer-term movements (foreign direct capital and portfolio investments) considered together achieved important levels with respect to the GDP of Spain: from 5 percent in 1990 to 13.4 percent in 1993.

A Policy Mix Made of Monetary Contraction and Fiscal Expansion

The Bank of Spain implemented tight credit policies during the whole inflow period in order to curb persistent inflation. At the same time, the government increased the amount of public expenditures, mainly with the aim of modernizing infrastructure and capital equipment, and to reduce the gap between Spain and the more advanced European countries in this respect. The result was a remarkable increase of nominal and real interest rates that attracted substantial amounts of foreign capital with short and medium maturities. As explained above, the fiscal deficit and the development of markets for public assets in the second half of the 1980s eased the way for this kind of inflow.

External Influences

The most important determinant here is the good economic prospects created by the integration of the Spanish economy with the European Community, and the new horizons opened in 1986 by the foreseen European single market. These institutional arrangements created expectations (a large part of which were realized) of a major change in the potential for trade in Europe, and raised the level of permanent income of the Spanish inhabitants.

Some empirical studies, such as Bajo and Torres 1992 and Martín 1992, show that the liberalization of trade, following the entry of Spain into the EC, gave rise to more creation than deviation of trade in manufactured goods during the five years following the enlargement of the EC. Although the results are not so evident in the trade of agricultural goods, it seems reasonable to think that trade integration with the EC brought about net welfare gains for Spain. Further evidence in this respect is provided by the evolution of the relative per capita general domestic product, measured in units of purchasing power; taking the base index of 100 for the EC 15 as a whole, the index for Spain increased steadily from 69.7 in 1985 to 76.9 in 1991.

The above considerations point to an increase of permanent income in Spain that could explain the sharp rise in both consumption and investment expenditures during the period analyzed. If this economic diagnosis is correct, most of the strong deterioration of the current account in Spain between 1986 and 1991 should be considered an equilibrium phenomenon.[8] The theoretical and empirical evidence provided by Beyaert, García Solanes, and Pérez Quirós (1994) and Alcalá and Peñarrubia (1995) completely confirm this interpretation.

Additional external influences could be found in the fact that the countries that are more closely and intensively linked with Spain by financial and trade flows shared with Spain the same expansionary cyclical phase during the period under consideration. This is the case with the remaining EC countries, and with Japan and the United States to a lesser extent. In both the EC as a whole and in Spain, the peak in the rates of real GDP growth during these years was achieved in 1987 (4.2 percent and 5.6 percent, respectively), whereas in Japan and the United States it occurred one year later (3.9 percent and 6.2 percent, respectively).

The above discussion about the causes of the surge of capital inflows in Spain is useful to evaluate the degree of sustainability and the risk of a reversal of those inflows in the future. It seems reasonable to assume that domestic structural changes and economic integration of Spain with the EU have been important determinants of foreign direct investment and other inflows with long and medium maturities, which by definition are highly sustainable and not very reversible movements. In fact, until 1988, the gap between gross investment and savings, that is, the current account, was perfectly financed with only foreign direct investment.

The period (1989–92) exhibits the highest current account deficits, which exceed the amounts of foreign direct investment inflows by 1.5 percent of the GDP as an annual average. To the extent that a sufficient proportion of other capital inflows (mainly portfolio and foreign direct credits) might be considered permanent enough to be added to direct investment flows for financing purposes of the current account, no problem of sustainability would be detected in the capital account of the Spanish balance of payments. In this case, the real appreciation of the Spanish peseta, the increase of the relative prices of nontradables, and the current account deficit of that period would be not signs of instability, but rather equilibrating and sustainable features.

However, if the bulk of the other kinds of inflows are temporary because they were provoked by the peculiar policy mix that was in force in Spain in those years or by other volatile causes such as foreign exchange speculation and economic expectations that are not well founded, a certain proportion of the increased domestic expenditures should be considered excessive with respect to the permanent budget constraint of the country, and part of the real appreciation of the Spanish peseta would be a deviation or misalignment with respect to its long-run equilibrium value.

Although there are no definitive and exact methods to determine the nature of all kinds of capital inflows, nor the long-run equilibrium value of main macroeconomic variables such as the real exchange rate and the current account, there is a broad consensus that the Spanish peseta was overvalued to some degree during the period 1989–92 and that part of the current account deficit of those years was unsustainable. According to this judgment, the devaluations of the Spanish peseta in 1992, 1993, and 1994 would be justified to some extent.

The above considerations indicate that for the authorities it is important to have reliable evaluations about the nature and effects of the international capital inflows. When the effects are likely to be destabilizing, a policy response is needed in order to contain or neutralize the inflows. On the contrary, if the effects are interpreted as stabilizing, policy can be more focused on improving the absorptive capacity of the economy than on containing destabilizing effects. In the next section I analyze the policy responses of the Spanish authorities to the surge in capital inflows of the second half of the 1980s.

Policy Responses

The choice between allowing the inflows to stimulate demand and growth and curbing their possibly destabilizing effects came to the fore in Spain during the first years after joining the EC.

Foreign Exchange Intervention and Capital Controls

Initially Spain responded to the surge in inflows by introducing some impediments to flows, and particularly by intervening in the foreign exchange market. This strategy was based on three kinds of arguments hinging upon the idea that the inflows were not likely to be permanent: first, the Spanish authorities thought that a market-determined appreciation would trigger speculative attacks against their currency; second, they desired to preserve a credible nominal anchor should the inflows reverse; and third, the Spanish government decided to shadow the exchange rate policy of the ERM countries before joining this mechanism in June 1989.

In order to make the exchange rate objective compatible with the gradual decline of the rate of inflation in a country where the nontradables sector has an important weight, these actions were combined with relatively aggressive sterilization. It was thought that this policy would allow the authorities to maintain an active monetary policy and to channel the capital inflows to the tradables sector. Sterilizing was attractive because it could be implemented quickly and allowed for time to consider the likely causes and persistence of inflows and to formulate a longer-term response.

The mechanisms most frequently employed by the Bank of Spain to limit the influence of capital inflows on money were open market operations and, especially, direct controls on credits to commercial banks. A reliable indicator of the intensity of sterilization is the deceleration or drop in the net domestic assets of the Bank of Spain as a proportion of its total assets. Table 9.8 offers the annual variation of this ratio for the years 1985–95. These figures confirm that intervention by the Bank of Spain was sterilized, for the amount of variation of those assets goes in the opposite sense than capital inflows. Thus, in 1987 and 1988 the proportion of domestic assets of the Bank of Spain fell by more than 16 percent per year, while short-term capital flowed significantly into the economy in net terms. As a result, the nominal exchange rate of the Spanish peseta with respect to the ecu did not change in the average during those years, despite the net inflows. A similar phenomenon was observed in 1990 and 1991, where net inflows and a decline of the ratio of domestic assets of the Bank of Spain were accompanied by only a small appreciation of the Spanish currency. On the contrary, in 1989 the peseta appreciated by more than 5 percent and sterilization was not necessary.

Estimates by the IMF of the offset coefficient, that is, the degree to which sterilization induces offsetting capital inflows, indicate that the Spanish monetary authorities enjoyed substantial monetary policy independence in those years.[9] However, in 1989 the Bank of Spain reduced its reliance on strong sterilized intervention for two important reasons: first, because these policy actions put upward pressure on domestic interest rates, weakening real activity and increasing government payments; second, because by forcing inflows into purchases of government bonds, sterilization channeled a

Table 9.8

Domestic Assets of the Bank of Spain, as a Proportion of Its Total Assets (Annual Variation Rates) (in percent)

Year	Series
1985	10,852
1986	−4,551
1987	−17,655
1988	−15,178
1989	6,803
1990	−14,155
1991	−7,918
1992	28,873
1993	−1,642
1994	28,607
1995	11,198

Source: Banco de España, Cuentas Financieras de la Economía Española (1984–1993) and 1987–1995).

Table 9.9

Foreign Loans to Spanish Residents (billions of Spanish pesetas)

Year	Direct financial long-term loans to the private sector	Foreign long-term investments in Spanish public assets	Foreign short-term loans to Spanish residents	
			Private Sector	Public Sector
1986	120.4	10.9	6.1	12.3
1987	475.9	174.5	45.4	164.1
1988	823.7	118.4	32.2	401.1
1989	387.7	899.6	58.5	805.9
1990	328.3	1,802.0	23.2	879.3
1991	948.9	10,218.8	179.6	4,800.4
1992	1,506.1	24,569.0	983.5	3,961.3

Source: Boletin Estadistico del Banco de España, 1993.

substantial share of foreign capital out of private utilization.

In order to make the final aim of controlling domestic liquidity and inflation compatible with the smaller recourse to sterilization, in June 1989 the Bank of Spain began to let the peseta appreciate more freely, according to market forces, in the frame of the ERM. At the same time, it implemented temporal complementary measures to alter the composition of

Table 9.10

Net Variations of the Foreign Reserves of the Bank of Spain (billions of Spanish pesetas)

Year	Net variations of the foreign reserves of the Bank of Spain
1986	318.6
1987	1,593.2
1988	961.8
1989	581.8
1990	689.3
1991	1,472.3

Source: Boletin Estadistico del Banco de España, 1993.

capital flows and intensified restrictions on the size of inflows while easing outflows. These restrictive actions also reflected concerns about the efficiency with which the economy could absorb the avalanche of funds, and were adopted in a context of increasing financial liberalization and capital account convertibility in the industrialized countries. Let me go into more detail about the whole set of capital restrictions put into place since 1987, and comment on their broad effects.

The impediments to inflows were quickly enforced through the following measures: In March 1987 the reserve requirements on Spanish bank accounts were extended to the increases of deposits in convertible pesetas held by nonresidents.[10] In April 1987 those coefficients were applied to the totality of deposits in convertible pesetas; furthermore, banks were prohibited from paying interest on convertible peseta balances exceeding 10 billion pesetas. In July 1987 short-term purchase agreements by nonresidents on domestic public assets, in the forward market or with buyback clauses, were forbidden.

In June 1988 the authorization procedure for foreign financial loans over 1.5 billion pesetas to resident borrowers, with average maturity less than three years, was reintroduced. Finally, in February 1989, a 30 percent non-remunerated reserve requirements was imposed on new foreign loans to resident physical persons and nonfinancial companies, with a 20 percent reserve requirement on increases in the short-term foreign currency positions of the banking system.

At the end of 1989, the Bank of Spain detected that the reasons for maintaining impediments to capital inflows were disappearing. Furthermore, the perception that the restrictions to international capital flows should be gradually eliminated in order to comply with the EC provisions

Figure 9.7 Difference Between the Three Months Domestic Interbank and Euromarket Interest Rate of the Peseta Deposits (in annual percent rate)

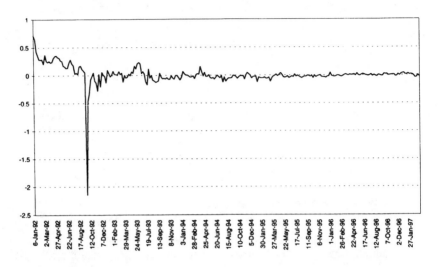

Source: Analistas Financieros Internacionales, Madrid.

Figure 9.8 Interest Rates of Swap Operations in Spanish Pesetas, Internet and External (weekly observations: Oct. 7, 1997, to Nov. 23, 1997)

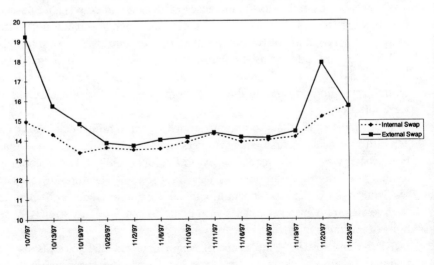

Source: Linde 1993.

became increasingly widespread. Consequently, it abandoned the impediments to inflows and pushed ahead with the gradual liberalizing process on the outflows side; this lasted until February 1992.[11] The most significant changes adopted in 1989 in the outflows direction consisted of permitting direct investments abroad in companies engaged in portfolio and real estate investment activities, and abolishing ceilings on real estate investments abroad. All those changes, combined with higher flexibility of the peseta exchange rate (although within the limits permitted by the ERM), put the domestic currency near the upper limit of the band and made it the strongest currency of the EMS during several episodes of this period.

The transitory restrictions on capital inflows were very effective in containing not only short-term movements but also flows with longer maturities as reflected in the following indicators. First, the intensity of the inflows decreased in those years, although a certain degree of evasion took place through subsidiaries of foreign companies, which made inflows through direct investment instead of loans or deposits. As seen in Table 9.9, direct financial loans to Spanish residents decreased substantially in 1989 and 1990 and picked up vigorously in 1991, when controls were abolished. Direct loans to the Spanish public sector remained modest before 1991 but increased spectacularly after that year. A similar evolution is observed in short-run foreign loans to both the private and public Spanish sectors.

Second, the positive variation of foreign reserves clearly decreased after 1987 and increased notably in 1990 and 1991 (Table 9.10). The third indicator is provided by the divergence with respect to the covered interest parity in the three-month Spanish interbank and Euro markets interest rates. As shown in Viñals (1992), this divergence was always positive in the period 1987–89, and attained higher values than in the preceding years.[12] Finally, the effectiveness of capital controls is also reflected in the fact that the variability of the interest rate of the short-term deposits denominated in pesetas was bigger onshore than offshore during that period, indicating that the Bank of Spain enjoyed higher autonomy in its monetary policy.[13]

In the fourth quarter of 1992 the EMS was shaken by the most important crisis since its inception at the end of the seventies. With the hindsight of experience accumulated in the past few years, we know more precisely the factors that triggered the speculative attacks against the Spanish peseta. In particular, concerns about the sustainability of the current account deficit, together with judgments that an important part of capital inflows was prone to reversal and that some structural changes would not be so deep as previously promised, contributed to the opinion that the Spanish peseta was overvalued. Political causes such as the difficulty approving the Maastricht

Treaty in Denmark added to the economic reasons to launch speculative pressures against the weaker currencies of the ERM.

In the face of the speculative turmoil, the Spanish government decided to keep the peseta in the ERM and adopted measures to reconcile this commitment with a modicum of monetary autonomy. Thus, on September 17, the central rate of the Spanish peseta with respect to the ecu was devalued by 5 percent, and some days later transitory measures were adopted to penalize the most important short-run speculative operations.

Aware of the fact that speculative sales (spot and forward) of the Spanish peseta must be matched by fresh provisions of the currency to nonresidents, the Spanish government imposed on domestic financial institutions the requirement of a nonremunerated one-year deposit in the Bank of Spain for the total amount of *new* lending to foreigners. In fact, the measures intended to make more expensive one specific way of lending to nonresidents, which is swap operations. For this reason, the deposit requirement was applied to the participation of domestic institutions in the two components of a short-run swap with nonresidents: the sale of pesetas against foreign currencies in the spot market and the inverted operation in the forward exchange market.[14] Furthermore, some ceilings were imposed on the foreign currency transactions of domestic banks with branches abroad, and on those of foreign banks operating in Spain. While the cost of this penalization was, in the first instance, borne by the (domestic) lending banks, part of it was subsequently translated to the (nonresident) potential borrowers.

It is worth noting that deposit requirements are in fact an implicit tax of the kind proposed by Tobin, but not a capital control in the form of administrative authorization or quantitative limitation, which are explicitly excluded by the OECD and EU regulations. Two additional features of these measures reveal the Spanish authorities' specific interest in fighting the new speculative attacks by foreigners. First, the measures were directed toward *increases* in bank positions and not toward the old financing. Second, they affected the whole set of swap operations by nonresidents, *independently of their term of maturity.* This implies that the hedging of international trade and other operations unrelated to speculation could in principle be affected.

This mechanism, adopted temporarily by the Spanish government to rebuff speculative attacks in late 1992, has been proposed recently by Eichengreen, Rose, and Wyplosz (1995) as a way of smoothing the transition to European monetary union, on the basis of its policy advantages with respect to other devices. The first advantage is that the opportunity cost of non-interest-bearing deposits increases with the interest rate, thus making this defense more powerful during periods of speculative pressure.[15] In connection with this, note also that the knowledge that the authorities possess more effective tools to defend the edge of the band in the ERM reduces the incentive for speculators to test it and, consequently, brings about a very positive stabilizing effect in the exchange rate.

The second advantage is that its distributive effects against long-term capital flows are likely small because the cost of borrowing will be little affected when it is spread over a long maturity. Finally, nonresident-bearing deposit requirements produce extra (nonofficial) depreciating effects in the domestic currency that are borne by speculators, although they are not reflected in the exchange market. This is tantamount to an implicit widening of the band, and consequently they relax the external constraints on domestic policy.[16]

The deposit requirements were in force between October 5 and November 23 of 1992. Since this measure affected the swap financing awarded only to nonresidents, its most direct effect was to create a negative wedge between domestic and offshore interest rates on swaps in pesetas during this period. Although the measure covered the whole range of contracts, the effects were more apparent for maturities between one day and one week. As can be seen in Figure 9.8, the differential between these two kinds of interest rates increased sharply at times when the speculative pressures were most intense, that is, during the first two weeks after the enforcement of the measure and the days preceding the second devaluation of the Spanish peseta (6 percent on November 22), as an indication that speculation was deterred to some extent. For longer maturities, the interest-rate wedge was smoothed by the arbitrage that took place through the London subsidiaries of Spanish banks. As argued by Linde (1993), this is not a bad result, because the operations with longer maturity are rarely related to speculative activities.

The presence of an implicit tax on certain kinds of capital outflows can also be detected by examining the covered parity condition (CPC) for the three-month interest rates on peseta deposits in the domestic interbank market, on the one hand, and the Euro market, on the other. As shown in Figure 9.7, there was a negative divergence during the two months of deposit requirements, an indication that investors could not take a higher profit on their funds abroad. However, and in agreement with what was stressed by Linde (1993), the CPC divergence corresponding to the three-month maturity was not sufficiently big (at least on a monthly average basis) for the measures to be really effective. In fact, the highest value achieved in this period (-0.41 percent in October) does not overcome the ±0.5 percent threshold dictated by the arbitrage transaction costs. As stressed earlier, the effectiveness of the measure is to be found in shorter maturities, where exchange rate speculation is more intense.

The non-interest-bearing deposit requirement was suppressed on November

23 in order for Spain to comply with the Maastricht Treaty, which contemplates these measures only for very short periods of time.[17] In compensation, the intervention interest rate of the Bank of Spain increased by almost 0.75 percent. Since then, international capital transactions have enjoyed complete freedom in Spain. This has contributed to link more narrowly the domestic financial markets to the foreign ones, as reflected in a more accurate fulfillment of the covered interest parity condition in the last years.[18] The peseta underwent two additional devaluations with respect to the ecu on May 14, 1993, and March 6, 1995, in amounts of 8 percent and 5.3 percent, respectively, in a context of much less intense speculative pressures.

According to some analysts, the last devaluation and part of the third one were not justified by fundamental economic reasons.[19] In fact, the market value of the Spanish peseta has almost completely recovered the rate against the ecu that prevailed before the last devaluation.[20]

Fiscal Policy

The reduction of the fiscal deficit is the most appropriate way to tackle the problem created by an erroneous and unsustainable financial policy mix. But this budgetary strategy is also recommended when other causes of the inflows are in play, because the fiscal restraints contribute to reduce the aggregate demand and then to contain inflation. Despite these considerations, fiscal adjustment was not a significant response of the Spanish authorities to capital inflows. As indicated before, in the years 1989–90 we simply detect the continuation of the previous fiscal consolidation that contributed to attract foreign capital flows, and between then and 1993, an important deterioration of the fiscal balance was clearly discernible.

According to Schadler et al. (1993), the minimal use of fiscal adjustment in most countries involved in recent surges in capital inflows results from the difficulty of garnering public support to reduce expenditures or increase taxes. In the case of Spain we find additional explanations in the high amount of public transfers to both unemployed workers and inefficient public enterprises, and in Spain's need to improve its capital endowments. These features explain in turn why the budget policy has played a significant stabilizing role in Spain since 1986, as shown by García Solanes (1995c). However, the stabilizing effects that imply higher revenues and lower public expenditures during expansion periods, such as the inflow episode, were not strong enough for the Spanish authorities to reorganize the public finances.

Since 1994, a gradual and pronounced fiscal consolidation has been observed in Spain, largely inspired by the convergence requirements of the Maastricht Treaty: The general public deficit as a percentage of the GDP declined from 7.4 percent in 1993 to 2.8 in 1997. These improvements should be permanent for two macroeconomic reasons: first, they are a key element for the relaxation of the monetary conditions, necessary to obtain lower rates of interest and inflation; and second, they are important for the Spanish government to gain the trust of the markets and establish its credibility with private agents.[21]

The 3 percent deficit with respect to GDP, imposed by the Maastricht Treaty and guaranteed by the stability agreement signed by the EU states in 1996, may be at first sight arbitrary and not sufficient to solve the problems stemming from asymmetric shocks. However, if we make a flexible interpretation of this limit, and apply it to the entire business cycle, the restriction would be sufficient to stabilize economic activity.

Monetary Policy

As explained before, the Bank of Spain's immediate and individual reaction to inflows was to impose tight credit conditions. However, once it was realized that in the present context of quasi-fixed exchange rates and free capital movements—corresponding to the second phase of the European monetary integration process—national monetary policies are not effective to control the aggregate demand, new monetary measures were framed by the coordinating rules of the European Monetary Institute.

The current coordinated monetary actions are aimed at gradually stimulating the economic activity in the EU as a whole, continuing the trend that was put in motion in August 1993, after the widening of the fluctuation bands of the ERM. They also intend to reduce both the average and the dispersion of the national rates of inflation. Obviously this second objective requires the collaboration of fiscal and supply policies.

In order to comply with those general rules, three technical and institutional policy innovations have been introduced in Spain recently. The first one is the approval of the independence statute of the Bank of Spain in August 1994; the second is the new strategy of the monetary policy, adopted by the Bank of Spain in 1995, based upon the direct control of the rate of inflation; and the third one consists of observing simultaneously several variables as indicators of the effectiveness of the monetary actions, such as narrower monetary aggregates and the yield curve.

Microeconomic Policies

Although, in general, the most important responses to the surge in capital inflows rely on the macroeconomic side, microeconomic measures play an important role as well. In the case of Spain, it suffices to remember four groups of measures already described. First, transitory impediments to inflows were imposed, and the financial sector was reformed. Second, existing market imperfections and implicit subsidies were eliminated, including easing restrictions on capital outflows. Third, imports of goods and services were gradually liberalized in the context of EC membership and export subsidies were eliminated. Furthermore, most nontariff trade barriers between Spain and the EC were suppressed upon accession. The surge in inflows eased this process. Finally, a wide range of measures was adopted to make the labor market more flexible and efficient.

Effects of the Inflows

The surge of capital inflows affected the main macroeconomic developments in Spain. In the absence of a complete general equilibrium model to evaluate the size of such influences, in the following lines I will make some general comments about the likely effects of these inflows on the basis of available macroeconomic series.

Interest Rates and Asset Prices

In principle, capital inflows should ease domestic monetary conditions and push down short-term interest rates. In Spain, short-term interest rates did not fall during the inflow episode except in 1988, when the average value of this variable came down to 11.6 percent. During the other years, the rates were never below 13.2 percent (Table 9.11). The reasons are to be found in the aggressive sterilization policy during the first years of the period, and in the monetary restrictions implemented by the Bank of Spain.

Equity prices increased gradually, compounding an upward trend that started vigorously in 1984. As shown in Table 9.12, the general index of Madrid's stock market rose steadily between 1984 and 1989 by a total of 400.85 percent. However, the increase was much lower during the second half of this period: only 41.6 percent between 1986 and 1989. After this last year a declining trend can be discerned, which lasted until 1992.

It can be argued that the developments in the stock market—as reflected by the gradual evolution of the general stock index—do not accurately reflect the intensity of the structural and policy changes in Spain during the inflow period. The explanation could be that the starting value of the stock index was already very high at the beginning of the inflow period.

Reserves and Money

Given that the tightening of domestic credit conditions to a large extent caused the short-term inflows, we should not expect important changes in the rates of growth of the broad monetary aggregates during the inflow episode in Spain. In fact, the figures in Table 9.11 indicate that the gradual decline in the rate of growth of the money supply, initiated in 1983, was not interrupted during the surge in inflows. The downward trend of this rate was sharply accentuated beginning 1991. Furthermore, sterilization caused a shift in the backing of the monetary base from domestic toward foreign assets.

The most relevant influence that insulated the money supply from the surge in inflows in Spain was the widening deficit of the current account. This is a normal outcome in countries where changes in fiscal and structural policies were relatively important causes of the inflows.[22] A direct implication of this is that the stock of foreign reserves cannot increase substantially. As can be seen in Table 9.13, the ratio of foreign reserves to imports of goods, which indicates the years of imports that could be bought in each year of the sample with the existing reserves, increased notably in 1987 with respect to the year before. Afterward, the ratio remained almost constant until 1991.

The degree to which official reserves provided a cushion against a reversal of the inflows is given by the ratio of official reserves to the cumulated flow of net foreign liabilities, excluding direct foreign investment, according to the method suggested by Schadler et al. (1993). Table 9.14 offers the results for Spain. As can be seen, the biggest cushion corresponds to 1987. In the following years it declined considerably, as a consequence of the lower proportion of direct investment in the total capital inflows.

Inflation and the Real Exchange Rate

In Spain, the inflow episode coincided with a noticeable decrease in the rate of inflation, which came down from 11 percent in 1986 to levels between 5.5 and 7 percent during 1987–91. This favorable outcome reflects both the limited impact of the inflows on the monetary aggregates and the effects of the appreciation of the peseta.

The real exchange rate of the peseta rose gradually, mainly as a result of nominal appreciation. As explained before, only a part of this real appreciation can be considered an equilibrating variation of the real exchange rate. According to our estimations, the peseta accumulated an excess of real appreciation of between 12 and 15 percent in effective terms before the first devaluation in 1992. Since the four devaluations supported by Spain, in the following

Table 9.11

Short-term Interest Rate and Growth Rate of the Broad Money Supply (M3) (millions of U.S. dollars)

Year	Interest rate	Growth rate of M3
1984	14.9	15.1
1985	12.2	13.8
1986	11.7	15.6
1987	15.8	13.5
1988	11.6	14.1
1989	15.0	14.3
1990	15.2	15.1
1991	13.2	9.9
1992	13.3	5.1
1993	11.7	7.6
1994	8.0	7.6
1995	9.4	8.8
1996	7.5	7.4

Source: European Economy, no. 62, 1996.

Table 9.12

Annual Average Index of the Madrid Stock Market (December 31, 1984 = 100)

Year	Series
1984	100.00
1985	135.78
1986	283.07
1987	308.75
1988	373.34
1989	400.85
1990	302.88
1991	339.53
1992	295.43
1993	445.06
1994	427.16
1995	402.09
1996	498.71

Source: Boletin Estadistico del Banco de España, 1996.

years largely outpaced these figures, I conclude that the peseta showed symptoms of undervaluation after the last devaluation, in March 1995.[23]

Domestic Activity, Savings, and Investment

In Spain, the surge in inflows was accompanied by higher rates of output growth, probably because these two phenomena were largely endogenous

Table 9.13

Ratio of Foreign Reserves to Imports of Goods PTA

Year	Series
1986	0.3906
1987	0.5945
1988	0.6561
1989	0.5855
1990	0.5989
1991	0.6968
1992	0.5527
1993	0.6051
1994	0.4676
1995	0.3168
1996	0.5137

Source: Anuario Estadistico del Ine, 1994; Boletin Estadistico del Banco de España, 1989, 1995, 1996.

Table 9.14

Proportion of Foreign Reserves with Respect to Cumulative Net Capital Inflows (Since 1984) of Each Year (Excluding Direct Investment), PTA

Year	Series
1987	4,397
1988	2,920
1989	1,732
1990	1,646
1991	1,173
1992	1,065
1993	1,361
1994	1,286
1995	1,430
1996	1,458

Source: Boletin Estadistico del Banco de España, 1990, 1997.

responses to the same causes, that is, structural and fiscal changes, and good productivity prospects for the near future.

Absorption also increased and outpaced production, giving rise to important current account deficits during the period 1989–92. This negative external balance did not raise serious concerns at least until 1991, because investment was the dominant force in the increased absorption, in opposition to what happens when the cause of the deficit is a fall in domestic savings. Table 9.15 shows that the rate of gross savings to GDP did not fall during the inflow period, and that it even increased in 1988. The downward

Table 9.15

Rates of Saving with Respect to GDP (annual percentage rates)

Year	Government rate of saving	Private rate of saving	Rate of gross saving
1984	−0.7	21.6	20.9
1985	−1.4	22.0	20.6
1986	−0.5	22.1	21.6
1987	1.7	19.9	21.6
1988	1.8	20.8	22.6
1989	2.9	19.0	21.9
1990	1.8	19.9	21.7
1991	0.8	20.2	21.0
1992	0.7	18.4	19.0
1993	−2.3	21.2	18.9
1994	−2.3	21.2	18.8
1995	−2.1	23.7	21.6
1996	−1.2	23.1	21.9

Source: European Economy, no. 62, 1996.

Table 9.16

Rate of Investment with Respect to GDP (annual percentage rates)

Year	Series
1984	18.7
1985	19.2
1986	19.5
1987	20.8
1988	22.6
1989	24.1
1990	24.5
1991	23.8
1992	21.9
1993	19.9
1994	19.8
1995	20.8
1996	21.3

Source: European Economy, no. 62, 1996.

evolution for this rate began in 1992, mainly as a consequence of the substantial reduction in the government savings rate. The rate of investment to GDP increased in the central years of the inflow period, achieving the highest values in 1989 and 1990 (Table 9.16). The degree of sustainability of the current account deficit may be calculated by applying the Dadush, Dhareshwar, and Johannes (1994) ratio, as proposed by Griffith-Jones (1995). This ratio measures the relative value of the current account with respect to annual variations of exports. Using average data for the last ten years, we obtain values below 2 (the upper threshold established by the authors) for this ratio in the period 1986–90, and over 2 in the years 1991–93.

The foreign direct investment (FDI) inflows that increased substantially just after Spain's accession to the EC played an important role in the evolution of both investment expenditures and real economic activity in Spain. The likely macroeconomic effects of these flows may be understood if we take into consideration the following aspects, derived from statistical data of the second half of the eighties, 1986–90[24] (see Tables 9.17–9.19):

1. Looking at the sector destination of the flows, the proportion absorbed by manufacturing activities (chemistry, motor vehicles, and machinery) decreased with respect to the five preceding years, 1981–85: 45.9 percent compared to 62.9 percent, respectively, to the benefit of services activities. This could indicate a shift in the preferences of foreign investors from commercialization of manufactures to commercialization of services.

2. During the period 1986–90, the FDI was directed mainly to activities of strong and medium demand. These activities absorbed 49.1 percent and 33.2 percent, respectively, of the total flows invested in manufactures.

3. Despite what is indicated in (1), the FDI attracted by the manufacturing industry represented almost 50 percent of the total fixed investment of this sector during the period 1986–90. The proportion was higher in activities of strong and medium demand: 96.5 percent and 57.2 percent, respectively. These features show that FDI was an important determinant of the industrial investments in Spain.

4. In general, the funds provided by the FDI were concentrated in tradables activities, where the weight of imports and exports is important. This explains why during the period 1986–90 the highest rates of growth in both exports and imports were found in FDI-intensive activities.

5. Production, demand, and employment have increased more in the economic activities that employ FDI more intensively.

Table 9.17

Foreign Direct Investment Sectorial Distribution in the Manufacturing Industry (in percent)

Sectors	1986	1987	1988	1989	1990
Strong demand					
Office machinery and computers	0.0	0.1	1.1	0.2	3.7
Machinery and electric material	5.5	2.6	7.5	2.9	4.1
Electronic material	2.5	1.7	3.1	3.8	1.4
Precision instruments	0.5	0.1	0.4	0.6	0.5
Chemistry	17.4	48.4	17.9	24.0	17.4
Medium demand					
Rubber and plastics	1.2	1.2	1.7	2.0	6.6
Vehicles	32.2	8.8	4.9	7.3	12.7
Machinery and mechanics' equipment	7.0	5.3	5.6	2.5	2.3
Other transport material	0.0	0.3	0.0	2.7	1.3
Food, drinks, and tobacco	13.9	9.8	23.3	18.2	11.5
Paper, graphic arts, and printing material	11.1	12.0	19.2	17.6	11.7

Source: Bajo and Torres 1992, p. 204.

Table 9.18

Foreign Direct Investment in the Manufacturing Sector, Proportion with Respect to Gross Capital Formation (in percent)

Sectors	1986	1987	1998	1989	1990
Strong Demand					
Office machinery and computers	0.81	14.45	122.20	116.38	1,921.46
Electric and electronic material	60.15	14.44	66.19	62.85	60.28
Chemistry	67.94	237.25	58.87	145.39	72.11
Medium Demand					
Rubber and plastics	12.09	15.42	13.75	26.72	79.78
Vehicles and other transport material	199.6	81.83	28.2	75.66	118.91
Machinery and mechanics' equipment	82.96	75.01	68.7	78.14	84.49
Food, drinks, and tobacco	33.65	27.77	49.45	57.43	41.24
Paper, graphic arts, and printing material	69.19	80.21	101.16	59.72	40.96

Source: Bajo and Torres 1992, p. 204.

Table 9.19

Foreign Direct Investment in the Manufacturing Sector Development and Structural Indicators

	% Real Y^ 1985–90	E Variation 1985–90	% E^ 1985–90	% AC^ 1985–90	AP^ 1990	% AP^ 1985–90
Chemistry	6.4	14.4	9.4	29.2	9.8	−1.4
Food, drink, and tobacco	13.4	23.3	6.0	35.4	14.3	23.3
Paper, graphic arts, and printing material	17.7	53.0	44.8	59.0	7.2	−1.9
Vehicles	47.8	39.9	28.4	118.6	16.4	47.3
Nonmetallic mineral products	32.8	40.5	28.0	75.8	7.3	29.7
Machinery and electric material	45.0	17.3	17.1	100.8	8.3	51.1
Machinery and mechanic's equipment	17.0	43.2	46.0	99.5	8.3	5.6
Intensive activities in foreign direct investment	21.3	231.6	20.3	58.0	11.1	19.5
Nonintensive activities in foreign direct investment	12.7	163.6	12.6	53.2	6.1	12.6

Source: Bajo and Torres (1992), pp. 206, 221.

Notes: Y, E, AC, and AP stand for production, employment, apparent consumption, and apparent productivity of labor, respectively.

^ indicates cumulative growth.

6. FDI has contributed decisively to the transmission of technology to the whole productive system. The subsidiaries of foreign companies realize the bulk of the imports of technology.

7. The sectors that are higher users of FDI have the highest levels of labor productivity.

8. The enterprises that received higher levels of FDI show better organizational capacity, and have a higher level of human capital and a more qualified labor force.

Summary and Conclusions

There is a wide range of factors that laid the basis for the substantial surge in international capital flows in the Spanish economy since the mid-1980s. Domestic structural changes and the economic integration of Spain with the EC attracted long-term capital inflows, especially foreign direct investment movements. These transformations improved remarkably the supply side of the Spanish economy and created expectations of increased productivity and higher incomes and revenues for Spanish residents in the near future. Since, by definition, long-term movements are highly sustainable and not likely to be reversible, Spain could rely on them to finance the ongoing economic transformations and increase the efficiency of the domestic productive system.

If we accept this interpretation, the derived appreciation of the real exchange rate and current account deficit in Spain during most of the second half of the 1980s and the beginning of the 1990s will be equilibrium phenomena. Some economic indicators give support to this diagnosis: the gap between gross investment and gross savings, that is, the current account, was to a larger extent due to investment increases rather than to savings reductions. Furthermore, factor productivity increased faster than in the more advanced countries of the EU during the period analyzed, and the share of profits of the manufacturing sector with respect to total profit of the economy augmented as well during those years.

This interpretation is also consistent with the fact that FDI has played an important role in increasing the fixed capital stock, incorporating technology in the manufacturing industry, and improving labor productivity in Spain.

However, part of the exchange rate and current account variations were due to portfolio investment and short-term capital inflows that were attracted by the particular policy mix of the Spanish authorities and by speculative considerations. Portfolio investment and short-term capital inflows accounted for around 75 percent of total flows in 1991 and in 1992 and more than 90 percent in 1993. Public bonds and short-term deposits were the most important vehicles in the money and capital markets that were developed some years earlier to help financing the public sector and to allow the Bank of Spain to implement an autonomous monetary policy. Given that these capital flows are generally not sustainable, they provoked some degree of misalignment in the peseta real exchange rate. In fact, the Spanish currency presented symptoms of overvaluation that triggered speculative attacks in the last quarter of 1992. Obviously, this phenomenon called for some kind of public intervention or controls in the foreign exchange market.

The initial response of the Spanish authorities to manage these inflows in the second half of the eighties was to intervene in the foreign exchange market and to sterilize the subsequent increase in the stock of foreign reserves, in order to keep control of the domestic monetary aggregates. They were right in interpreting the transitory nature of the bulk of capital inflows, but were wrong in not understanding or not correcting the source of those movements. Thus the same policy mix was sustained until 1992 without taking deeper corrective measures, and as a consequence of that, the need to sterilize did not decrease along with the inflow episode. When the Bank of Spain decided to escape from the negative effects of sterilization, it had to either impose controls over capital inflows or let the peseta float more freely, as in 1989 and since 1993, although within the limits of the ERM.

It seems to me that the broad lines of the policy reactions of the Spanish authorities, including the order and timing of the liberalization process, fit in general terms within the recommendations of Williamson (1995) and McKinnon (1986).[25] The liberalization steps begun in 1986 in the field of long-term movements, and the abolition of the last controls, affecting only the more volatile short-term flows, took place in 1992, in compliance with the deadline set by the European Community.

The Spanish experience in managing international capital flows during the second half of the eighties may serve as useful lessons for the Central and East European countries (CEECs) that are undergoing deep economic transformations and accelerating the process of economic integration with the most industrialized countries.[26]

First of all, it gives support to the academic view concerning the order of liberalization. In the first steps, when the financial markets are little developed and/or strongly segmented, there is scope for liberalizing only trade flows and direct investments. Under those circumstances, the distinction between sustainable and reversible inflows is not difficult to make, and controls over very short-term movements can be easily implemented. During this period, it is expected that the inflows of direct investment bring about important positive effects on investment, productivity, and growth. For this reason, the authorities should devise appropriate strategies to keep or even to increase the size of these flows. Some kind of gradual exchange rate adjustment is advised in this stage in order to cope with persistent inflation rate differentials and divergences in productivity with respect to the more advanced economies.

Further developments in financial markets and institutions, and more strengthened links between them, require higher degrees of liberalization. At the same time, these transformations reduce the effectiveness of durable capital controls and end up making full financial integration with the rest of the world an avoidable outcome.

The case analyzed here also indicates that the latest liberalizing steps must be preceded by sound macroeconomic policy and not by an erroneous policy mix. Otherwise, the remedies against undesirable capital flows will not produce any positive effect. It is true, however, that macroeconomic stabilization confronts very particular difficulties in the post-Communist economies, which prevent the full implementation of the approach followed by the Western industrialized countries.[27]

Since the strategy explained above does not guarantee accurate diagnosis, and also because the exchange market is not protected from self-fulfilling speculation, transitory controls and penalties for movements of short maturity should not be ruled out. They may be important tools to deal with temporal crisis in the balance of payments, providing both more independence to domestic macroeconomic policies, especially when complemented with sterilization, and time for the multilateral government consultations that precede exchange rate adjustments. Here the case of Spain offers a very good illustration.[28] However, it is important that capital controls not be used as a substitute for necessary financial and macroeconomic reforms.

In broad terms, the step-by-step approach followed in Spain some years ago seems desirable for the CEECs, since most of them are still in the process of establishing basic market mechanisms and institutions without which sound macroeconomic policies cannot be implemented. In fact, in some of those countries organized capital markets are still lacking, and the banking reforms are just now being tackled. However, gradualism should not be imposed on a uniform basis everywhere. Attempts to fine-tune an ideal sequencing of reforms would entail the risk of losing the local economic and political perspective of each country. Rather, the speed of reforms should be tailored according to the structural features of each country, taking into account the economic changes undertaken in those economies in recent years.

There are other elements derived from the experiences of Spain and other OECD countries that seem advisable for the economic transformations of the CEECs. The OECD report on exchange control policy gives an excellent picture of the main points.[29] In particular, it is important that the program for progressive liberalization be announced and duly accomplished by the authorities. Furthermore, this program should be built on the official recognition that the final outcome will be permanently beneficial for the economy. Otherwise, liberalization measures could be perceived as easily reversible and could thus trigger speculative attacks against the domestic currency.

Finally, the experience of the Spanish economy provides useful lessons concerning the effects that should be expected on the main macroeconomic variables of countries that receive considerable amounts of foreign capital during a period of increasing economic openness and integration with the rest of the world.

Notes

1. In 1989 the strictest restrictions addressed the short-term outflows. For instance, purchases of assets in foreign money markets and opening financial accounts in nonresident banking institutions required previous official authorization. As for portfolio movements, the restrictions affected purchases of assets issued in pesetas by nonresidents in foreign markets, purchases of assets issued in foreign currencies in the Spanish capital markets, and operations with assets that are not transacted in stock markets. For a detailed analysis of the restrictions on capital movements prevailing in Spain in 1989, see Ortega Regato (1989).

2. As described more extensively in this work, these restrictions consisted mainly of limits on forward purchases of public debt (mid-1987) and requirements of nonbearing interest deposits in the Bank of Spain (February 1989).

3. Viñals (1992) examines the general content and the most salient aspects of the convergence program.

4. Most nontariff barriers between Spain and the EC were eliminated in 1986; tariffs on industrial imports from EC countries were reduced by 22 percent in 1987.

5. For a more detailed analysis of the transformations of the Spanish financial system during the seventies and eighties, see García Solanes 1989.

6. This does not imply that exchange controls for short-term capital flows were always very effective. As shown by Viñals (1992) and García Solanes (1995a), using tests based on the interest parity condition, the degree of mobility of short-term capital was higher during some periods, like 1982–85, where controls were supposed to be intense, than in other more recent episodes with more permissive legislation in this respect.

7. See, for instance, *European Economy* 60 (1995), Table 37. The share of profits and the index of unit labor costs can be considered indicators of productivity and competitiveness. For a discussion of the pros and cons of the competitiveness indicators most frequently used in the literature, see Lipschitz and McDonald 1991.

8. The current account balance in proportion of GDP changed progressively from 1.6 percent in 1986 to -3.6 percent in 1991. See, for example, *European Economy* 60 (1995), Table 46.

9. See Schadler, Carkovic, Bennett, and Kahn 1993, Appendix I. In any case, the difficulties of implementing sterilization measures depend on the causes of capital inflows. See in this respect, Frankel 1994.

10. Convertible pesetas could be freely converted into foreign currencies, on the basis that they were created through foreign funds. They were maintained by foreigners as deposits in domestic banks, for current purposes in Spain. Obviously, conversions of this kind of pesetas did not feed speculative pressures in the foreign exchange market.

11. In November 1989 the 20 percent nonremunerated reserve requirement on short-term foreign currency positions of the banking system was suppressed. In April 1990 nonresidents were allowed to maintain remunerated deposits in the Spanish banking system to undertake all kind of financial operations with public debt assets, and to lend to Spanish residents with less restrictive bounds. In January 1991 the 25 percent fiscal prepayments over the interest of public debt held by nonresidents disappeared. The 30 percent nonremunerated reserve requirements for residents were suppressed in March

1991. One month later, the constitution of sight deposits in foreign currency in banks operating in Spain was completely liberalized. New measures were adopted in February 1992 to completely liberalize all capital transactions.

12. The positive sign indicates that nonprofitable margins existed favorable to the Spanish deposits, due precisely to capital controls and/or fears of investing in Spain. The monthly averages of the divergences on an annual percent basis were 1.74, 0.75, 1.51, and 0.80, for the years 1987–90, respectively. (See Viñals 1992, p. 434).

13. See Viñals 1992, pp. 441–47.

14. For a more detailed analysis of these measures, see Linde 1993.

15. This means that the domestic interest rate does not need to jump to levels not politically and/or economically supportable, as in the cases of Sweden and Ireland during some episodes of the 1992 and 1993 exchange rate crisis.

16. The reason is as follows: The fact that the cost of the deposit requirements imposed on domestic banks is partially translated to nonresident borrowers amounts to considering that the latter obtain a lower quantity of borrowed pesetas. In other words, the "effective" price of the strong currency that they get in exchange in the spot market may exceed the official band. Eichengreen, Rose, and Wyplosz (1995) put special emphasis on this property and remark that deposit requirements are more appropriate than the explicit widening of the band, in the sense that the former bind only in periods of speculative pressure, thus giving the government the opportunity to implement the desired macroeconomic policies the rest of the time.

17. According to Article 73f of the Maastricht Treaty, the signatory national countries are allowed to impose *temporary* discretionary measures in capital transactions (in this case against loans to nonresidents) in case of emergency (crisis of balance of payments).

18. See García Solanes 1995a in this respect.

19. See, for instance, the economic explanations provided by García Solanes 1995b.

20. The central rate before the last devaluation was 154.25 pesetas per ecu. After the devaluation of March 6, 1995, the central rate was established at 162.49 pesetas per ecu. The market value of the ecu in terms of pesetas on April 9, 1996, was 155.55.

21. The general lines proposed to achieve a significant fiscal consolidation in Spain in the coming years are described in García Solanes 1995c.

22. Otherwise, the permanent income would not increase notably, and, consequently, expenditures would not increase to provoke current account deficits. According to Schadler et al. (1993), in the countries where the fundamental causes of the inflows are changes in structural and fiscal policies, some 60 to 80 percent of the cumulative inflows over three to four years was absorbed by the widening of the current account deficit.

23. My calculation takes into account the changes in productivity of the domestic and foreign traded goods sector and the decomposition of the real exchange rate series of the peseta into transitory and permanent components.

24. The following comments are based on work by Bajo and Torres (1992).

25. The sequencing of the adjustments proposed by these authors is as follows. First, macroeconomic stabilization, through fiscal consolidation and tight monetary policy; second, product market deregulation, including trade liberalization and labor market reform; third, internal financial reform; and, finally, opening up of the capital account.

26. Most CEECs have expressed a desire to model their economic structures and regulations on those of Western and more industrialized countries. Also, they share the main objectives of macroeconomic policy that prevail in developed countries, and have been quick to adhere to the modern view that wide and efficient capital markets and a competitive banking sector are key ingredients to foster economic growth.

27. For instance, the transmission channels of monetary policy are less effective than

those of the more industrialized countries. Furthermore, in the CEECs the demand for money is made highly unstable by currency substitution and financial reform.
28. The effectiveness of temporary capital controls in Spain goes in the direction of the evidence presented by Johnston and Ryan (1994) for the industrialized countries.
29. See OECD (1993), in particular Chapter V of part II on policy options and priorities.

References

Alcalá, F., and D. Peñarrubia (1995). "Crecimiento, convergencia, cuentas exteriores y la experiencia española reciente," *Revista Española de Economía,* vol. 12, no. 1, pp. 89–115.

Bajo, O., and A. Torres (1992). "El comercio exterior y la inversión extranjera directa tras la integración de España en la CE (1986–90)." In *La economía española ante el Mercado Unico Europeo,* ed. J. Viñals. Madrid: Alianza Editorial.

Beyaert, A., J. García Solanes, and G. Pérez Quirós (1994). "Consumo intertemporal y balanza por cuenta corriente en la economía española," *Revista Española de Economía,* vol. 11, no. 1, pp. 27–48.

Dadush, V., A. Dhareshwar, and R. Johannes (1994). "Are Private Capital Flows to Developing Countries Sustainable?" World Bank, International Economics Department.

Devlin, R., R. Ffrench-Davis, and S. Griffith-Jones (1994). "Surges in Capital Flows and Development: An Overview of Policy Issues." In *Coping with Capital Surges: Latin American Macroeconomics and Investment,* ed. R. Ffrench-Davis and S. Griffith-Jones. Boulder and London: Lynne Rienner. A modified Spanish version was published in *Pensamiento Iberoamericano,* no. 27 (enero-junio 1995), pp. 77–114.

Dolado, Juan, and Viñals, Jose. 1991. "Macroeconomic Policy, External Targets and Constraints: The Case of Spain," in *External Constraints on Macroeconomic Policy: The European Experience,* ed. George Alogoskoufis, Lucas Papademos, and Richard Portes. Cambridge: Cambridge University Press, 1991.

Edwards, S. (1984). "The Order of Liberalisation of the External Sector in Developing Countries," *International Finance Section,* Princeton University, Essay no. 156.

Eichengreen, B., A.K. Rose, and C. Wyplosz (1995). "Is There a Safe Passage to 5 EMU? Evidence on Capital Controls and a Proposal," Working Paper No. C95–047, CIDER, University of California, Berkeley.

Frankel, J. (1994). "Sterilisation of Money Inflows: Difficult (Calvo) or Easy (Reisen)?" IMF Working Paper no. 94/159, Research Department, December.

García Solanes, J. (1989). "The Implications of Financial Integration for the Spanish Financial Sector." In *European Financial Integration and Monetary Cooperation,* ed. P. Van den Bempt and M. Quintyn. London: IFR Publishing Ltd., pp. 149–78.

García Solanes, J. (1995a). "Movilidad internacional de capital en la Unión Europea," *Pensamiento Iberoamericano,* no. 27 (enero-junio), pp. 235–90.

García Solanes, J. (1995b). "La unificación monetaria europea desde la pespectiva española," in *La economia española en un escenario abierto,* Fundación Argentaria and Visor Distribuciones, pp. 199–245.

García Solanes, J. (1995c). "Los márgenes d ela ploítica fiscal y presupuestaria en la Unión Monetaria Europea," *Presupuesto y Gasto Público,* no. 17, pp. 67–84.

Griffith-Jones, S. (1995). "Capital Flows to Latin America and Asia: Lessons for Central and Eastern Europe." Workshop on Managing Capital Flows in Central and Eastern Europe, Prague, 15–16 June 1995.

Johnston, R.B., and C. Ryan (1994). "The Impact of Controls on Capital Movements on the Private Capital Accounts of Countries' Balance of Payments: Empirical Estimates and Policy Implications," IMF Working Paper /94/78, Monetary and Exchange Affairs Department, July.

Linde, L.M. (1993). "Las medidas del Banco de España de septiembre y octubre de 1992 penalizando la especulación cambiaria," *Papeles de Economía Española,* no. 54, pp. 301–308.

Lipschitz, L., and D. McDonald (1991). "Real Exchange Rates and Competitiveness: A Clarification of Concepts, and Some Measurements for Europe," IMF Working Paper no. 91/25, European Department, March.

Martín, C. (1992). "El comercio industrial español ante el Mercado Unico Europeo," in *La economía española ante el Mercado Unico Europeo,* ed. J. Viñals. Madrid: Alianza Editorial, pp. 119–166.

McKinnon, R. (1986). "Financial Liberalisation in Retrospect: Interest Rate Policies in LDCs." Economic Growth Center, Yale University.

OECD (1993). *Exchange Control Policy.* Paris: OECD.

Ortega Regato, E. (1989). "Controles sobre los movimientos de capital. Situación actual y perspectivas de liberalización," *Boletín Económico,* Banco de España, abril, pp. 11–21.

Schadler, S., M. Carcovic, A. Bennett, and R. Kahn (1993). "Recent Experiences with Surges in Capital Inflows," Occasional Paper no. 108 (December), IMF.

Viñals, J. (1992). "Del control de cambios a la libre circulatión de capitales." In *La economia española ante el Mercade Único Europeo. Las claves del proceso de integración,* ed. J. Viñals. Madrid: Alianza Economía.

Williamson, J. (1995). "El manejo de los flujos de entrada de capitales," *Pensamiento Iberoamericano,* no. 27, pp. 197–218.

10

Summary and Conclusions

Managing Capital Flows in Central and Eastern Europe

Zdeněk Drábek and Stephany Griffith-Jones

In the mid-1990s, the East European countries in transition faced a new and unexpected challenge—the challenge of absorbing massive inflows of foreign capital. As if "transition" did not bring enough difficulties, the Central and East European countries (CEECs) began to attract so much foreign capital that monetary authorities were put to severe tests. The inflows were somewhat unexpected, as most observers had originally predicted a rather different picture—that the countries would probably have difficulties attracting foreign capital. The surprising developments were further complicated by the rise of globalization of financial markets in recent years. The speed of globalization has been unprecedented in modern times as private capital flows have been much more dynamic than the provision of funds under official development assistance and, in general, foreign capital has played a much more active part in a growing number of countries.

But the fruits of financial globalization have also brought difficulties. The "Mexico crisis" is still fresh in our minds and so are the "tequila effects" resulting from it. Most recently, we have witnessed speculative attacks on the baht—the Thai currency—which have quickly spread to other parts of Southeast Asia, including the Philippines, Korea, and Indonesia. The region of Central and Eastern Europe has also not been spared as speculators undermined the stability of the Czech crown in the spring of 1997. These events have exposed the vulnerability of policy makers, who have found themselves subject to different and sometimes conflicting policy advice. There is no consensus among academics and other experts on how to cope with such events even though agreement on what to do has been growing. It is also arguable whether the relevant public international institutions have been in a position to cope with the pace of globalization. The recent initiatives of the IMF, BIS, G-20, and others to improve the quality of financial information and its availability and to strengthen prudential regulations indicate that the problems have been recognized and that we are moving in the right direction, though large questions can be asked whether this progress is sufficient and sufficiently quick.

The attacks on the Czech crown as well as the growing exposure to external capital flows in the other CEECs have taken place against the background of all these developments. This book provides detailed information on the origins of the difficulties faced by the CEECs, evaluates the seriousness of the problems, and, in particular, shows how individual governments in these countries have coped with these capital inflows. The individual papers in the book cover the three most exposed CEECs—Hungary, Poland, and the Czech Republic. In addition, we have also included in the book a paper on Spain which provides a comparative perspective on the events in the CEECs since Spain has experienced similar difficulties in the past.

In this chapter, we shall start by emphasizing the scale and relevant features of global capital flows. This will provide the key elements for analyzing the challenges facing policy makers in transition economies. The challenges are essentially of two types—those related to attempts to attract foreign capital and those of managing foreign capital flows. We will then try to extract the main lessons from the recent rich literature about policy responses in countries that have been subject to "capital surges." These lessons became visible after the Mexican peso crisis and have strong implications for managing capital flows in the so-called emerging markets. Next we turn to an evaluation of the size and types of capital flows into the CEECs. The management of capital flows in the Czech Republic, Hungary, and Poland is then discussed under three separate headings—government objectives, policy responses, and effectiveness of the policies. We will finalize this chapter with recommendations based on our assessment of the policies and other responses to capital surges and their volatility. These recommendations draw on the contributions to this book and on other theoretical and empirical literature.

Management of Capital Flows in a Broad Context

Key Features of Global Capital Flows

The explosion in the growth of private capital flows in the last decade or so, both globally and to the so-called emerging markets (which include both transition and developing economies), has different origins. Perhaps the most important factor has been the financial and capital account liberalization in most of the countries of the world. The process started in the developed economies, but spread later to the developing countries and most recently to the transition economies.[1] Another factor has been technological developments in communications that have enabled rapid interactions between markets, the virtually instantaneous spread of information around the globe, and rapid implementation of financial transactions. A third factor has been the rapid growth of institutional investors, who are both willing and able to invest internationally as a result of measures to deregulate their industries.[2]

The pace of capital flows has been breathtaking. The flows to emerging markets reached $230 billion in 1996 (World Bank 1997). This was a level nearly six times greater than at the start of the 1990s, and four times larger than in their previous peak (1978–82), during the commercial bank lending surge. It is particularly noteworthy that private capital flows to emerging markets (after a brief and rather sharp fall) continued growing rapidly after the Mexican peso crisis, which started in December 1994; indeed, according to IMF data, capital flows to developing and transition economies grew by almost 29 percent for the whole of 1995, which was a rate higher than in any previous year.

In contrast to previous trends in capital flows, the most recent growth in private capital flows has had a number of structural specifics. In particular, transition and developing economies have begun to attract a far larger share of global capital flows. Thus, their share in global foreign direct investment grew from 15 percent in 1990 to almost 40 percent in 1996; the growth in their share of global portfolio equity flows was even more spectacular, rising from less than 2 percent in 1990 to 30 percent in 1996. True, the distribution of capital flows has been uneven among these countries, but the growth of these flows in emerging economies has been striking in countries such as China, Indonesia, Malaysia, Brazil, Chile, and many others.

During the 1990s the economic importance of private capital flows for the economies of transition and developing countries has also sharply increased. For example, the share of foreign capital in domestic investment increased from less than 4 percent in 1990 to almost 17 percent in

1996. Similarly, the shares have also increased in the case of the host countries' GDP, money supply, domestic savings, and so on.[3] The fact that private capital flows represent such a high proportion of the domestic economy of some transition countries is one of the key reasons why they have such a large impact on economic fundamentals and on key economic variables of these economies, and why the issue of properly managing these flows is so central to a successful transition.

The second reason why it is both important and complex for governments in transition economies to manage capital flows carefully is the volatility of capital flows and—above all—the potential vulnerability to large reversals, as experienced by Mexico and more recently by Asian economies. In this context, it is very important for policy makers to know the extent to which capital flows are likely to be permanent or temporary, since the desirable policy response will be qualitatively different in either case. For example, if it is known that the flows are permanent, then national economic authorities can be far more relaxed about allowing the real exchange rate to appreciate, as the ensuing current account deficit could be financed not only in the present but also in the future. However, if it is known that a particular surge of flows is temporary, then national economic authorities would be wise to resist appreciation—at least partially—of the real exchange rate, as an increasing current account deficit would not be financed in the future and could pose the risk of a costly foreign exchange crisis.

Naturally, one of the difficulties for policy makers in an open economy is that they have very imperfect information on this matter, as it is difficult to know *ex ante* whether and to what extent capital flows will be permanent or temporary, and indeed to what extent there could be reversals. To a large extent, the answers to both questions will depend on the country's economic performance and on trends in the international economy. The importance of these distinctions has become less relevant in the sophisticated financial markets that have been recently expanded with the introduction of derivatives, options, introduction of hybrid financial instruments, and so on.

In addition, the volatility of capital flows also seems to depend on the type of flow—foreign direct investment (FDI) tends to be less volatile than portfolio investments. The types of foreign capital have regained an important place in the debate about management of capital flows, particularly since the Mexican crisis, which illustrated so clearly the large negative impact of rapid capital outflows on the host country's economy in 1995. In contrast, the emerging economies of Southeast Asia appeared to be relatively stable till the early 1990s, and this was often attributed to a much greater reliance of these countries on FDI rather than on portfolio investment. As a result, there has been renewed interest in establishing whether one can determine a ranking of volatility by category of flow.

The intuitively logical view is that volatility differs among different instruments, and that FDI and long-term bank loans are less volatile than portfolio flows and short-term bank loans. FDI is more costly to reverse and thus responds more to fundamentals than to short-term interest rates, while portfolio flows are far more responsive to short-term changes in interest rates. Furthermore, portfolio investors can sell their existing stock of paper from a particular country far more easily than foreign direct investors can.

It was surprising, therefore, that a recent econometric study by Claessens et al. (1995) concluded that different categories of capital flows did not appear to reflect systematic differences in volatility and that it is not therefore possible to tell the "temperature" of flows just from their name. However, Claessens and colleagues based their analysis only on net, not gross flows; hence they did not fully reflect the risk of flow reversals, which is the main concern of the countries' economic authorities. From a methodological point of view, the econometric tests were limited by the fact that they were only univariate tests. A more comprehensive analysis is the recent work of Chuhan et al. (1996), which provides a strong empirical evidence that short-term flows are "hotter" than foreign direct investment. Chuhan and colleagues used a multivariate analysis to take account of interactions between types of flows and between flows to different countries. One of the most important empirical conclusions of this work is that it confirms that the "tequila effect" (or contagion effect) of the Mexican peso crisis was clearly transmitted to other emerging markets via changes in short-term flows, but that there was little effect from variations in FDI in Mexico on FDI in other emerging markets.

An important study in the context of this book was that of Frankel and Rose (1996). The study provides econometric evidence of a crucial link, as it shows that the greater the proportion of FDI in total capital flows, the smaller the probability that the recipient country will suffer a foreign exchange crisis, like that of the Mexican peso. This study is important not only because it backs the dominant view that there is a hierarchy to volatility, but because it links volatility to the likelihood (or not) of crisis.

We can extract two relevant conclusions and policy recommendations from this brief review of the recent empirical literature on the volatility of capital flows. First, there seems to be a hierarchy of volatility; as a consequence, the type of flow does matter. Second, there are some doubts about the relevance of the distinction between short- and long-term flows. The distinction is often blurred as a result of the evidence provided by econometric studies and by the fact that the global capital markets are increasingly more sophisticated in terms of generating product innovations and hybrid financial instruments. Therefore, it is not just the type of flow that matters, but also the level of flows (and that of the current account deficit) and the capital sophistication. As a consequence, transition countries should follow policies that encourage long-term flows. Occasionally, they may have to discourage surges of short-term capital if they are "excessive," and avoid a ratio of total capital inflows to GDP (and above all a ratio of current account deficit to GDP) that is too large and may, therefore, prove unsustainable once market sentiment changes. This may not be the optimal policy in terms of microeconomic efficiency but we are convinced that such a policy will be prudent if combined with sound macroeconomic and structural policies that maintain strong fundamentals.

Main Challenges for Policy Makers

Naturally, it is not just the type of capital inflows and their level that determine their impact on the transition economy. It also matters a great deal whether the macroeconomic management of these flows is sensible and how strong and well regulated the domestic banking sector and capital market are. If macroeconomic management of the flows is prudent (subject to which we return in more depth below) and if the domestic financial system is relatively strong and well regulated, it is far more likely that capital flows will lead to increased and more efficient investment and higher growth, as well as adding momentum to market reforms. However, if macroeconomic management of the flows is inadequate and financial systems are weak and badly regulated, the impact of the flows may lead to lower growth and to higher potential instability of growth.

This dichotomy is particularly true of transition economies. On the one hand, the potential positive effects of capital flows in terms of higher and more productive investment, higher growth, and stimulating market reforms, especially in the financial sector, are particularly significant for these economies, as the needs in those areas are especially important. On the other hand, the risks of negative impact of these flows on growth and its volatility are also high. This is because in transition economies banking systems and capital markets suffer from various shortcomings: from incomplete and asymmetric information, poor supervision, shortage of skilled personnel, limited competition, problematic balance sheets, thin capital markets, and various other problems.[4] Transition economies are also quite new in the portfolios of international investors, making them particularly prone to fluctuations in international financial conditions (Calvo and Mendoza 1995; World Bank 1997). As a result, transition economies may be vulnerable to a greater degree of volatility of capital flows, especially in the initial stages.[5]

We can distinguish three levels of challenges facing the economic authorities in Central and Eastern Europe with regard to capital flows:

(i) Attracting capital flows
(ii) Managing surges of large inflows
(iii) Managing volatility of capital flows, and especially declines of capital flows

Attracting Foreign Capital

Countries in need of foreign capital have to be concerned about the attractiveness of their economies to foreign investors. This is, of course, a major issue in the transition economies. All transition economies started the process with a large inflationary gap and weak balance of payments, requiring both a domestic adjustment effort and external assistance. The economic adjustment of these countries has been threatened by declining savings (reflected in a drop in the average propensity to save) and a large technological gap. In addition, all these countries had to maintain a relatively high investment rate, needed for restructuring of industry and to build an efficient infrastructure. A more long-term reason why it is important for all transition economies to attract foreign direct investment is that there is growing empirical evidence that in transition economies, firms with foreign investment had a far higher propensity to invest in tradables (and export a higher proportion of their output) than purely indigenous firms.[6] The introduction of currency convertibility has clearly played a major role in encouraging FDI in the region. In this respect, the compliance with Article VIII of the IMF was basically a good move on the part of these countries (Cooper 1997).

The problem is that the desire to attract foreign investment may be inconsistent with efficient management of capital flows. For example, the decision to privatize (and thus attract foreign capital) may come at the time when the authorities are already facing a foreign capital surge. Under such circumstances the privatization decision may exacerbate the balance-of-payments management problem and the conduct of monetary policy. Of course, attempts to attract foreign capital may not always be inconsistent with a prudent balance-of-payments policy. Using the example of privatization above, the decision to privatize could be highly effective as an indirect balance-of-payments management tool if it came at the time of rising current account deficits and diminishing foreign capital inflows. These examples document the interlinkages among policy interventions. The question of policy timing and sequencing is, therefore, very important.

How should the authorities attract foreign capital under such circumstances? In general, the empirical evidence is quite clear—what matter most to foreign investors are factors such as political stability, stable macroeconomic environment, little "red tape," no relevant foreign exchange restriction, no danger of nationalization, and nondiscriminatory treatment.[7] The evidence also shows that fiscal incentives and other fiscal privileges have little or no effect on the decisions of potential investors (e.g., EBRD 1994). The rejection of fiscal incentives can also be based on what we have just said about the need for consistency among different policy interventions. It would be much more difficult to remove fiscal incentives at the time of capital surges.

Managing Surges of Foreign Capital

The second major challenge for monetary authorities is the management of surges of large capital inflows. As pointed out above (see also chapter 1), one of the key difficulties for policy makers is to determine when a surge of capital inflows is likely to be permanent or temporary, and whether flows are likely to be "cool" or "hot." Useful hints can be found from the type of flow (as we have seen above), the source country of flows, and the causes of flows, but policy makers cannot be completely sure of the permanence of large inflows. Only *ex post* will policy makers know that a surge of capital will remain for several years (e.g., Chile and several Asian countries in the 1990s) or that it will be fairly short-term (e.g., Mexico in the mid-1990s, and more recently Thailand).

In particular, if there are indications that the surge will be temporary (or even more important, if there is the possibility that capital flows may be reversed), a crucial problem is to fight pressure toward excessive strengthening of the real exchange rate (above productivity improvements), which discourages exports and encourages imports. From a long-term perspective, an excessively strong exchange rate will be particularly damaging for relatively small and open economies, whose main dynamism should come from export-led growth.[8] Indeed appreciation of the exchange rate may contradict one of the key aims of the import liberalization carried out by transition economies, which is to eliminate the bias against exports, which had originated in protection of imports! At the same time, such an appreciation weakens the competitive ability of domestic producers vis-à-vis foreign producers, as the latter's goods will have significantly lower prices, due to the simultaneous reduction of tariff barriers and the strengthening of the real exchange rate. Therefore, an overvalued exchange rate may give the wrong signals, for long-term comparative advantages, at a crucial moment of the transition.

Furthermore, a very strong exchange rate is likely—after a lag—to lead to rapid increases in current account deficits. Large current account deficits are not bad in theory, as they imply a clear easing of a country's external constraint, but in practice they are deeply problematic, particularly due to problems of moral hazard and adverse selection.[9] Moreover, there are limits to how much countries can borrow and—above all—these limits can change rapidly, due to rapid changes in the perceptions of financial markets (Griffith-Jones 1998). Especially as a result of the Mexico crisis, there is consensus that current account deficits should not be excessive (see chapter 1 and below).

The second danger of large capital surges becomes evident in situations when they are not effectively "absorbed." In such cases, the capital inflows will be inflationary if the growth of money supply exceeds the growth in demand for money.[10] *Pari passu,* foreign capital will be absorbed if the surge reflects an increase in the demand for domestic money. The additional money supply generated by the inflows will be held by domestic agents in the form of higher real money balances, and therefore not spent or spent on imports; as a consequence, the surge will not put upward pressure on prices. No policy response is required. In general, whenever capital inflows reflect either a change in international conditions or other changes (rather than the corresponding increase in the demand for money) in the national economy, a policy response is required.

The optimal mix of instruments to manage a capital surge depends on the country's institutional structure and past policies. However, a certain consensus is emerging internationally about the effectiveness of different policies. First, from the point of view of economic analysis, the policy that most reliably removes overheating without reducing competitiveness is seen to be fiscal contraction. It should be emphasized (as Begg [1996] correctly does) that the primary aim of fiscal contraction is not to reduce aggregate demand in order to offset the expansionary impact of capital inflows. The main reason for fiscal contraction is to reduce public borrowing and thus the incentive for short-term inflows to occur.[11] As capital inflows are reduced, so is the resulting exchange rate appreciation. The problem with fiscal policy contraction in practice is that it is somewhat unwieldy for short-term demand management, due to lags linked to the budgetary processes; furthermore, politically it is often far more difficult to cut government spending—or raise taxes—than to tighten monetary policy. This is clearly illustrated by the experience of Poland in 1997 and that of Brazil in the mid-1990s.

Moreover, cuts in expenditures beyond certain limits would be particularly damaging in countries in transition, as the government may need to play key roles in the transition (e.g., retraining people, building infrastructure), particularly in sectors where the private sector may be unwilling to finance such activities. Thus, there may be a difficult trade-off between the scale of government spending cuts needed for purposes of macroeconomic management and the optimal size of government needed to help meet the challenges of transition; a similar objection relates to proposals to increase taxes due to their negative impact on labor incentives ("supply side") at a time when the private sector needs to be particularly dynamic.

However, as empirical evidence for a number of emerging markets shows, countries that managed to follow a policy of fiscal contraction in the face of capital surges tended to have not only lower current account deficits but also a mix of absorption more oriented toward investment, as well as faster economic growth (World Bank 1997). This is in contrast with countries that used the exchange rate as a nominal anchor and relied more heavily on monetary than on fiscal policy. The latter countries often tended to experience consumption booms and larger real exchange rate appreciations, as well as lower growth.

In practice, the first reaction of most countries to capital surges has been to try to sterilize them. Sterilization can be defined either narrowly, as neutralizing the effect of foreign exchange intervention on the monetary base (by placing government paper), or more broadly, as offsetting the implications for the wider money supply (by increasing reserve requirements).

In advanced countries, where capital mobility is high, sterilization has for a long time been regarded as almost pointless, though it may have some short-term effect (Obstfeld 1982, 1995). The literature on the effectiveness of sterilization in developing countries is somewhat more inconclusive. However, it would seem that their more limited financial integration into the world economy implies that there is more space in developing countries for monetary autonomy (World Bank 1997). *Pari passu,* there is a consensus that sterilization in emerging markets can be effective for limited periods of time. However, sterilization has led to at least two difficulties: high quasi-fiscal cost and higher interest rates than they would have been had sterilization not been undertaken. As a result, economic authorities tend to abandon it after a period of time.

In the case of transition economies, Begg (1996) argues that—because, for example, risk aversion was greater among investors—sterilization was relatively more effective. This was the case particularly when the inflow was temporary, as was the sterilization. However, where the cause of inflows was related to high real interest rates and the expected evolution of real exchange rate being very profitable for speculators, sterilization was far more problematic.

With regard to exchange rate policies, there is evidence that countries that aim at maintaining competitive real exchange rates (broadly, the Asian ones, especially till the early 1990s) have a better performance than those that do not (such as most Latin American ones). Though reliance on exchange rate anchors can be vital during early disinflation, such a policy becomes inappropriate or even unsustainable at a later stage. At the other extreme, free floating can also be problematic, particularly when financial markets are thin, banks are fragile, and money demand is difficult to predict. As a result, intermediate solutions, such as wide exchange rate bands (where the middle point may either be fixed or "crawl") seem to provide a valuable halfway house for transition economies.

The ultimate way of coping with capital surges is by discouraging or limiting inflows (for example, by imposing nonremunerated deposit requirements) as well as liberalizing capital outflows or early repayment of public debt. In the early 1990s discouraging or limiting inflows (usually of short-term capital) was viewed with some skepticism by international financial organizations, though it was already supported by some studies (Ffrench-Davis and Griffith-Jones 1995). There is also some disagreement about the effectiveness of measures to discourage capital inflows, though there is growing recognition of their value, especially in the short term. The longer the measures are in place, the less effective they are likely to be, as investors find ways around them. However, the IMF, World Bank, and BIS all concluded in their studies after the Mexican crisis that discouraging excessive surges of short-term capital inflows, as countries such as Spain in the late 1980s (see chapter 7) or Chile and Colombia in the early 1990s (see chapter 8) did, can play a very positive role in managing such flows, if complemented by appropriate macroeconomic policies.[12] Indeed, it is interesting that a recent IMF publication (Lee 1997) suggests that such nonremunerated deposit requirements on a part of short-term inflows should not be regarded as a form of capital control, but can be seen as a sterilization instrument, as it directly sterilizes a fraction of the capital inflows and thus reduces the cost of other sterilization measures. Some transition economies, such as Slovenia, have in the mid-1990s also discouraged inflows by similar measures.

Managing Volatility of Capital Flows

The third and perhaps the major challenge facing policy makers in transition economies is to manage declines of capital outflows, above all avoiding costly foreign exchange crises (as occurred in Mexico in December 1994).

This could be particularly damaging to the process of economic reform (Griffith-Jones 1996).

In this context, two different situations can be distinguished:

(a) One is a relatively gradual decline of capital flows, but only when net capital inflows are at a level similar to that of the current account deficit: thus international reserves do not fall.

(b) The other is a situation characterized by a sharp decline of capital inflows leading to a level of net capital inflows significantly below that needed to finance a persistent, large, and possibly growing current account deficit; if the difference is large, this can lead to a large loss of foreign exchange reserves. In such a situation, there is a risk—particularly in the presence of political instability or if the country has a large short-term foreign debt—that a major speculative attack will occur on the currency. This would, in turn, lead to a large devaluation and, possibly, to "overshooting" the equilibrium exchange rate. An exchange rate adjustment will be ultimately unavoidable and costly in terms of output and inflation, and may also endanger the stability of the financial sector. The financial costs can be increased if banking systems are fragile, poorly managed, or supervised. A large devaluation can threaten the solvency both of bank borrowers and of banks, as credit risk shoots up whenever liabilities are denominated in foreign exchange and assets are in local currency. In such a case, the authorities would be faced with the difficult dilemma of a fiscally expensive bailout (e.g., Mexico in 1995) and/or a banking crisis followed by a costly bailout (Chile in the early 1980s, Norway and Sweden in the early 1990s).

Clearly the preferred option must be for the authorities to adopt an adjustment package whenever the current account deficit is rising rapidly and is large. One of the problems is to encourage politicians and economic authorities to move soon enough and drastically enough so as to stem any decline in reserves before it becomes excessive. Unfortunately, politicians often exhibit an outlook known in the literature as "disaster myopia." If a crisis has not occurred for a long time or ever in that country, this is taken by politicians and economic authorities as evidence that it will never happen. Experiences of other countries are often ignored, even if known, due to the "our country is different" argument.[13] International financial institutions, academics, and advisers face a difficult but important challenge in persuading economic authorities that a timely adjustment (with small costs in terms of reduced output growth and higher inflation up front) is far better than a "wait and see" attitude, which will normally lead to much higher costs (in terms of both lower output growth and investment and higher inflation).

Policy makers do face a difficult trade-off, as the adjustment package needs to be large enough to avoid crisis but not so large as to stifle growth. The options are not clear-cut, as much will depend on how the financial markets as well as foreign investors perceive an adjustment package. There is here a strong element of self-fulfillment; if "the markets" receive a package well, then it will be successful. If "the markets" think it is too little and/or too late (or the wrong policy mix), the package will not be successful. As a consequence, economic authorities in transition countries (as in other emerging markets) need to monitor very closely the likely reactions of markets and foreign investors, and need to present the package in a clear and consistent way. To a certain extent, the package has to be based not only on sound economic analysis, but also on what the markets see as sound economics. As Eatwell (1997), drawing on Keynes (1936), rightly points out, this may introduce a deflationary bias to policy making; however, small transition countries that have open capital markets and thus are integrated into a globalized economy have little choice but to adapt macroeconomic policy to avoid negative perceptions from the international financial markets and direct investors.

Naturally, the policy mix of an adjustment package should vary depending on initial circumstances. An important consideration is whether the economy is well below the production frontier or close to it. If the economy is well below the production frontier (as, for example, Poland may indeed have been in late 1997 and early 1998), an optimal policy mix would combine expenditure switching measures (e.g., devaluation or accelerating crawl if there is a crawling peg) with expenditure reduction measures (e.g., tightening monetary and fiscal policy). This policy mix will reduce the deflationary impact of the package on output and investment, but may lead to higher inflation due to the weakening of the exchange rate. However, fears that limited nominal depreciation encourage rapid exchange rate pass-through to prices are not supported by the international experience. As Begg (1996) points out, a high pass-through to prices occurs only in exceptional circumstances, such as in countries with a history of very high inflation and extensive indexation. Obstfeld (1995) presents an analysis that rigorously reviews the empirical evidence of recent decades and concludes that nominal depreciation need not lead to domestic inflation, particularly if unemployment is relatively high. Leiderman and Bufman (1995) provide further support for this conclusion, with evidence from countries such as Israel and Chile, where the introduction of crawling bands did not increase persistence of inflation.

A final issue is the scale and timing of an adjustment package, once a country's foreign exchange reserves start falling rapidly. Forecasting the risk of a foreign exchange crisis is an imprecise science. However, in the wake of the Mexican peso crisis, an important literature has emerged (both empirical and analytical) on criteria for vulnerability or "early warning signals."[14] Consensus has emerged that early warning signals of vulnerability to foreign exchange crises in emerging markets include the following: (i) Large current account deficits for several years, particularly if funded to an important extent by reversible short-term flows. For economies growing at around 4 to 5 percent, a "reasonable" scale of current account deficit seems to be not higher than 4 to 5 percent of GDP (see Williamson 1995). (ii) Overvalued exchange rate in relation to an "equilibrium" exchange rate. (iii) Very high proportion of government debt paper that is short-term and/or held by foreigners; the situation is worsened if the government paper is denominated in foreign currency, as the government would need to bear the cost of any devaluation. (iv) Constraints (posed, for example, by fragilities within the banking system) on the willingness of economic authorities to increase domestic interest rates if reserves decline significantly as a result of a reversal of capital flows. This again is a major issue in transition economies, where banking systems are often fragile and poorly regulated (see, for example, Griffith-Jones and Drábek 1995). (v) Last but not least, the likelihood or reality of rising international interest rates, particularly in industrial countries, which are a major source of capital for the transition economy. In 1997, again—as in 1994—this was a factor.

The Impact of Foreign Capital Flows on the Economies of the CEECs

Size and Type of Capital Inflows

The size of capital inflows has been very large in three countries of the region—the Czech Republic, Hungary, and, beginning in 1995, Poland. Hungary has been by far the most important recipient of foreign investment, followed by the Czech Republic and Poland. Slovakia, for the time being, has been relatively on the sidelines of foreign investors' activities in the region. There have also been significant differences in the composition of capital inflows. While the bulk of foreign capital inflows in the Czech Republic have been in the form of portfolio investment, FDI has dominated the capital inflows scene in Hungary. A significant expansion of portfolio investment took place in Hungary in late 1995 and in 1996. In Poland, there has also been a rapid expansion of both portfolio investment and FDI, with a dramatic expansion taking place in 1996.

This report only covers in detail the period 1990–95, with additional comments also provided about the developments in 1996 and 1997. The Czech experience is instructive. The Czech Republic experienced a massive inflow of foreign capital in 1995 and in early 1996, but these capital inflows had almost dried up by the second half of 1997. Thus the country has been facing not only a problem of a rapid surge of foreign capital but also a relatively dangerous volatility of foreign capital flows.

Positive Impact of Capital Inflows

As noted above, the positive aspects of capital inflows are very important. While the main focus of this study is on the impact of capital surges and governmental responses, it is important to keep the positive dimension of capital flows in mind when evaluating government policies.

Even though the evidence is only sketchy, there is no doubt that capital inflows have played a major positive role in the CEECs. Foreign capital has significantly contributed to the expansion of domestic demand at the time of recession (see Gáspár's chapter in this volume) and has played a crucial role in filling the savings-investment gap (see, again, Gáspár's chapter and also Drábek's). Capital inflows have helped the governments concerned to meet their privatization objectives, since a large number of privatization deals in the region have involved foreign investors. Foreign capital has facilitated the management of balance of payments, since all of these countries have lately been running current account deficits and have required external financing to maintain external equilibrium. Furthermore, according to official government estimates, more than 70 percent of Hungarian exports originate in factories wholly or partially owned by foreign companies, and the corresponding figure for the Czech Republic is not much lower (about 50 to 60 percent).[15] In addition, capital inflows have been vital for these countries to build up their international reserves. Capital inflows have, therefore, enabled a higher level of domestic activity without the need for additional and even more drastic domestic adjustment than that the countries actually undertook. Last, but not least, foreign capital inflows have also been instrumental in helping the governments develop financial markets in their countries, introducing modern know-how in management and technology as well as facilitating access to foreign markets.

Dangers of Capital Inflows: Warning Signals

These positive effects notwithstanding, capital inflows have also led to serious dangers. These dangers were signaled through a number of indicators that we have used in monitoring these flows. The problems of selecting among different indicators are discussed by Drábek in this volume and also in Portes and Vines 1997.[16]

The indicators signaled five dangers of capital inflows. The first danger was a level of capital inflows that may have been too high and unstable, and could have brought about costly changes in government macroeconomic policies. Judging from the available evidence from the CEECs, it is clear that the level of capital inflows was indeed already very high both in Hungary and the Czech Republic, as evidenced by the shares of foreign capital in GDP, domestic savings, and money supply. As noted above, there have also been signs of significant instability in capital inflows in the Czech Republic and in Hungary. In Poland, the level of capital inflows remains relatively small but rising rapidly.

The *second related danger* was that foreign capital inflows increased inflationary pressures. Here again, the evidence provided in this book indicates that inflationary pressures from foreign capital were building up in the Czech Republic and most recently also in Poland and to some extent Hungary. As shown in the chapter by Drábek, changes in net foreign assets have played a major role in the expansion of the domestic money stock in the Czech Republic. Similar phenomena have been also observed by Gomulka and Gáspár in their chapters on Poland and Hungary, respectively. Whether or not the inflows have actually generated higher inflation remains subject to dispute. Using the empirical material presented in this volume, it is difficult to establish that capital inflows have been inflationary or that they had any other direct impact on other domestic economic variables. Two chapters included in this volume make such attempts—those of Klacek and Gáspár. Klacek addresses the question of the impact of capital inflows on domestic monetary expansion and finds that capital inflows had a direct impact on domestic credit in the Czech Republic. Given the size of the capital surge, his finding is not entirely surprising.

Gáspár tries to evaluate the impact of capital inflows on interest rates. He finds very little empirical support for the thesis that capital inflows had a direct impact on interest rates. Nevertheless, he goes on to suggest that the level of interest rates was more powerfully affected by forces other than capital inflows, such as government borrowing and market segmentation. This suggestion is very plausible since it is consistent with the findings of other empirical studies. In addition, the bulk of foreign capital inflows into Hungary have been in the form of FDI, and these are less likely to be affected by changes in interest rates or by expected changes in exchange rates. As a result, and as pointed out by Begg (1996), capital flows based on

FDI are easier to manage than those that are strongly sensitive to changes in interest rates.

The third danger, as pointed out by García Solanes in this volume, was the possibility that foreign capital might be diverted to finance public sector deficits. If this were to happen, the private sector could have been "crowded out." The Central European papers in this volume are not specifically dealing with this issue and therefore do not provide evidence to test the hypothesis for the CEECs. According to indirect evidence provided by the authors of the country papers, however, the problem did not appear to be serious—the fiscal deficits were either small or declining in all of the countries under consideration. The exception was Hungary in the mid-1990s, as pointed by Gáspár.

The fourth danger of capital inflows is that they may have increased the fragility of the financial sector in these countries. This is partly because the increased liquidity of the banking sector increases incentives to banks to lend, which in turn may lead to an expansion of higher-risk credit. This could turn out to be a particularly serious problem given the high rates of inflation and, therefore, higher level of interest rates, as was the case in the countries in question. In addition, capital inflows may also increase the currency-maturity mismatch on banks' balance sheets and hence their vulnerability—a problem that can emerge particularly in countries with inexperienced bank management and inadequate supervision.[17] The financial problems experienced in the Czech Republic and, to a lesser extent, in Hungary can be partially attributed to the speed of financial liberalization and capital inflows.[18] At the same time, the fragility of the financial system was probably another factor in the instability of capital inflows.

Finally, the capital inflows into the region displayed a certain degree of other undesirable characteristics. For example, capital inflows have been highly concentrated. If foreign investors perceive that their share in the host country economy exceeds what they consider a "safety threshold" (e.g., they have become a dominant force in the stock market), they may withdraw or dramatically reduce their exposure. This is indeed what appears to have happened in Hungary and in the Czech Republic, which experienced sharp swings in the Budapest and Prague stock markets in 1993 and 1996, respectively, which were due to foreign investors' rising nervousness. Furthermore, the capital inflows in the Czech Republic have been concentrated in portfolio flows, in contrast to those in Hungary, where FDI plays a much larger role. As we noted above, the latter tend to be more stable than the former. In comparison to Hungary, therefore, the access to relatively more stable and long-term financing was more limited in the Czech Republic.

Government Objectives

Before assessing government policies toward capital surges, the first important question is the extent to which the governments in these countries have been concerned about the inflationary impact of capital inflows, their sustainability, and the other dangers noted above.

If inflation was indeed the matter of concern, the authorities would respond as soon as they felt that monetary expansion begins to dangerously accelerate. The message coming from these countries has been virtually uniform—inflation control has been policy objective number one in these countries. According to Klacek, for example, inflation control has been the top priority in the Czech Republic. The same point has been also made by Gomulka for Poland, and one could hear the same arguments for Hungary.

However, it is arguable whether the concern about inflation has been actually as powerful as we have been made to believe by politicians and, *pari passu,* whether anti-inflationary policies have received such absolute priority. The evidence is quite telling and suggests a rather different story. Neither the Czech nor Polish government has been able to reduce the level of inflation very significantly since 1994. Moreover, the failure to successfully combat inflation in these countries has clearly been related to serious mistakes in government policies. Both countries have experienced an excessive growth of wages, for which the governments have partially been responsible. The evidence coming from Hungary also suggests that government preoccupation with capital inflows was relatively less important in comparison to the government concerns about unemployment and access to external resources. Nevertheless, as we shall argue further below, the Hungarian authorities have taken the dangers of capital surges more seriously than their Czech counterparts.

The second important question about the capital surges in the CEECs is the extent to which demand for money concurrently expanded in these countries or whether it has remained unchanged. As we discussed above, if the growth of capital inflows were to reflect a corresponding expansion in the demand for money, there would have been no need for the authorities to respond. Indeed, such a response would have been clearly unwise, as it would tend to increase interest rates and choke off demand for investment. While we have a priori reasons to believe that demand for money in these countries actually expanded, there is, unfortunately, no hard empirical evidence to support this conjecture. Several attempts have been made elsewhere in the literature to estimate demand for money functions, but these attempts have usually suffered from weak data (such as short and inconsistent time series) in addition to serious econometric difficulties. We can report only some indirect evidence, such as changes in interest rates, that can provide indications of changes in money markets. For example, judging from the relatively stable level of interest rates in the Czech Republic, it would seem that the growth of capital inflows was at least partially offset by a simultaneous expansion in the demand for money. It appears that the level of interest rates continued to be pulled upward despite the relatively strong inflow of foreign capital.[19] But, clearly, this conclusion is premature until we analyze the responses by individual governments.

Following again our argument above, the third consideration for governments is whether capital inflows are temporary or persistent. If they are temporary, no action may be necessary, or the measures that need to be taken should be maintained over a long period. In practice, however, the distinction between temporary and persistent is difficult, and policy makers have to choose. The Czech authorities have treated capital inflows as if they were there to stay, and therefore they were initially reluctant to change the direction of their policies.[20] The Hungarian and Polish authorities appeared to have been more willing to change their policies as soon as they faced pressures of capital inflows.[21]

Policy Responses: Types of Instruments

Since governments were not initially preoccupied with the impact and dangers of excessive capital inflows, they did not immediately respond to any significant degree to the pressures in the markets. When the capital inflows persisted, each of the four governments took some actions.

(a) *Sterilization.* Both the Czech government and, to some extent, the other governments actively engaged in "sterilization" (see Klacek's, Dědek's, and Gáspár's chapters in this volume, and Begg 1996). Using data on changes in net domestic assets and in international reserves of the central banks, Begg provides the most comprehensive review of sterilization policies in the region so far. He shows that the monetary authorities have used a variety of instruments, ranging from simple purchases of foreign currency (nonsterilized intervention) to mopping up the excess liquidity through sales of official paper in open market operations or through repurchase agreements (in Hungary) or increased reserve requirements. Most of these instruments have been also used by the Czech and Polish authorities (see Klacek's and Gomulka's chapters).

(b) *Tightening of fiscal policy.* Fiscal policy has been relatively tight throughout this period in the Czech Republic, while the other two countries were running deficits. However, the other countries have undertaken much greater fiscal tightening in recent years, while the fiscal position of the Czech Republic has been slightly deteriorating. In order to cope with the capital surge, the only fiscal measure of significance was the decision by the Czech government to use the central bank more actively for deposits of other state institutions. Thus, the authorities have made recourse to measures such as compulsory deposits of the Fund for National Property with the central bank or of proceeds from privatization of Czech Telecom. Similar measures were taken in Hungary. Whether these measures should be treated as parafiscal or monetary may be immaterial, but the effect was the same—a sterilization of a large amount of liquidity. The costs of these policies were, of course, different, as we shall see further below.

(c) *Exchange rate changes.* Exchange rates were not originally used as an instrument of absorbing or slowing down the capital inflows in these countries. On the contrary, all governments initially relied on pegging exchange rates—either nominal or real—and have thus eliminated the possibility of freely using exchange rate changes as a "shock absorber." This feature was particularly pronounced in the Czech Republic, where the authorities maintained a fixed nominal rate. The policy eliminated virtually all foreign exchange risk for foreign currency speculators and provided additional stimulus for capital inflows. However, the policies subsequently have been changed in all of these countries. The Czech Republic introduced wider bands on exchange rates in February 1996 to allow greater fluctuations of nominal rates, and in May 1997 floated it under pressure from the markets. Poland and Hungary moved to a more flexible regime earlier; the countries initially allowed a currency appreciation before they moved to a sliding peg with a band. Moreover, both countries were prepared to use even these policies much more flexibly (see, for example, Gomulka's chapter).

In the countries studied here, there has also so far not been much of an attempt to throw "sand in the wheels"—into the capital inflows—by introducing capital controls. One exception has been the Czech Republic, which has introduced measures to reduce the inflow of capital with maturities shorter than twelve months (see Dědek's chapter). While the profession is not entirely united as to the effectiveness of such measures, the reluctance to use selective capital controls in the CEECs is not entirely out of place. The main reason is that capital controls are sometimes thought to be ineffective and costly instruments of government policy, especially if they are maintained too long.[22] Nevertheless, even the staunchest supporters of the "pure" market solutions now recognize that temporary, transparent nontraditional measures may be necessary in extreme situations, as noted above.

Effectiveness of Policies: An Evaluation

Elements of Optimal Government Intervention

So far we have asked the question whether the authorities should have responded to foreign capital inflows. The answer depends on whether the authorities are concerned about inflation, and whether the capital inflow is considered temporary or permanent. The answer also depends on whether capital inflows reflect an expansion in demand for money. For Central Europe, we have made the point that the authorities should have responded in view of the persistent inflationary pressures and the growth of money demand, which was unlikely to match the growth of domestic money supply. The problem was particularly acute in the Czech Republic in the second half of 1995 and in the first half of 1996, and it was less serious in the other countries. The answer will also depend on the origins of capital, that is, whether capital inflows have external or internal origins. Furthermore, the concern about capital inflows also depends on the way foreign capital is absorbed and utilized in the host country. If foreign capital is not used effectively because, for example, foreign loans are not "translated" into an effective expansion of production capacities because new production capacities are poorly utilized or for some other reason, then the return on foreign capital may be lower than the rate of interest. In other words, foreign capital would only increase the country's indebtedness without the corresponding increase in the ability to service the country's debt. Perhaps most important, the need to respond depends on whether the capital flows lead to large current account deficits, due to the overvaluation of the currency.

Once the decision has been taken to respond, the next question is whether the policies are optimal in protecting the countries against "excessive" capital inflows and their instability. The answers to this question crucially depend on a satisfactory answer regarding the above elements of optimal intervention. Unfortunately, the answer is not clear-cut, and the choice of policy instruments is complicated. While it is possible to provide a theoretical ranking among different instruments (see, e.g., Ul Haque et al. 1997), their implementation in practice can be constrained by other factors. For example, the effectiveness of sterilization policies will partially depend on the sophistication of financial markets. The use of fiscal policy will depend on the ability of governments to carry out the fiscal reform with speed, and so on. The evaluation of government responses will therefore have to consider all these elements.

Moreover, the answers will also depend on other government objectives. For example, the general reluctance of the authorities to use measures to discourage surges of capital flows was understandable in the context of the government policies to liberalize the capital account (see Dědek's chapter in this volume). Rapid liberalization of the capital account had important advantages, such as helping to attract much-needed FDI, giving a clear signal to markets about commitments to market reforms and their determination to join the EU (with the latter being perhaps the most important). However, the liberalization of the capital account at such an early stage of market reforms was contrary to the broad conclusions of the then-current literature on timing and sequencing of economic reforms, which recommended leaving the liberalization of the capital account to the end of the reform process, and doing it only once certain preconditions were met.[23]

The liberalization has complicated the macroeconomic management in these countries, particularly as it happened during a period of rapid global growth of capital flows to emerging markets (Griffith-Jones 1998; World Bank 1997). The problem was especially serious in the case of the Czech Republic in the mid-1990s (see chapter 3). It would now be inappropriate to reverse this process, but it is important to maintain that existing provisions—as, for example, those existing in the Foreign Exchange Law of the Czech Republic—allowing in the case of a major surge the imposition of nonremunerated deposit requirements on short-term inflows (see chapter 4). This practice would be similar to the measures successfully implemented in Chile and Colombia.

Timing of Policy Responses

By using nonsterilized intervention, the Czech authorities were able to build up relatively fast and effectively the country's international reserves, which had been depleted since the pre-1989 period. Initially, there was not much concern about the inflationary impact, which was to some extent understandable. Many economists believed at the time that the financial markets were "overreacting" and that foreign investors would adjust their expectations in time. Under such circumstances, the initial "wait and see" policy was, therefore, to be expected.

However, the rationality of this argument is somewhat questionable given the empirical evidence provided by Gomulka in this volume. In trying to explain the changes in portfolio capital inflows into Poland, he shows that return on capital was a powerful determinant, in addition to changes in net international reserves.[24] Thus, his paper confirms the well-established phenomenon that portfolio investments are highly sensitive to changes in interest rates. The policy implication is that capital inflows could become dangerous provided they reach a significantly high level. At the time of writing this summary, as Gomulka points out, the level remains relatively low and makes Poland therefore less vulnerable than, say, the Czech Republic.

Nevertheless, the speed of policy response was too slow in the Czech Republic. There are several reasons to believe that the response of the Czech authorities to the inflationary impact and to the current account imbalance came too late. The response came only once the current account deficit was already too large and threatening. No warning signals were heeded by the authorities, irrespective of whether they signaled a sharp deterioration in domestic "fundamentals" or a highly risky pattern of foreign capital inflows and a rapidly deteriorating current account. Yet the "red lights" had been flashing for some time. In contrast, Poland was responding much earlier in the process and much faster, partially learning from the Czech experience and partially pursuing a different policy. Gomulka argues in this volume that the "safe" level of current account deficit should not exceed 4 to 5 percent of GDP—that is consistent with our recommendation above. Hungary had also responded in 1995 to a rapidly rising current account deficit, and avoided a foreign exchange crisis.

Moreover, the transition economies—particularly those perceived as successful, such as the Czech Republic in the mid-1990s—faced a particularly difficult challenge as the foreign capital inflows (and their effect on the exchange rate) followed almost immediately after the import liberalization. If the authorities allowed the exchange rate to appreciate, this meant that the appreciation in the real effective exchange rate very quickly eliminated a large part of the benefits from import liberalization. The latter, as we noted above, had as one of the main objectives the encouragement of exports, which was weakened by the strengthening of the exchange rate.

The Worst-Case Policy Choice

While the evidence is still relatively limited about the effectiveness of policies, we can make a few firm conclusions based on their qualitative assessment. First, the policy of the Czech Government was the least effective and efficient.[25] The Czech government pursued a policy of fixed nominal exchange rate combined with a relatively tight monetary policy. The combination of a preannounced fixed nominal exchange rate combined with relatively high interest rates led, not surprisingly, to a strong inflow of short-term foreign capital. Without doubt, this policy mix was the worst combination of policies that could have been adopted in the face of the foreign capital surge. The policies were a mix of little foreign exchange uncertainty (and thus virtually no foreign exchange risk to foreign investors) and high fiscal and other costs to the monetary authorities, as we shall see further below. The dangers of these policies have been widely discussed and are now well known, as we have argued above. Predictably, this led to precisely what has happened in other countries in similar situations—a dramatically deteriorating current account deficit. This happened in the Czech Republic in 1994–96, in Hungary since 1994 (before the adjustment), and in Poland since 1996. In contrast, judging from the most recent experience of Poland described by Gomulka and in Hungary discussed by Gáspár, the exchange rate policy of Polish and Hungarian authorities was more flexible.

Second, the Czech policy of a fixed nominal exchange rate was highly inappropriate for another reason. The policy has been one of the main factors of the rapidly deteriorating current account imbalance and the recent slowdown in economic growth. During the period between 1991 and 1996, the real effective exchange rate of the Czech koruna appreciated by about 40 percent.[26] During the same period productivity also increased, by most accounts of independent observers, but at a considerably slower pace. Clearly, the competitiveness of Czech sectors producing tradables deteriorated, and this adversely affected the current account balance. Moreover, the loss of competitiveness was to a large extent due to "excessive" wage settlements, which were "monetized" by the central bank's monetary policy and thus inflationary, without corresponding changes in the external value of the currency.[27]

Limited Use of Fiscal Policy

The recourse to fiscal policy has been very hesitant and its impact underestimated in the Czech Republic. The authorities were clearly reluctant to tighten the budget, which would have been the most effective economic instrument in the long run. It would have reduced the expansionary impact of the budget on aggregate demand and thus reduced demand for imports and trade deficit. It would have reduced inflationary pressures that forced the Central Bank to maintain a fairly restrictive monetary policy and thus high interest rates. This, in turn, generated additional incentives for capital inflows. Without the necessary fiscal tightening, the government was, therefore, unable to defend itself more effectively against capital surges.[28] In contrast, Hungary and Poland took in the course of 1995–96 more significant steps to tighten the government budgets.

Of course, the problem with fiscal tightening, apart from political sensitivities, was that fiscal measures take time to implement, while foreign capital moves with great speed. However, the fiscal policies in the Czech Republic could have been used more effectively since capital inflows *persisted* over a relatively long period of time and the monetary responses were quite clearly not sustainable.

The Impact of Policies: Empirical Evidence

What was the impact of the policies? The answer to this question is not straightforward because empirical evaluations of the policies are difficult. One reason for these difficulties is that the capital surges did not last long enough for us to provide a basis for a reasonably long time-series. As noted above, the surge was relatively short-lived in the Czech Republic and weak in Poland and Hungary. Another reason is the difficulty of measuring the policy impact. On a broad level, all three countries have been able to slowly reduce their inflation rates but the level of inflation remains uncomfortably high in all of these countries. All three countries have been able to increase the level of international reserves but all of them have also recently seen the levels dropped, mainly as a result of increasing current account deficits. In Poland, the process of dollarization of domestic savings has been reversed and FDI substantially increased. Output growth was either slow (Hungary) or slowing down (Czech Republic and Slovakia). Thus, with the exception of the Polish GDP growth, all performance indicators of these countries tend to indicate considerable economic difficulties that were most likely made worse by capital surges and their fluctuations.

The empirical evidence of the impact of policies going beyond the analysis of these broad indicators is equally sketchy and ambiguous. Although there have been fluctuations in changes of capital inflows, the empirical evidence fails to support the idea that these fluctuations can be attributed to changes in domestic policies. As noted above, two papers included in this volume make such attempts—the papers by Klacek and Gáspár. Since he finds a close relationship between capital inflows and domestic credit, Klacek suggests that "the sterilization policies did not contain the inflationary impact of capital inflow on money stock." Bank credit is determined in Klacek's model by two factors—changes in net foreign assets (NFA) and industrial output (a proxy for domestic activity). Since NFA is a component of banks' liquidity, a relationship between NFA and domestic credit must be expected. But the real question is the extent to which changes in bank credit reflected the impact of other factors on demand for credit and on banks' liquidity (such as interest rates and thus the impact of sterilization policies) in addition to changes in bank liquidity due to inflows of foreign capital. This additional step has been partly considered by Begg (1996), who tries to estimate it in broad terms by separating the impact of sterilization policies. He finds that the government sterilization policies have not been fully effective, and confirms to some extent Klacek's findings, but he also discerns a certain degree of success from these policies. Similarly Gáspár estimates that about 75 percent of foreign capital was effectively sterilized in 1995–96.

Relatively more convincing evidence has been provided in this volume and elsewhere on the impact of privatization and other policies on foreign investment. For example, in April 1997 the Czech Republic took several policy measures, such as accelerating its program of privatization in sectors like banking, to an important extent with the specific objective of encouraging foreign investment. This was linked to the fact that the current account deficit was growing rapidly, and capital inflows had fallen precipitously.[29] As regards policies to attract FDI into Central Europe, Lansbury, Pain, and Smidkova (1996) provide empirical evidence that both macroeconomic policies as well as the form and timing of privatization have a strong influence on the level of FDI to different Central European countries; they also show that structural factors such as availability of skilled workers and research intensity play an important role.

Costs of Policies

It is very clear that the policies of sterilization have been costly in the countries concerned. This, obviously, would also explain why sterilizations have not been used as widely and as intensively as might have been expected in the light of the size of capital inflows. According to Begg, using IMF estimates, the costs of sterilization in the Czech Republic amounted to 0.3 percent of GDP in 1994 and the beginning of 1995 alone. Gáspár also argues in this volume that the costs of sterilization were "high," particularly if measured in terms of fiscal costs. For Poland, Gomulka estimates the costs of sterilization was 0.6 percent of GDP in 1995 and 0.8 percent in 1996—also high despite the relatively smaller amount of capital inflows than in the Czech Republic.

The fiscal costs of government policies would have been even higher had they relied exclusively on standard monetary instruments. By deciding to use nonstandard instruments such as the recourse to compulsory deposits by state institutions, as noted above, they were able to shift the costs of their policies to other institutions. By insisting on direct deposits with the central bank, for example, the Czech authorities have thus partially avoided the need for sterilization through open market operations that would have been more costly. In doing so, they shifted the costs to institutions such as Telecom (a major affected party) or the National Property Fund (another affected party). Alternatively, the authorities could have reduced their costs by relying more extensively on increased minimum reserves of commercial banks. The result would have been higher costs to the banks, and it is an open question whether this alternative would have been more efficient.

Policy Recommendations

There is now a growing consensus among experts that, whenever a room for maneuver exists, governments should respond to capital surges with measures that affect current rather than capital account rather than with those measures that affect capital movements as a result of changes in interest rates and exchange rates.[30] This means that the emphasis should be placed on measures and policies that affect the growth of exports and imports of goods and services rather than capital movements. In other words, the measures must affect domestic fundamentals—the balance between savings and investments, changes in employment and in capacity utilization, inflationary pressures, etc. This, in turn, calls for the distinction between short- and long-term measures. Despite several influential voices to the contrary, there also seems to be a majority support for the idea that the causes of foreign investment differ, which will also call for a different treatment of different types of capital surges (Ul Haque, Mathieson, and Sharma 1996).

The lessons to be learned by the CEECs from other countries are limited in one important respect. All four CEECs opened their capital accounts considerably faster than many other countries that have experienced similar surges such as Spain, as shown by García Solanes in this volume, or countries in Southeast Asia, except for Hong Kong. This has enabled the latter countries to respond to capital surges through gradual liberalizations rather than a rapid one. By the same token, those latter countries have sequenced the liberalization steps differently; first opening the current account and only much later the capital account. In contrast, the CEECs have liberalized their foreign exchange in a "big bang," which has deprived them of a more gradual and sequential reform.

Short-term Measures

The room for a new regulatory framework that would restrict capital outflows in times of "crisis" is fairly limited and could well be counterproductive (see also Portes and Vines 1997). Since the countries have already eliminated the bulk of foreign currency restrictions, any reversal of these policies could be damaging to the credibility of their policies and may be also in contradiction with their international commitments.[31]

The first serious proposal that should be made is that the system of monitoring capital flows must be improved. The central banks in the CEECs have reasonably good information and data systems, but even these institutions should work on further improvements of the systems. One area deserving special attention is the need to qualitatively assess foreign investments, in order to evaluate better and faster the types of foreign investments, their end use, and the degree of associated risk.[32]

The second recommendation is that short-term adjustments typically require a suitable policy mix. A reliance on a single instrument is likely to lead to an "overadjustment" in that instrument.[33] This is closely related to the third recommendation. It is necessary to recognize that sterilization must be seen as an instrument that can only have a temporary impact but is unlikely to be sustainable without a simultaneous, fiscal tightening and changes in the exchange rate regime (Ffrench-Davis et al. 1993). The lessons from the CEECs, as documented by individual contributions to this study and from elsewhere, only confirm that the authorities cannot rely on monetary measures alone since they only encourage speculative "bubbles" (Portes and Vines 1997, Ul Haque et al. 1997). Sterilization can help central banks to accumulate reserves while it will restrain inflationary pressures only temporarily. The problems with sterilization have been discussed above and they include high costs and, ultimately, they are ineffective because of their impact on interest rates. When used, it is also important to keep in mind that open market operations involving foreign investors are risky in that they can increase volatility of capital flows. It is clear that the limits of sterilization policies were exhausted relatively fast in the Czech Republic. The defense against capital surge had to draw on other instruments and policies. In contrast, the room for sterilization policies was much wider in Poland and Hungary.

The third recommendation concerns the exchange rate policy. As a very short-term measure, a real currency revaluation may be necessary. However, unless the currency appreciation reflects a relative improvement in productivity, such measures should only be seen as giving enough time and room for taking other measures, discussed further below. One of these measures should include a currency depreciation.[34] There was a great reluctance in the Czech Republic to devalue the currency but the attitude had to change, forced by the markets. The change is necessary mainly because devaluation is the *first*-best policy compared to import surcharges or import currency deposits, which the Czech Government introduced as an alternative. These measures are not only inferior but could be WTO-inconsistent.

The change is also necessary because it is vital for these countries to reestablish the level of long-term competitiveness that has been eroded through the gradual appreciation of their effective exchange rates. Of course, to the extent that pegging the exchange rate played an important stabilization instrument it will be also necessary to find a new "discipline device," such as inflation targeting. An alternative measure would be a further widening of bands around "downward crawl" in order to avoid an outright devaluation which many politicians see as humiliating. Indeed, it is noteworthy that the Czech Republic, Poland, and Hungary—as well as other transition economies—tended to move toward such this intermediate option, though at different paces. However, after the May 1997 speculative attack, the Czech Republic introduced a float.

The fourth recommendation is that fiscal tightening will have to play a much greater role in future management of capital surges than in the past. Lower fiscal deficits or higher fiscal surpluses will not only reduce aggregate spending and thus current account imbalances but also the stock of money and the pressures for interest rates to rise, *ceteris paribus*. Since fiscal policies have been inflationary in all CEECs, tighter budgetary policies would be anti-inflationary as well as conducive to better coping with capital surges. Moreover, fiscal tightening should come from much greater emphasis on higher tax revenues than has been contemplated so far. Expenditure reductions—which has been the standard approach by all CEECs—is under present circumstances far less advantageous. The expenditure cuts usually come from a reduction of public investment expenditures or by cutting social programs, neither of which is desirable.

Finally, we need to address the question of measures to discourage excessive surges of short-term capital flows. Which measures to use or not may depend on the institutional specifics of each country. The specific rules that should be followed, however, are that such measures should be seen as temporary, fair and transparent. Ideally, they should be time-bound or linked to *ex-ante* criteria under which they will be relaxed or abandoned.

Long-term Measures

If capital inflows persist over a longer period, the governments will have to take steps that affect domestic fundamentals but will take time to have an impact. In particular, this will mean that the countries will have to reduce their current rates of inflation even further than they have achieved until now. They will also have to increase their savings rates—partly to reduce domestic spending and inflation and partly to avoid the traps of "foreign investors dominance." Last but not least, the countries will have to increase productivity of capital if they want to have a continuous access to foreign capital. This means that they have to attract foreign capital not only through attractive interest rates but also through high returns in the productive sectors.

A number of measures to increase domestic savings should be considered. Reform of pension schemes and further institutionalization of domestic savings (health insurance, mutual funds) can play a positive role. Such a step would be useful for at least two reasons in relation to balance-of- payments management. It would tend to encourage domestic savings, which in turn would be conducive to the strengthening of domestic financial markets. In addition, the establishment of strong pension, mutual, and insurance funds would also enable these funds easier access to foreign markets and hence be conducive to capital outflows. Furthermore, and most important, pension fund reform could encourage the development of a domestic long-term capital market.

The increased emphasis on domestic savings will also call for a significant improvement in the process of financial intermediation. It is clear that the banking sectors in all CEECs have been under strain and will have to be strengthened. In general, it is questionable whether countries with weak banking sectors are even in the position to open up to foreign capital flows or whether the opening of capital accounts should not go hand in hand with a reform of the banking sector. Various proposals have been already made in the professional literature to strengthen the financial sectors in the CEEC by various experts (e.g., Griffith-Jones and Drábek 1995), and these reforms will have to be accelerated in light of the most recent crises that have affected these countries.

The increased exposure to foreign capital flows will also necessitate other institutional changes toward greater flexibility of factor and product market. These changes are typically vital in order to stimulate the growth of productivity and returns to capital. The rapid speed with which capital can move across borders has so far not been accompanied by comparable adjustments in other markets. As a result, the volatility of foreign capital movements has put a great strain on domestic capital markets, on the financing of government deficits, labor markets, and others. Each of these markets is typically affected by a variety of legislative, governmental, and other measures, the effect of which may be to impede the operations of these markets. The point that needs to be emphasized here is that countries cope with volatile capital flows better if they themselves are better equipped—through efficient rules and flexible institutions—to adjust to sudden changes in capital flows. This study has identified a number of shortcomings and bottlenecks in the CEECs, such as weak financial supervision, ineffective courts and judicial support, lack of transparency, and other problems. All of these shortcomings will call for additional measures of structural nature that must become part and parcel of the overall policy package.

Notes

1. See, for example, Drábek and Laird 1997.
2. See, for example, Griffith-Jones 1998.
3. See Drábek in this volume for detailed figures on these ratios for transition economies.
4. Arguably, the problems are more serious than in industrial country markets, and even than in some of the more advanced markets in the developing world. For more details, see Griffith-Jones and Drábek 1995.
5. There is, however, a factor that may favor transition economies, especially in Eastern Europe. This is also related to differential volatilities, but in this case of source countries. Capital flows to Eastern Europe originate mainly from Western Europe, unlike capital flows to Latin America, which originate mainly from the United States. Many distinguished economists, and in particular Keynes (1936), have argued that traditionally capital flows originating from Western Europe are more stable than those originating in the United States. Several senior policy makers in Eastern Europe share this view. Though there is no firm empirical evidence to back this view, this may provide some comfort to policy makers in Eastern Europe. However, not too much should be made of this, as increasingly globalized and integrated markets (especially in portfolio and bank flows) make distinctions based on national origins increasingly blurred, and therefore diminish any potential differentials of volatility that could have existed in the past, between countries of origin.
6. See, for example, Lane 1994 or Lansbury, Pain, and Smidkova 1996 for empirical evidence on this link in Hungary.
7. See, for example, Bartolini and Drazen 1997.
8. This is clearly our value judgment. But even if we concede that production incentives should be neutral, it is still true that small open economies will crucially depend on exports.
9. See also Begg 1996.
10. This would be particularly serious for transition countries in view of their interest in joining the EU and possibly the EMU.
11. In practice, however, the objective may not be fully accomplished if fiscal contraction has no or only a limited impact on interest rates. This would happen if government and central bank policies do not have a sufficient impact on money markets due to the lack of proper policy instruments and institutions.
12. See, for example, World Bank 1997 and also the recent pronouncements of high-ranking economists and policy makers such as Stiglitz, Wolcker, and others.
13. Interview material.
14. For a useful synthesis, see Goldstein 1996. An alternative approach has been proposed in this book by Drábek.
15. See also Lansbury et al. 1996 for more empirical residence.
16. The choice of the indicators was our own and therefore subjective. However, there was no alternative due to the absence of unambiguous indicators.
17. This point is strongly emphasized in Calvo, Sahay, and Vegh 1995. The problem is discussed in the case of the Mexican crises by Griffith-Jones 1996.
18. For more details, see Griffith-Jones and Drábek 1995.
19. The level of interest rates is likely to fall if the origin of capital inflows is mainly external, such as a drop in foreign interest rates. The opposite holds true if the origin is domestic, such as in the case of a shift in the demand for money function. For a discussion of these issues, see, for example, Ul Haque, Mathieson, and Sharma 1997. Obviously, the matter becomes even more complicated when both external and internal factors interact.

20. This was reflected, for example, in the government insistence on pegging the nominal exchange rate.

21. Viz., the willingness of the authorities to revalue the nominal exchange rate or to introduce a more flexible exchange rate regime. For more on this, see the discussion further below.

22. See Dooley 1995. As pointed out above, other countries in the region that have also introduced measures to discourage short-term capital were Hungary and Slovenia.

23. In contrast, the liberalization of current account transactions has been generally applauded as a positive step. As Cooper (1997) pointed out, countries that have moved rapidly to comply with Article VIII performed rather better on balance than those that have adopted a gradual approach.

24. Methodologically, the use of NIR as an independent variable is not ideal. The level of NIR is partially explained by changes in portfolio investment, and some simultaneous equation bias must, therefore, be suspected. Gomulka suggests, we think correctly, that the bias is probably small since other factors played an important role in building the level of NIR-capital outflows, current account surplus and, to a lesser degree, FDI. The use of interest rates as the other independent variable is appropriate in view of the relative independence of domestic monetary policy, as pointed out by Gáspár and discussed above.

25. The exchange rate policies in the region have been reviewed by Rosati 1997.

26. The exact figure is subject to dispute, and it depends on the price index used and whether one uses the wholesale or retail prices as the base.

27. The same experience has been observed in other countries that pursued similar policies at some time in the past. See, for example, Gurria 1993.

28. It is perhaps ironic that the fiscal tightening by the Czech government came in April 1997, when it was already under the intense pressure of looming current account deficits.

29. In 1995 the Czech Republic had a major surge of foreign capital inflows (which peaked at around 18 percent of GDP in 1995), and the central policy issue was whether and how best to discourage excessive capital inflows, particularly, of course, those with short-term maturities.

30. See, for example, Begg 1996.

31. The recent introduction of various import restrictive measures in these countries (Drábek 1996) have not been well received by the European Union, which regards them as a possible violation of the Europe Agreement. Even though the conflict may be clarified, the measures have been controversial.

32. See, for example, the discussion in Griffith-Jones, Marr, and Rodriguez 1992.

33. This recommendation is based on pragmatic assessment rather than on a rigorous analysis. The pragmatic approach comes from policy makers with considerable experience in this area. See, for example, French-Davis, Agostin, and Uthoff 1993.

34. This approach has been adopted very successfully by Chile. See Ffrench-Davis et al. 1993.

Bibliography

Bartolini, Leonardo, and Allan Drazen. 1997. "Capital Account Liberalization as a Signal for Foreign Investment." *The American Economic Review* 87, no. 1 (March), 138–54.

Begg, David. 1996. "Monetary Policy in Central and Eastern Europe; Lessons after Half a Decade of Transition." Washington, D.C., IMF Working Paper no. 96/108 (September).

Calvo, Guillermo, Ratna Sahay, and Carlos A. Vegh. 1995. "Capital Flows in Central and Eastern Europe: Evidence and Policy Options." Vienna: Institute for International Economics, Oesterreichische Nationalbank (7–9 September).

Calvo, Guillermo, and Enrice Mendoza. 1995. "Reflections on Mexico's Balance of Payment Crisis." Mimeo, October, University of Maryland.

Chuhan, Punam, Gabriel Pérez Quirós, and Helen Popper. 1996. "International Capital Flows, Do Short Term Investment and Direct Investment Differ?" Policy Research Working Paper no. 1669 (October).

Claessens, S., Michael Dooley, and Andrew Warner. 1995. "Portfolio Capital Flows: Hot or Cold?" *The World Bank Economic Review* 9, no. 1.

Cooper, Richard N. 1997. "Currency Convertibility in Transforming Economies: Was It a Mistake?" In Zecchini 1997, 463–79.

Drábek, Zdeněk. 1996. "The Stability of Trade Policy in Countries in Transition and Their Integration into the Multilateral Trading System." *The World Economy* 19, no. 6 (November), 721–745.

Drábek, Zdeněk, and Sam Laird. 1997. "The New Liberalism: Trade Policy Development in Emerging Markets." Geneva, WTO, Research Department Working Paper No. 97–005 and *Journal of World Trade*, forthcoming.

Eatwell, Jonathan. 1997. "International Financial Liberalization: The Impact on World Development." *UNDP Office of Development Studies Discussion Paper Series.*

Ffrench-Davis, Ricardo, Manuel Agostin, and Andreas Uthoff. 1993. "Capital Movements, Export Strategy and Macroeconomic Stability in Chile." Paper prepared for a conference of ECLAC, Santiago, 6–7 December 1993.

Ffrench-Davis, Ricardo, and Stephany Griffith-Jones, eds. 1995. *Coping with Capital Surges: The Return of Finance to Latin America.* Boulder, Colorado: Lynne Rienner.

Frankel, Jacob, and Andrew Rose. 1996. "Currency Crashes in Emerging Markets: An Empirical Treatment; Board of Governors of the Federal Reserve." International Financial Discussion Paper 534 (January).

Goldstein, Maurice. 1996. "Risks of Foreign Exchange Crises." Paper presented at I.I.E./Austrian National Bank, September 1995 Conference.

Griffith-Jones, Stephany. 1996. "The Mexican Peso Crisis." Brighton, Sussex, I.D.S. Discussion Paper, No. 354.

———. 1998. *Global Capital Flows: Should They be Regulated?* Macmillan.

Griffith-Jones, Stephany, and Vasile Papageorgiou. 1993. "Globalization of Financial Markets and Impact on Flows to LDCs: New Challenges for Regulation." In *Pursuit of Reform: Global Finance and Developing Countries,* ed. J. Teunissen. The Hague: FONDAD (November).

Griffith-Jones, Stephany, A. Marr, and Andreas Rodriguez. 1992. "The Return of Private Capital to Latin America: The Facts, an Analytical Framework and Some Policy Issues." In *Fragile Finance: Rethinking the IMS,* ed. J. Teunissen. The Hague, FONDAD, 13–41.

Griffith-Jones, Stephany, and Zdeněk Drábek, eds. 1995. *Financial Sector Reform.* London: Macmillan and St. Martin's Press.

Guria-Trevino, José Angel, 1995. "Capital Flows: The Mexico Case." In *Coping with Capital Surges: The Return of Finance to Latin America,* ed. R. Ffrench-Davis and S. Griffith-Jones. Boulder, Colorado: Lynne Rienner.

Keynes, John M. 1936. *The General Theory of Employment Interest and Money.* London: Macmillan.

Lansbury, Melanie, Nigel Pain, and Katerina Smidkova. 1996. "Foreign Direct Investment in Central Europe since 1990: An Econometric Study." *National Institute Economic Review,* May.

Lee, Jang-Yung, 1997. "Sterilizing Capital Inflows." Washington, D.C. Private Financing; IMF Occasional Paper, Economic Issues, no. 7.

Leiderman, Leonardo, and Gil Bufman. 1995. "Searching for Nominal Anchors in Shock-Prone Economies in the 1990s: Inflation Targets and Nominal Exchange Rate Bands." In *Stability in Latin America,* ed. R. Hausman and H. Reisen. IDB and OECD.

Obstfeld, Maurice, 1982. "Can We Sterilize? Theory and Evidence." *American Economic Review,* 72, no. 2 (May), 45–50.

Obstfeld, Marice, 1995. "International Currency Experience: New Lessons and Lessons Re-learned." Brookings Papers on Economic Activity.

Portes, Richard, and David Vines. 1997. "Coping with International Capital Flows." London: A Report for the Economic Affairs Division of the Commonwealth Secretariat, Occasional Paper 1.

Rosati, Dariusz. 1997. "Exchange Rate Policies in Post-Communist Economies." In Zecchini 1977, 481–502.

Ul Haque, Nadeen, Donald Mathieson, and Sunil Sharma. 1997. "Causes of Capital Inflows and Policy Responses to Them." *Finance & Development* (March), 3–6.

World Bank 1997. *Private Capital Flows to Developing Countries.* Washington, D.C.: The World Bank.

Zecchini, Salvatore, ed. 1997. *Lessons from Economic Transition.* Dordrecht/Boston/London: Kluwer for OECD.

Index